Workshop on Computational Approaches to Linguistic Code Switching (CALCS 2023)

Singapore
7 December 2023

ISBN: 978-1-7138-8597-9

Printed from e-media with permission by:

Curran Associates, Inc.
57 Morehouse Lane
Red Hook, NY 12571

Some format issues inherent in the e-media version may also appear in this print version.

Printed with permission by Curran Associates, Inc. (2024)

For permission requests, please contact the Association for Computational Linguistics
at the address below.

Association for Computational Linguistics
209 N. Eighth Street
Stroudsburg, Pennsylvania 18360

Phone: 1-570-476-8006
Fax: 1-570-476-0860

acl@aclweb.org

Additional copies of this publication are available from:

Curran Associates, Inc.
57 Morehouse Lane
Red Hook, NY 12571 USA
Phone: 845-758-0400
Fax: 845-758-2633
Email: curran@proceedings.com
Web: www.proceedings.com

CALCS 2023

Computational Approaches to Linguistic Code-Switching

Proceedings of the Workshop

December 7, 2023

The CALCS organizers gratefully acknowledge the support from the following sponsors.

Gold

Bloomberg

Engineering

Introduction

Bienvenidos to the proceedings of the sixth edition of the workshop on computational approaches for linguistic code-switching (CALCS-2023)! Code-switching is a common phenomenon in the multilingual communities where multilingual speakers communicate by moving back and forth between the languages they speak when communicating with other multilingual speakers. This year the workshop is being held in Singapore on December 7th, 2023 at EMNLP.

This workshop series brings together experts and practitioners that are currently working on different aspects of code-switching with a special focus on motivating tighter collaborations between speech and text researchers. We received 15 regular workshop submissions, of which we accepted 8 and 1 non-archival. Our workshop also aims to motivate new research and energize the community to take on the challenges posed by code-switching data.

The workshop program includes short talks from regular workshop submissions and keynote speakers. We also have a stellar invited speaker program with a keynote talk by Preethi Jyothi and Haizhou Li. We would like to thank the EMNLP workshop organizers for their help during the organization of the workshop. It would have been great to see everyone face to face in Singapore and we hope that you join us on December 7th and that you enjoy the program we put together.

Let's talk code-switching in December!

The Workshop Organizers

Organizing Committee

Organizer

Sudipta Kar, Amazon
Genta Indra Winata, Bloomberg
Marina Zhukova, University of California, Santa Barbara
Thamar Solorio, University of Houston and Mohammad bin Zayed University of Artificial Intelligence
Mona Diab, Carnegie Mellon University
Sunayana Sitaram, Microsoft Research
Monojit Choudhury, Microsoft Turing
Kalika Bali, Microsoft Research

Program Committee

Program Committee

A. Seza Doğruöz
Abhinav Arora
Dama Sravani
David Vilares
Elena Álvarez-Mellado
Els Lefever
Holy Lovenia
François Yvon
Ganesh Jawahar
Gustavo Aguilar
Kellen Gillespie
Manuel Mager
Parth Patwa
Salim Sazzed
Segun Aroyehun
Shuguang Chen
Suman Dowlagar
Suraj Maharjan
Tanya Roosta
Vivek Srivastava
Xingzhi Guo
Yihong Theis

Invited Speakers

Haizhou Li, The Chinese University of Hong Kong and National University of Singapore
Preethi Jyothi, IIT Bombay

Keynote Talk: Modeling Code-Switch Languages Using Bilingual Parallel Corpus

Haizhou Li
The Chinese University of Hong Kong, Shenzhen; National University of Sinagapore

Abstract: Language modeling is the technique to estimate the probability of a sequence of words. A bilingual language model is expected to model the sequential dependency for words across languages, which is difficult due to the inherent lack of suitable training data as well as diverse syntactic structure across languages. We propose a bilingual attention language model (BALM) that simultaneously performs language modeling objective with a quasi-translation objective to model both the monolingual as well as the cross-lingual sequential dependency. The attention mechanism learns the bilingual context from a parallel corpus. We will discuss the study of multilingualism in South East Asia and how code-switch language models can be useful for language processing.

Bio: Haizhou Li is the X.Q. Deng Presidential Chair Professor in the School of Data Science, The Chinese University of Hong Kong, Shenzhen, China. He is also an Adjunct Professor at the National University of Singapore, Singapore and a Bremen Excellence Chair Professor at the University of Bremen, Germany. Prior to joining CUHK (Shenzhen), Professor Li has taught at Nanyang Technological University and National University of Singapore (2006-2016) in Singapore, University of Eastern Finland (2009) in Finland, and University of New South Wales (2011-2016) in Australia. He was the Principal Scientist and Research Director at the Institute for Infocomm Research (2003-2016), the Agency for Science, Technology and Research, Singapore. Professor Li is an IEEE Fellow, and ISCA Fellow.
He has served as the Editor-in-Chief of IEEE-ACM Transactions on Audio Speech and Language Processing (2015-2018), Associate Editor of Computer Speech and Language (2012-2021), Springer International Journal of Social Robotics (2008-2021), and a Member of IEEE Speech and Language Processing Technical Committee (2013-2015), Awards Board (2021-2023), and Publications Board (2015-2018) of IEEE Signal Processing Society. He was the President of the International Speech Communication Association (ISCA, 2015-2017), the President of Asia Pacific Signal and Information Processing Association (APSIPA, 2015-2016), the President of the Asian Federation of Natural Language Processing (AFNLP, 2017-2018). He was the General Chair of major scientific conferences including ACL 2012, INTERSPEECH 2014, and ICASSP 2022.

Keynote Talk: Resource-efficient Computational Models for Code-switched Speech and Text

Preethi Jyothi
IIT Bombay

Abstract: Code-switching, i.e., the linguistic phenomenon of switching between languages within and across sentences, is widely prevalent in multilingual societies. Code-switched inputs pose a serious challenge to existing speech and NLP models. The challenge mainly emerges due to the limited availability of natural code-switched data and the inherent diversity in code-switching. In this talk, we will discuss techniques that aim to effectively address these dual challenges. These techniques will cover how to exploit monolingual speech and text for code-switching, how to generate synthetic and diverse code-switched text to augment real data and how to judiciously use existing real code-switched speech and text in conjunction with other linguistic resources.

Bio: Preethi is an Associate Professor at IIT Bombay. She joined the department in September 2016. Prior to that, she was a Beckman Postdoctoral Fellow at the University of Illinois at Urbana-Champaign. She obtained my Ph.D. from the CSE Department at The Ohio State University in 2013. Her research interests are broadly in the areas of automatic speech recognition and machine learning as applied to speech, and code-switching.

Table of Contents

Program

Thursday, December 7, 2023

09:10 - 09:00 *Opening Remarks*

09:05 - 10:35 *Paper Oral Presentation 1*

Towards Real-World Streaming Speech Translation for Code-Switched Speech
Belen Alastruey, Matthias Sperber, Christian Gollan, Dominic Telaar, Tim Ng and Aashish Agarwal

Text-Derived Language Identity Incorporation for End-to-End Code-Switching Speech Recognition
Qinyi Wang and Haizhou Li

TongueSwitcher: Fine-Grained Identification of German-English Code-Switching
Igor Sterner and Simone Teufel

CONFLATOR: Incorporating Switching Point based Rotatory Positional Encodings for Code-Mixed Language Modeling
Mohsin Ali Mohammed, Sai Teja Kandukuri, Neeharika Gupta, Parth Patwa, Anubhab Chatterjee, Vinija Jain, Aman Chadha and Amitava Das

Prompting Multilingual Large Language Models to Generate Code-Mixed Texts: The Case of South East Asian Languages
Zheng Xin Xin Yong, Ruochen Zhang, Jessica Zosa Forde, Skyler Wang, Arjun Subramonian, Holy Lovenia, Samuel Cahyawijaya, Genta Indra Winata, Lintang Sutawika, Jan Christian Blaise Cruz, Yin Lin Tan, Long Phan, Long Phan, Rowena Garcia, Thamar Solorio and Alham Fikri Aji

10:25 - 11:00 *Break*

11:00 - 11:45 *Invited Talk - Preethi Jyothi*

11:45 - 12:15 *Paper Oral Presentation 2*

Multilingual self-supervised speech representations improve the speech recognition of low-resource African languages with codeswitching
Tolulope Ogunremi, Christopher Manning and Dan Jurafsky

Language Preference for Expression of Sentiment for Nepali-English Bilingual Speakers on Social Media
Niraj Pahari and Kazutaka Shimada

12:15 - 12:30 *Findings Paper Code-Switching with Word Senses for Pretraining in Neural Machine Translation*

Thursday, December 7, 2023 (continued)

14:00 - 12:30 *Lunch Break*

14:00 - 12:15 *Paper Oral Presentation 3*

Unified Model for Code-Switching Speech Recognition and Language Identification Based on Concatenated Tokenizer
Kunal Dhawan, KDimating Rekesh and Boris Ginsburg

14:15 - 15:30 *Panel Discussion - Sudipta Kar, Genta Winata, Marina Zhukova*

15:30 - 16:00 *Coffee Break*

16:00 - 16:45 *Invited Talk - Haizhou Li*

16:45 - 16:50 *Best Paper Announcement*

16:50 - 16:55 *Closing Remarks*

TONGUESWITCHER: Fine-Grained Identification of German–English Code-Switching

Igor Sterner
Department of Engineering
University of Cambridge
United Kingdom
is473@cam.ac.uk

Simone Teufel
Department of Computer Science and Technology
University of Cambridge
United Kingdom
sht25@cam.ac.uk

Abstract

This paper contributes to German–English code-switching research. We provide the largest corpus of naturally occurring German–English code-switching, where English is included in German text, and two methods for code-switching identification. The first method is rule-based, using wordlists and morphological processing. We use this method to compile a corpus of 25.6M tweets employing German–English code-switching. In our second method, we continue pretraining of a neural language model on this corpus and classify tokens based on embeddings from this language model. Our systems establish SoTA on our new corpus and an existing German–English code-switching benchmark. In particular, we systematically study code-switching for language-ambiguous words which can only be resolved in context, and morphologically mixed words consisting of both English and German morphemes. We distribute both corpora and systems to the research community.

1 Introduction

A large proportion of the world's population is multilingual, and that naturally means that a large proportion of the world is code-switching daily, frequently and routinely (Harris and McGhee Nelson, 1992; Grosjean, 2010; Grosjean and Li, 2013). Code-switching occurs when speakers alternate between languages; this can happen at the sentence, word, or even subword level. For many multilingual speakers, code-switching is a natural part of informal language, either as a matter of convenience or possibly because it allows them to express their intended meanings more precisely. Several psycholinguistic and sociolinguistic theories of code-switching exist (Poplack, 1980; Joshi, 1982; Myers-Scotton, 1997; Muysken, 2000; Green and Abutalebi, 2013; Filipović and Hawkins, 2019). The dominant language is called the matrix language, while the subordinate language that is included is

Tweet: ich glaub ich muss echt $_{M}$rewatchen $_{E}$like i feel so empty was soll ich denn jetzt machen
Translation: I think I really have to rewatch it like i feel so empty what should I do now

Figure 1: German–English code-switching

called the embedded language (Joshi, 1982). We refer to any text segment in the embedded language as an island. In the example of code-switching shown in Figure 1, $_{E}$like i feel so empty is an island.

Many NLP systems are currently developed to be capable of handling text from informal contexts. Code-switching places new pressure on these, particularly for applications that require the recognition and precise extraction of meaning from code-switched text, or even the generation of such text. Available NLP tools lag behind in this respect (Aguilar and Solorio, 2020; Doğruöz et al., 2021); in particular large language models perform best when fine-tuned on natural code-switching data (Santy et al., 2021). Our work is aimed towards NLP tools that can better understand and manipulate code-switched language.

We are interested in studying *naturally occurring* code-switching. Social media, where mostly informal conversation take place, is an ideal source of such texts. We study code-switching between English and German, two closely related languages. We encounter many high-frequency words of identical form in both languages, such as "was" in Figure 1, which is a WH-pronoun in German. If the same string "was" appeared in English, it would be the past form of 'to be'. Importantly, the two meanings are entirely unrelated. Such cases constitute an interesting corner case for code-switched text, and are called interlingual homographs (IHs, Dijkstra et al., 1999). A second interesting phenomenon is that, because German is a morphologically rich language, its morphology can act on English mor-

Proceedings of the 6th Workshop on Computational Approaches to Linguistic Code-Switching, pages 1–13
December 7, 2023 ©2023 Association for Computational Linguistics

phemes, creating intra-word codeswitching, such as in the past participle $_{\text{M}}$rewatchen in Figure 1. A third property of the German–English language pair is the high frequency of English loanwords in German. Loanwords are words of foreign origin that have been fully assimilated into the main language. Loanwords and code-switching constitute a grey area in language change: whether something is a loanword or part of an island is a hotly debated topic in linguistics (Deuchar, 2020; Treffers-Daller, 2022). While we do not directly address the loanword distinction in this work, we believe that our theory-neutral methods can contribute to an empirical way of addressing this in the future.

In this paper, we study German–English code-switching with an analytic interest in fine-grained phenomena (e.g. short islands, mixed morphology and interlingual homographs). This introduces new aspects to the automatic study of code-switching. At the same time, we bring scale to the analysis; the TONGUESWITCHER Corpus includes 25.6M German-English code-switching tweets with automatic code-switching identification. We release our corpus and the two code-switching identification methods we developed, one rule-based, one neural[1].

2 Related work

Code-switching identification and language identification are closely related tasks, but traditional language identification (LI) tools can only determine which languages are present in a given text, not the precise beginning and end of each island. For instance, the LI tools provided by Chen and Skiena (2014) and Joulin et al. (2016b; 2016a) rely on character-based n-gram models. FastText (Joulin et al., 2016b,a) uses a character-based n-gram method to compare statistical properties of the input text with a pre-compiled frequency profile of each language. It distinguishes 176 languages, including English and German, alongside similar languages such as Luxembourgish and Afrikaans. Polyglot is another such tool, which is able to identify more than one single language per document (Chen and Skiena, 2014). It is built from the CLD2 tool from Riesa and Giuliani (2013), which uses quadgram ranking. Lingua (Stahl, 2023) is a blackbox LI tool that also offers code-switching identification for many language pairs, including German–English. It combines a language modelling approach with hard-coded rules. Its code-switching identification performance has never been experimentally evaluated.

Nguyen et al. (2020; 2021) present rule-based code-switching identification systems for Vietnamese–English and Hindi–English mixed text, which is based on specially-created wordlists for each of these language pairs. All words that appear in both wordlists are manually disambiguated by a human annotator. This is a simple approach to the task that affords the researchers control over their system, as it does not require any training.

Osmelak and Wintner (2023) detect code-switching at a finer-grained level. In their Denglisch system, tagging proceeds at token-level, and the following labels are used: **D** and **E** for German and English tokens respectively; **SD, SE** and **SO** for loanwords imported from German into English, from English imported German, and from other languages. There is also an **O**ther category for unclassifiable items, such as punctuation and emojis, and a **M**ixed category for words of mixed morphology.

Several other code-switching approaches also model mixed morphology. Nguyen and Cornips (2016) perform morphological analysis with the Morphessor tool to address Dutch-Limburgish-English code-switching, and Mager et al. (2019) detect intra-word code-switches in German–Turkish and Spanish–Wixarika text using RNNs. Osmelak and Wintner (2023) use CRFs, a supervised machine learning framework, in combination with manually curated features, such as orthography, n-gram, morphology, function words, frequency, lexical components and wordlists. The training material consists of 950 Reddit comments containing 60K tokens, balanced between English and German. They also use automatically-tagged silver-standard data to the tune of a further 31,500 comments (5 million tokens). In contrast, our solution does not require any human-annotated training material.

For neural code-switching identification, the use of word embeddings from a multilingual language model such as mBERT (Devlin et al., 2019) is one possible approach. mBERT is an encoder-only transformer-based model which embeds each token into a 768-D vector. Santy et al. (2021) found it is best suited when fine-tuned on naturally occurring code-switching material. Nayak and Joshi (2022)

[1]Code, models (neural tagger and code-switching language model, both with demos) and corpus are all online.

pretrain and fintune a BERT-based model for code-switching identification in Hinglish. They use an existing tool to collect and automatically label a large corpus of tweets.

When it comes to gold-standard datasets, the majority of code-switching datasets are between (1) languages spoken in India with English (Gupta et al., 2021; Nguyen et al., 2021; Adda-Decker et al., 2008), (2) Mandarin with English (Lyu et al., 2010) and (3) Spanish with English (Mave et al., 2018; Samih et al., 2016). For German–English code-switching other than Osmelak and Wintner (2023), Rijhwani et al. (2017) use a mini-corpus consisting of 99 Twitter tweets, which is not publically available. Our corpus is much larger.

3 Corpus construction

The German tweets we use as input were collected at scale by Kratzke (2022, 2023). The Twitter language identification algorithm assigns a probable language at the time of writing of each tweet; Kratzke chose those that were deemed German. This resulted in 149.2M input tweets written between April 2019 to February 2023. We clean the tweets (URLs are replaced with <URL>, emojis, emails, phone numbers and mentions are removed) and run FastText language detection on them, only keeping tweets that are re-assigned the German tag or instead assigned an English language tag. This step eliminates many tweets in Luxembourgish and other languages too similar to German for Twitter's language identifier to catch. 123.7M tweets remain after this step. In contrast, Osmelak and Wintner (2023) filter their input to remove those examples for which Polyglot's prediction is not *both* English and German.

To establish a testset, code-switching annotation was performed by the authors of this paper on 1252 tweets. We used the Prodigy annotation tool (Montani and Honnibal, 2018). To use annotation time efficiently, we wanted to make sure that a good proportion of the cases seen had reasonably high code-switching occurrences. The tweets were therefore processed and pre-filtered by a precursor of TONGUESWITCHER. This system differed from the final version only marginally, e.g. in the ordering of the rules and the quality of the multilingual stemming algorithm. We then random-sampled from two subsets: all input tweets (25%), and those with a high proportion of code-switching (75%). System annotations were not removed before human annotation. There were no explicit guidelines. Annotators discarded tweets in German dialects such as Swiss German, made sure that German indeed acted as the matrix language, and then marked island start and end points in each surviving tweet. In 63.5% of cases, boundaries were moved; this means that annotators did not simply accept the system's suggestions. Regarding the annotation of loanwords, each annotator followed their own intuition about which words were so common as to be used as loanwords, additionally using a context-sensitive definition of loanwords. To establish consistency of the annotation, we randomly sampled 36 tweets consisting of 1172 tokens, which both annotators labelled. Inter-annotator agreement was measured at κ=0.68 (N=1172, n=3, k=2; Cohen, 1960). The annotators agreed fully on all tokens in 15 out of the 36 tweets. The distribution of island sizes in the resulting testset is given in Figure 2.

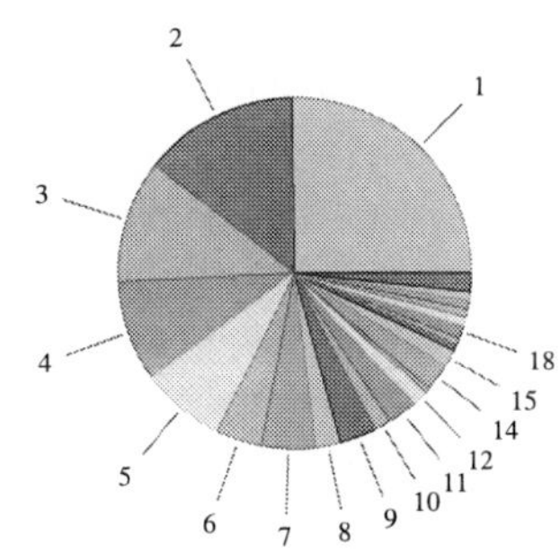

Figure 2: Proportion of island sizes in testset. Each field expresses the total number of tokens occurring in islands of that size.

4 TongueSwitcher

Our rule-based method takes as input German tweets and produces labels indicating the language of each word, or sub-word if the word is of mixed morphology. The main algorithm applies several wordlist-based filters to make the decision. Additional processing applies if a) the word is genuinely a possible word in both languages or b) it is an intra-word code switch. All processing in this method is performed on lowercased words.

4.1 Constructing wordlists

We first compile formal and informal wordlists for English and German. Our strategy given the resources we have is to compile pure wordlists which contain words that are guaranteed to be contained in only one of the two languages (for instance, "parser" should not be in either pure list), and a big wordlist to cover as many words as possible from the matrix language, German. For the "Pure English" wordlist, we combine the WortSchatz Leipzig News Corpora (WL, 15K words, Biemann et al., 2007) and a scraped version of the online Urban Dictionary (UD, 13K words, Bierner, 2022), which contains many informal words and phrases used in English slang. We remove words that appear 5 times or fewer in the WL corpus and words that appear 10 times or fewer in the UD.

For German, we use the WL corpora (65K words), and add Swiss (37K words) and Austrian (34K words) as we could not automatically filter out many input tweets written in these dialects. We also add the more informal online German dictionary dict.cc (583K words, Hemetsberger, 2023). This list is the basis for our "Big German" wordlist. For our multilingual stemming, we also need a wordlist of pure German roots. We start by collecting a smaller wordlist of words appearing more than twice only in the German WL corpus.

English loanwords need to be removed from the German lists. Ideally, we would have an exhaustive list of loanwords to handle such words separately, but in reality we have access only to a small list of 3367 known English loanwords in German, created by Seidel (2010) from an analysis of the German magazine Der Spiegel. We remove these from "Big German"[2]. We remove an additional set of suspected loanwords automatically from the German wordlists, namely all entries from dict.cc (Hemetsberger, 2023) where the English word and its German translation are identical and vice versa. We also remove a large list of boys', girls' and city names (Weiss, 2022a,b; OnTheWorldMap, 2023) from both wordlists. Names in our approach are handled based on the surrounding language in our n-gram processing (step **7** of our algorithm coming up in §4.2).

Finally, we also want to remove the many non-language-specific one or two letter words in our wordlists (e.g. "eh"), which we consider noise. Such words can arise from typos, abbreviations, and general processing problems. Unless such ultra-short words were included in hand-selected lists[3], we removed them from all wordlists.

Wordlist	Words
Big German	709,979
Pure German	92,099
Pure English	20,203
Interlingual homographs	120

Table 1: Wordlists compiled, with number of words

Even after all these stages, there are still words appearing in both wordlists (many purely English words in the German wordlists and vice versa). Many of these are noise. One could whittle them down entirely manually, as Nguyen and Bryant (2020) do. We instead first ask the large language model (LLM) `text-davinci-003` (Brown et al., 2020) for its guess of the primary language of each word with the following prompt: `In one word, what language is the word: {}?` The LLM may introduce a bias towards English. We therefore do not accept the LLMs predictions blindly, but manually review all classifications. Knowing the model's choice still saved time. We removed the German ones from the English wordlist, and the English ones from the German wordlists.

When going through this list manually, we also find some words that are graphically identical and have the *same* meaning in both languages (e.g. 'diverse')[4]. If such a word is found, it is removed from *all* wordlists. We will treat these based on the surrounding language later.

Finally, we compiled a list of IHs. Under the assumption that IHs have different POS in the two languages, we compute a list of such IHs by tagging an English and a German WL corpus, looking for shared words with at least one different POS, modulo capitalisation.

The sizes of the resultant wordlists are given in Table 1.

4.2 Code-switching identification algorithm

Our code-switching identification algorithm is defined as follows. We first tokenize and POS-tag each cleaned tweet using the Flair `upos-multi` multilingual uPOS tagger (Akbik et al., 2018; Petrov et al., 2012). Then we apply the following steps to classify each token. These steps are also visualized as a flow chart in Figure 3; examples of tokens handled by each step are given in Appendix

[2]Another reason for removing these loanwords is that some display mixed morphology. Our algorithm will not detect mixed morphology if the full word is already in "Big German". By removing them, these words are automatically handled by our mixed word detection steps.

[3]The hand-selected lists contain 28 English one or two-character words (e.g. 'of' and 'if') and 24 German one or two-character words (e.g. 'zu' and 'um').

[4]These words are not IHs, because IHs are defined as having different meanings.

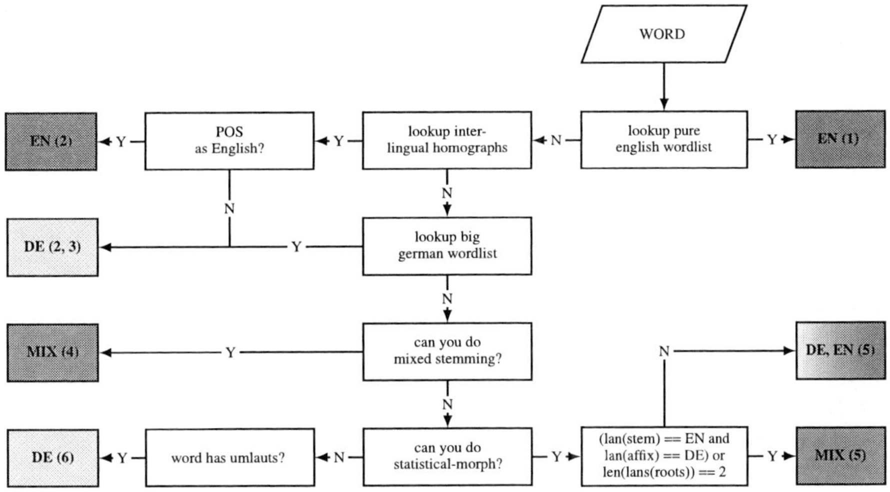

Figure 3: The word-level classification subroutine

Table 9. The proportion of tokens in our corpus identified using each step is given in brackets.

1 (5.8%) If a word is in our pure English wordlist, it immediately receives an English tag.

2 (9.3%) If a word is a interlingual homograph (IH), language identification is attempted using the words' part of speech tag.

3 (74.6%) Else, we look the word up in our big German wordlist and assign a German tag if found.

4 (0.2%) If the word is still not identified, a multilingual stemming system we developed recursively strips affixes (lists taken from Osmelak and Wintner, 2023) from words until a word (or simple variations: adding a missing trailing 'e' or removing a double last letter) is found in our pure English wordlist or no more affixes are found. If an English stem is found with purely German affixes, the word is given a Mixed label.

5 (1.4%) We next look for known subwords using a statistical morphological segmentation subsystem based on HanTa (Wartena, 2019), a trainable second-order autoregressive model, where each morpheme depends on the previous two morphemes to predict the most likely morpheme sequence. We train HanTa on the (a) Tiger Corpus (Brants et al., 2002) for German (b) Brown Corpus (Francis and Kucera, 1964) for English and (c) a mixture of both, and attempt segmentation in turn with these three systems, looking for roots in our pure English or pure German wordlists. This subsystem also detects fully monolingual compound word creations, hence the increase in proportion compared to 0.2% for the previous step.

Split	Tweets	Sentences	Tokens	Eng. tokens
Train	24.6M	57.8M	741.9M	82.6M
Dev	1.1M	2.6M	32.9M	3.6M
Test	1.3K	3.0K	37.5K	2.8K
Total	25.6M	60.4M	774.8M	86.2M

Table 2: TONGUESWITCHER Corpus statistics

6 (0.5%) If the unknown word contains an umlaut, it receives a German tag.

7 (8.2%) Words unknown at this stage which occur inside single-language islands are assigned the language of their neighbours. Words at an island boundary assume the language of the most probable bigram on either side, based on the frequencies of the most likely 10,000 bigrams of German and English we compiled from the WL Corpora for each language. Otherwise, tokens assume the language of their nearest identified token.

We implement this algorithm using the framework of Lin and Byrne (2022), resulting in the TONGUESWITCHER (TS) system. Using this system, we next automatically labelled all 123.7M cleaned input tweets, creating our silver-annotated data. Based on the silver labels, we excluded tweets that do not contain at least 50% German tokens, and at least one English or Mixed token. We split this corpus by allocating the last two months of data (Jan, Feb '23) to a development set. A summary of the corpus with its silver-standard training/development data is given in Table 2. Our silver-standard data has 11% English tokens.

We sanity-check our corpus and the silver-standard annotations by sampling 5 tweets each for different island sizes (1 to 20 tokens). Out of the 100 tweets, 64 were true code-switching. Of the remaining, 9 were translations and 27 were monolingual. Most of the monolingual mistakes arose due to the erroneous identification of single-token loanwords or named entities[5]. Overall, we find the precision acceptable, given that the recall is likely to be higher than in any currently available corpus. If we had chosen a stricter condition for tweets that are selected for our corpus, perhaps to exclude tweets with only a single-token island as Nayak and Joshi (2022) do, we could easily raise precision, but would have missed many interesting border cases of either code-switching insertions or loanwords. It is precisely these instances that are valuable to linguists and lexicographers who study the process of loanwording.

Of the code-switching tweets, we then counted how many of the system-predicted islands were correctly identified[6]. We found that single-token English islands had a precision of 62.5 (40 predicted), two-token islands 87.5 (8 predicted), three-token islands 80.0 (10 predicted) and all island sizes greater than this (65 predicted) had a precision of 100.0.

Two examples of particularly dense code-switching are shown in Table 3. TS labels example (1) perfectly, but for example (2) it incorrectly tags 'performed', 'pushen', 'Time-to-Market' and 'Relaunch' as German[7]. 'Top-of-mind-Awareness' is not segmented correctly by Flair and hence incorrectly identified as the language of the surrounding tokens, which is German.

5 BERT-based system

We also wanted a neural system that is fine-tuned for German–English identification, so we could investigate to which degree neural word embeddings are suited to the task. To that end, we pretrain a neural language model on the TONGUESWITCHER Corpus and fine-tune it for token classification. We then learn the classification layer using the human-labelled examples from the Denglisch Corpus. This system is called tsBERT.

[5]The TS system does not include any named entity recognizer, or special handling of loanwords, except using the wordlists and surrounding language.

[6]We used a lenient definition of boundaries where overlap between system-predicted islands and real islands was sufficient.

[7]It did so because these words all happen to make their way into our "Big German" wordlist, and are also not in our "Pure English" wordlist.'

6 Experiment

Systems, Competitors, Baselines We evaluate our systems, TONGUESWITCHER (TS) and tsBERT, against two competitors from the literature, Denglisch CRF (Osmelak and Wintner, 2023) and Lingua (Stahl, 2023). The Denglisch system is not provided as a trained system, so we follow their procedure in training it. To interpret Denglisch's output, we match Denglisch labels onto our reduced set as follows: English, German, Mixed are taken directly. SE becomes English, and SD becomes German. Denglisch's SO labels and punctuation labels are ignored in evaluation.

We construct a strong baseline by prompting the GPT-4 LLM (OpenAI, 2023) with the prompt given in Appendix §A.3. We also train baseline neural classification models by learning the classification layer directly on (English) BERT (*eBERT*), German BERT (*gBERT*, DeepsetAI, 2019) and multilingual BERT (*mBERT*) models.

Datasets We use the TONGUESWITCHER Corpus as pretraining data, and the human-labelled examples from the Denglisch Corpus (Osmelak and Wintner, 2023) as finetuning data (after removing emojis, replacing out-of-vocabulary punctuation tokens, and removing entries longer than 100 tokens).

Our main evaluation uses our own corpus (§3) with its 1252 tweet testset. We also report results for our systems and the Denglisch CRF system on the German–English subpart of the Denglisch Corpus (15% of their corpus sentences, using the same definition as before). While our BERT-based system is trained on their data in the cross-validation setup, TONGUESWITCHER cannot be trained. We use this evaluation as a sanity check: if our systems performed much below the Denglisch system on this corpus, this would be a cause for alarm.

Training We initialize our BERT-based models with the `bert-base-multilingual-cased` (mBERT) pretrained model (Devlin et al., 2019). Unlike our rule-based system, this model distinguishes between upper and lowercase words. We continue pretraining for 1 epoch on all 24.6M code-switching tweets in the TS training corpus. We finetunne for our task on the Denglisch Corpus (Osmelak and Wintner, 2023). For evaluation on their corpus, we train models for the same 10-fold cross-validation setup as they do. For evaluation on our testset, we train on 100% of their corpus,

(1) Pronouns: he/him Height: 1,83m Zodiac: Virgo Smoke: nope Tattoo: 3 Piercings: Ohrringe (mehr will ich auch nicht, allerhöchstens noch mehr Ohrlöcher) Fav colour: grün Fav drink: Kaffee und oolong milk tea, heiß, mit einem quarter süss und tapioka bei meinem bubble tea laden **Translation:** Pronouns: he/him Height: 1.83m Zodiac: Virgo Smoke: nope Tattoo: 3 piercings: earrings (I don't want more, at most more ear piercings) Favorite colour: green Favorite drink: coffee and oolong milk tea, hot, with a quarter sugar and tapioca at my bubble tea shop
(2) Wenn wir unsere Skills elevaten und die Units gemeinsam performen, werden wir die Sales auf ein neues Level pushen. Außerdem können wir so den Time-to-Market für den Relaunch shorten. Das bringt zusätzliche Top-of-mind-Awareness und pushed die Brand in der Community. Ok? Go! **Translation:** If we elevate our skills and perform the units together, we will push sales to a new level. This also allows us to shorten the time-to-market for the relaunch. This brings additional top-of-mind-awareness and pushes the brand in the community. Ok? Go!

Table 3: Examples from our TONGUESWITCHER Corpus sanity check

as they do when labelling their silver-standard material. Training details are given in the Appendix §A.2.

Metrics We report results separately in token-based micro-averaged F_1 measure (shown as F_t), and in entity-based F_1 measure (shown as F_e). F_e is defined based on the number of islands of English inside the German matrix text, with strict boundaries. We use the BIO format (Ramshaw and Marcus, 1995) for entity representation. Because code-switching segments are coherent entities inside a text, using an entity-based metric should be more informative than a token-based one, which ignores the code-switching context of each token. We report performance on all islands, and we also introduce a new metric which measures the performance of systems for short islands only, namely those consisting of 2-4 tokens according to our gold standard. The statistical test we use throughout this paper is the two-tailed paired permutation test, approximated by $R = 10,000$, with significance threshold at $\alpha = 0.05$.

7 Results

	German	English	Mixed	Overall
	9907	*1972*	*192*	*12071*
Denglisch	97.5	89.1	25.6	95.5
TS	96.9	87.7	32.4	94.5
tsBERT	98.9	95.5	60.1	97.8

Table 4: Results on Denglisch corpus; in F_t

Table 4 gives results in F_t on the G–E subset of the Denglisch corpus. Our trained tsBERT model outperforms trained Denglisch in all categories (differences significant; 4x p<0.01), setting a new SoTA on this benchmark. The superiority of tsBERT in the English category (95.5 vs. 89.1), which is the core of the task of German–English code-switching identification, is particularly satisfying. In mixed word detection, our system achieves a 135% improvement over Denglisch.

Revisiting example (2) from Table 3, where TONGUESWITCHER (TS) made multiple mistakes, tsBERT fixes all of these mistakes and perfectly identifies the code-switching. Denglisch predicts 'Skills', 'elevaten', 'Units', 'performen', 'Relaunch', 'shorten', 'pushed' are all German, and wrongly suggests that 'Time-to-Market' is mixed.

Meanwhile, TS is not trained on any Denglisch data, as it is rule-based[8]. In the English and Mixed categories, TS is statistically indistinguishable from Denglisch (p=0.19, p=0.09); in the German category, it is significantly outperformed by Denglisch.

We consider both our systems to pass the sanity check; we will now turn to our main results on our own corpus, where no new human-annotated training material is available to any of the systems.

Table 5 shows the results in precision, recall and F_t for our corpus.

TONGUESWITCHER (F_t=97.1 overall) and tsBERT (F_t=97.0 overall) are indistinguishable from each other, and significantly better than all baselines and competitors, with the exception of the category Mixed. In the mixed category, TS is better than tsBERT (p<0.01), and tsBERT is indistinguishable from all BERT-based baselines. All other differences are significant, which means that GPT-4 (F_t=94.3 overall) is inferior to our two TS systems, as least with our prompting strategy. This means that TS has established SoTA on our corpus.

TS outperforms all others in the mixed category; the BERT-based models are the next best. Although

[8]Note that our treatment of Denglisch's gold standard (collapsing all 'Shared German' tokens to be German) hurts only TS. For example, TS would say named entities like 'Berlin' are English in an otherwise English constituent.

	German			English			Mixed			Overall		
	29761			*2757*			*129*			*32647*		
	P	R	F_t	P	R	F_t	P	R	F_t	P	R	F_t
Lingua	95.8	97.3	96.5	66.5	57.6	61.7	0.0	0.0	0.0	93.6	93.6	93.6
GPT-4	99.2	95.2	97.2	66.2	93.7	77.5	12.2	16.3	14.0	94.8	94.8	94.8
Denglisch CRF	98.4	97.4	97.9	75.1	85.5	79.9	19.0	6.2	9.4	96.0	96.0	96.0
eBERT	98.7	97.4	98.0	78.1	86.7	82.2	23.1	38.0	28.7	96.3	96.3	96.3
gBERT	98.8	97.0	97.9	73.9	87.6	80.1	27.7	34.1	30.6	95.9	95.9	95.9
mBERT	98.7	97.5	98.1	78.1	87.3	82.4	24.9	32.6	28.2	96.4	96.4	96.4
TONGUESWITCHER	99.3	97.6	98.4	79.0	93.8	85.8	48.0	38.0	42.4	97.1	97.1	97.1
tsBERT	99.0	97.9	98.5	81.5	89.1	85.1	25.5	38.8	30.8	97.0	97.0	97.0

Table 5: Results on our testset

	Island			Short Island (2-4)		
	1192			*365*		
	P	R	F_e	P	R	F_e
Lingua	25.4	14.0	18.1	27.8	34.5	30.8
GPT-4	44.5	70.1	54.4	50.7	74.5	60.4
Denglisch	49.0	55.5	52.0	53.2	72.3	61.3
eBERT	54.0	61.5	57.5	63.1	70.7	66.7
gBERT	49.2	58.4	53.4	55.3	71.0	62.2
mBERT	54.8	62.0	58.2	63.4	73.7	68.2
TS	58.9	75.7	66.2	57.3	77.3	65.8
tsBERT	60.5	66.5	63.4	66.7	75.9	71.0

Table 6: Island-based results

mixed word identification might be seen as a niche task given the low occurrence frequency of mixed words, we are happy to see this result because we think that the mixing of morphologies is an understudied phenomenon. Linguists and cognitive scientists requiring empirical data can profit from a system such as ours that is able to automatically detect these cases reasonably well.

It is nice to see the small, but significant improvement of our tsBERT system over the other BERT-based models in most categories (those other than Mixed). This shows that pretraining with the TONGUESWITCHER code-switching corpus helps. This language model trained on code-switching data may be useful to other researchers working on German–English tasks other than ours, too.

7.1 Islands

So far, we have presented results in a token-based metric, but this ignores the fact that code-switching is a context-sensitive phenomenon: we care less about how many tokens are of which language overall, and more about which textual material forms an island.

Table 6 gives results for P, R and F_e for islands and short islands. Again, the two TS systems beat all competitors and baselines. Lingua is left far behind. The success of TS on islands is a surprising result, as the majority of tokens are handled by this system without any context. One explanation may be that step **7** in our algorithm (§4.2) performs contextual smoothing by assigning the labels of neighbouring tokens to unknown tokens. This handles spelling mistakes and other word creations by favouring coherent islands.

For short islands, tsBERT and mBERT are joint winners with F_e=71.0 and F_e=68.2, respectively, beating TS (65.8), GPT-4 (60.4) and Denglisch (61.3). TS is better than GPT-4 (p=0.02), while GPT-4 and Denglisch are indistinguishable. Lingua's performance, meanwhile, is poor at F_e=30.8. We suspect Polyglot (Chen and Skiena, 2014) would have similar problems with this task[9]. Denglisch (Osmelak and Wintner, 2023) use Polyglot as a filtering tool for all their data and therefore many cases of short islands of code-switching may have been lost when the Denglisch corpus was created.

7.2 Post-analysis: interlingual homographs

We next performed an analysis of how well the systems perform on IHs. We compiled a separate small testset specifically for such cases: tweets containing real IHs. We sorted our previous list of IHs by the frequency of the less frequent language of the two (e.g. English 'war' rather than the German verb), and then manually checked up to 100 tweets in each language for each word. We discarded words if they show any of the following problems: the word was only ever encountered as a proper name in one or both languages (e.g. English "los"),

[9]We base this on the assertion by Lingua's authors that Lingua beat Polyglot experimentally (see GitHub). We have not verified Polyglot's performance; it was unsuitable as a baseline for us, as it cannot predict token-level labels.

	German *146*	English *130*	Overall *276*
Lingua	70.9	55.7	64.9
GPT-4	92.8	92.0	92.4
Denglisch	74.9	72.0	73.6
eBERT	80.0	80.3	84.1
gBERT	85.4	81.5	83.7
mBRET	84.4	83.7	84.1
TS	84.5	82.8	83.7
tsBERT	89.3	89.1	88.8

Table 7: IH disambiguation results (in F_t)

(3) Tweet: I don't get $_{\text{IH}}$was er damit erreichen will. **Translation:** I don't get what he wants to achieve with that.
(4) Tweet: fang über nächstes jahr mit abi an but no problem zeugnis durchschnitt $_{\text{IH}}$was 1.5 letztes halb jahr wird schlechter sein dieses halbjahr tho cuz mental health yk **Translation:** no problem the average result of the end-of-year report was 1.5 last half-year will be worse this half-year tho cuz [because] mental health yk [you know]

Table 8: Examples from our IH testset

or the word was so infrequent in German–English code-switching in the target sense that it didn't occur in the top 100 tweets (e.g. English "stark"). We found 29 true IHs with at least one tweet of true English and German usage[10]. For each IH, 2-10 tweets were added to the testset. We attempted to balance the tweets between German and English occurrences and prioritised examples where the IH was at a borderline of an island. This resulted in a testset of 253 tweets with 276 IH tokens, 47% of which were in English.

Results are given in Table 7. For IHs, our rule-based TS (overall F_t=83.7) and neural tsBERT (overall F_t=88.8) outperform trained Denglisch (overall F_t=73.6) and Lingua (overall F_t=64.9; all Denglisch and Lingua results significantly different from all other systems). For the BERT systems, in all categories, eBERT is indistinguishable from mBERT, which is indistinguishable from gBERT. TS is indistinguishable from eBERT, gBERT, and mBERT in all categories. Overall and for German tokens, it is also indistinguishable from tsBERT. GPT-4 and tsBERT are indistinguishable in all categories (p=0.21, 0.13, 0.08).

The "strong baseline" GPT-4 and our neural system tsBERT turn out to be best at the hard task of disambiguating these words. Table 8 gives two examples for the IH 'was'. In German, this string is a WH-pronoun, whilst in English it is the past form of 'to be'. All systems except Lingua correctly identify (3) as German. In contrast, the only system to identify the IH in (4) as English is GPT-4.

[10] Namely *war, bin, bad, see, die, man, was, made, ran, toll, falls, hat, dick, drum, links, still, these, fast, hell, handy, fort, positives, tag, sage, seen, lose, rum, will, not*

8 Conclusion

We have presented two methods for German–English code-switching identification. Our rule-based system enabled us to collect the largest corpus of naturally occurring code-switching. Our BERT-based model, trained on this corpus and fine-tuned on human-annotated data, established SoTA on an existing German–English benchmark. We also established SoTA on our newly formed corpus using token and entity-based metrics. A post-analysis on interlingual homographs revealed that neural language models are the best systems for disambiguating these words. Overall, our study combines two aspects we think are important for the future of code-switching: a) the use of large-scale empirical methods on naturally occurring data and b) an analytic interest in fine-grained linguistic phenomena.

9 Future work

We are interested in providing a more objective definition of loanwording, as opposed to genuine code-switching, in the light of the debate in linguistics, lexicography and cognitive science. Our future contribution to this topic will centre around the fact that the distinction can only be made *in context*, more specifically in island-context. Therefore, it is useful to employ the best tool for island detection, and we have demonstrated here that our systems for German–English are very effective. Frequency also plays a role; loanwords which can be considered part of German will be far more frequent in German matrix text than any naturally occurring English words in English islands. We release frequency-sorted data of the top 10,000 islands of each island length in the TONGUESWITCHER Corpus. This may serve as a starting point for empirical studies of this challenge.

Limitations

There may be some bias in our gold standard due to the pre-selection of tweets found by TS. In the future, we plan to create a new gold standard entirely from scratch, even if this requires more annotation effort and guidelines. Our current definition relies on annotators' intuition too much.

Evaluation of systems such as ours is also difficult, partly because code-switching language identification is subjective. In particular, annotators and NLP systems often introduce English bias (Anastasopoulos and Neubig, 2020; Garrido-Muñoz et al., 2021).

In our rule-based system, we do not implement a named entity recognizer. As such, in our corpus, named entities containing English words are often incorrectly labelled as English.

The quality of the multilingual part of speech tagger, alongside its tokenization, also constrains our method. Tagging all our input tweets with this tagger required intensive GPU computation.

In terms of our mixed identification methods, our TONGUESWITCHER system over-segments words (e.g. verrate), which is a particular problem for misspelt words.

Ethics Statement

Working with and releasing large corpora of social media posts raises data privacy concerns. We do not collect any personal information about the authors of the tweets. We release our corpus to the research community only.

Acknowledgements

We thank Alexander Bleistein and Constanze Leeb for their early support of this work. We also thank Louis Cotgrove, Chris Bryant, Li Nguyen and our three reviewers for their insightful comments.

References

Martine Adda-Decker, Thomas Pellegrini, Eric Bilinski, and Gilles Adda. 2008. Developments of "Lëtzebuergesch" Resources for Automatic Speech Processing and Linguistic Studies. In *Proceedings of the Sixth International Conference on Language Resources and Evaluation (LREC'08)*, Marrakech, Morocco. European Language Resources Association (ELRA).

Gustavo Aguilar and Thamar Solorio. 2020. From English to Code-Switching: Transfer Learning with Strong Morphological Clues. In *Proceedings of the 58th Annual Meeting of the Association for Computational Linguistics*, pages 8033–8044, Online. Association for Computational Linguistics.

Alan Akbik, Duncan Blythe, and Roland Vollgraf. 2018. Contextual string embeddings for sequence labeling. In *COLING 2018, 27th International Conference on Computational Linguistics*, pages 1638–1649.

Antonios Anastasopoulos and Graham Neubig. 2020. Should All Cross-Lingual Embeddings Speak English? In *Proceedings of the 58th Annual Meeting of the Association for Computational Linguistics*, pages 8658–8679, Online. Association for Computational Linguistics.

Chris Biemann, Gerhard Heyer, Uwe Quasthoff, and Matthias Richter. 2007. The Leipzig corpora collection-monolingual corpora of standard size. *Proceedings of Corpus Linguistic*, 2007.

Matt Bierner. 2022. Urban Dictionary List. Original-date: 2016-03-10T07:51:42Z.

Sabine Brants, Stefanie Dipper, Silvia Hansen, Wolfgang Lezius, and George Smith. 2002. The tiger treebank. In *Proceedings of the workshop on treebanks and linguistic theories*, volume 168, pages 24–41.

Tom B. Brown, Benjamin Mann, Nick Ryder, Melanie Subbiah, Jared Kaplan, Prafulla Dhariwal, Arvind Neelakantan, Pranav Shyam, Girish Sastry, Amanda Askell, Sandhini Agarwal, Ariel Herbert-Voss, Gretchen Krueger, Tom Henighan, Rewon Child, Aditya Ramesh, Daniel M. Ziegler, Jeffrey Wu, Clemens Winter, Christopher Hesse, Mark Chen, Eric Sigler, Mateusz Litwin, Scott Gray, Benjamin Chess, Jack Clark, Christopher Berner, Sam McCandlish, Alec Radford, Ilya Sutskever, and Dario Amodei. 2020. Language Models are Few-Shot Learners. ArXiv:2005.14165 [cs].

Yanqing Chen and Steven Skiena. 2014. Building sentiment lexicons for all major languages. In *Proceedings of the 52nd Annual Meeting of the Association for Computational Linguistics (Short Papers)*, pages 383–389.

Jacob Cohen. 1960. A coefficient of agreement for nominal scales. *Educational and psychological measurement*, 20(1):37–46.

DeepsetAI. 2019. bert-base-german-cased · Hugging Face.

Margaret Deuchar. 2020. Code-Switching in Linguistics: A Position Paper. *Languages*, 5(2):22. Number: 2 Publisher: Multidisciplinary Digital Publishing Institute.

Jacob Devlin, Ming-Wei Chang, Kenton Lee, and Kristina Toutanova. 2019. BERT: Pre-training of Deep Bidirectional Transformers for Language Understanding. In *Proceedings of the 2019 Conference of the North American Chapter of the Association for Computational Linguistics: Human Language Technologies, Volume 1 (Long and Short Papers)*, pages 4171–4186, Minneapolis, Minnesota. Association for Computational Linguistics.

Ton Dijkstra, Jonathan Grainger, and Walter JB Van Heuven. 1999. Recognition of cognates and interlingual homographs: The neglected role of phonology. *Journal of Memory and language*, 41(4):496–518.

A. Seza Doğruöz, Sunayana Sitaram, Barbara E. Bullock, and Almeida Jacqueline Toribio. 2021. A Survey of Code-switching: Linguistic and Social Perspectives for Language Technologies. In *Proceedings of the 59th Annual Meeting of the Association for Computational Linguistics and the 11th International Joint Conference on Natural Language Processing (Volume 1: Long Papers)*, pages 1654–1666, Online. Association for Computational Linguistics.

Luna Filipović and John A Hawkins. 2019. The complex adaptive system principles model for bilingualism: Language interactions within and across bilingual minds. *International Journal of Bilingualism*, 23(6):1223–1248.

W Nelson Francis and Henry Kucera. 1964. A standard corpus of present-day edited american english, for use with digital computers. *Brown University, Providence*, 2.

Ismael Garrido-Muñoz, Arturo Montejo-Ráez, Fernando Martínez-Santiago, and L. Alfonso Ureña-López. 2021. A Survey on Bias in Deep NLP. *Applied Sciences*, 11(7):3184. Number: 7 Publisher: Multidisciplinary Digital Publishing Institute.

David W Green and Jubin Abutalebi. 2013. Language control in bilinguals: The adaptive control hypothesis. *Journal of cognitive psychology*, 25(5):515–530.

François Grosjean and Ping Li. 2013. *The psycholinguistics of bilingualism*. John Wiley & Sons.

François Grosjean. 2010. *Bilingual: Life and Reality*. Harvard University Press.

Yogesh Gupta, Ghanshyam Raghuwanshi, and Aprna Tripathi. 2021. A new methodology for language identification in social media code-mixed text. In *Advanced Machine Learning Technologies and Applications: Proceedings of AMLTA 2020*, pages 243–254. Springer.

Richard Jackson Harris and Elizabeth Marie McGhee Nelson. 1992. Bilingualism: Not the exception any more. In Richard Jackson Harris, editor, *Cognitive Processing in Bilinguals*, volume 83 of *Advances in Psychology*, pages 3–14. North-Holland.

Paul Hemetsberger. 2023. dict.cc | German-English dictionary.

Aravind K. Joshi. 1982. Processing of sentences with intra-sentential code-switching. In *Coling 1982: Proceedings of the Ninth International Conference on Computational Linguistics*.

Armand Joulin, Edouard Grave, Piotr Bojanowski, Matthijs Douze, Hérve Jégou, and Tomas Mikolov. 2016a. FastText.zip: Compressing text classification models. *arXiv preprint arXiv:1612.03651*.

Armand Joulin, Edouard Grave, Piotr Bojanowski, and Tomas Mikolov. 2016b. Bag of Tricks for Efficient Text Classification. *arXiv preprint arXiv:1607.01759*.

Nane Kratzke. 2022. Monthly Samples of German Tweets. 10.5281/zenodo.7528718.

Nane Kratzke. 2023. Monthly Samples of German Tweets. 10.5281/zenodo.7708787.

Weizhe Lin and Bill Byrne. 2022. Retrieval Augmented Visual Question Answering with Outside Knowledge. ArXiv:2210.03809 [cs].

Dau-Cheng Lyu, Tien-Ping Tan, Eng Siong Chng, and Haizhou Li. 2010. Seame: a mandarin-english code-switching speech corpus in south-east asia. In *Eleventh Annual Conference of the International Speech Communication Association*.

Manuel Mager, Ozlem Cetinoglu, and Katharina Kann. 2019. Subword-Level Language Identification for Intra-Word Code-Switching. ArXiv:1904.01989 [cs].

Deepthi Mave, Suraj Maharjan, and Thamar Solorio. 2018. Language Identification and Analysis of Code-Switched Social Media Text. In *Proceedings of the Third Workshop on Computational Approaches to Linguistic Code-Switching*, pages 51–61, Melbourne, Australia. Association for Computational Linguistics.

Ines Montani and Matthew Honnibal. 2018. Prodigy: A new annotation tool for radically efficient machine teaching. *Artificial Intelligence*.

P. Muysken. 2000. *Bilingual Speech: A Typology of Code-Mixing*. Cambridge University Press.

C. Myers-Scotton. 1997. *Duelling Languages: Grammatical Structure in Codeswitching*. Clarendon Press.

Ravindra Nayak and Raviraj Joshi. 2022. L3Cube-HingCorpus and HingBERT: A code mixed Hindi-English dataset and BERT language models. In *Proceedings of the WILDRE-6 Workshop within the 13th Language Resources and Evaluation Conference*, pages 7–12, Marseille, France. European Language Resources Association.

Dong Nguyen and Leonie Cornips. 2016. Automatic Detection of Intra-Word Code-Switching. In *Proceedings of the 14th SIGMORPHON Workshop on Computational Research in Phonetics, Phonology, and Morphology*, pages 82–86, Berlin, Germany. Association for Computational Linguistics.

Li Nguyen and Christopher Bryant. 2020. CanVEC - the Canberra Vietnamese-English Code-switching Natural Speech Corpus. In *Proceedings of the Twelfth Language Resources and Evaluation Conference*, pages 4121–4129, Marseille, France. European Language Resources Association.

Li Nguyen, Christopher Bryant, Sana Kidwai, and Theresa Biberauer. 2021. Automatic Language Identification in Code-Switched Hindi-English Social Media Text. *Journal of Open Humanities Data*, 7:7.

OnTheWorldMap. 2023. Maps of all cities of the World | List of all cities in the World alphabetically.

OpenAI. 2023. GPT-4 Technical Report. _eprint: 2303.08774.

Doreen Osmelak and Shuly Wintner. 2023. The denglisch corpus of German-English code-switching. In *Proceedings of the 5th Workshop on Research in Computational Linguistic Typology and Multilingual NLP*, pages 42–51, Dubrovnik, Croatia. Association for Computational Linguistics.

Slav Petrov, Dipanjan Das, and Ryan McDonald. 2012. A universal part-of-speech tagset. In *Proceedings of the Eighth International Conference on Language Resources and Evaluation (LREC'12)*, pages 2089–2096, Istanbul, Turkey. European Language Resources Association (ELRA).

Shana Poplack. 1980. Sometimes i'll start a sentence in spanish y termino en espaÑol: toward a typology of code-switching1. *Linguistics*, 18(7-8):581–618.

Lance Ramshaw and Mitch Marcus. 1995. Text chunking using transformation-based learning. In *Third Workshop on Very Large Corpora*.

Jason Riesa and Ivan Giuliani. 2013. Compact language detector 2.

Shruti Rijhwani, Royal Sequiera, Monojit Choudhury, Kalika Bali, and Chandra Shekhar Maddila. 2017. Estimating Code-Switching on Twitter with a Novel Generalized Word-Level Language Detection Technique. In *Proceedings of the 55th Annual Meeting of the Association for Computational Linguistics*, volume 1, pages 1971–1982, Vancouver, Canada. Association for Computational Linguistics.

Younes Samih, Suraj Maharjan, Mohammed Attia, Laura Kallmeyer, and Thamar Solorio. 2016. Multilingual Code-switching Identification via LSTM Recurrent Neural Networks. In *Proceedings of the Second Workshop on Computational Approaches to Code Switching*, pages 50–59, Austin, Texas. Association for Computational Linguistics.

Sebastin Santy, Anirudh Srinivasan, and Monojit Choudhury. 2021. BERTologiCoMix: How does code-mixing interact with multilingual BERT? In *Proceedings of the Second Workshop on Domain Adaptation for NLP*, pages 111–121, Kyiv, Ukraine. Association for Computational Linguistics.

Uwe Seidel. 2010. The usage and integration of English loanwords in German a corpus-based study of anglicisms in Der Spiegel magazine from 1990–2010. Master's thesis, The University of Alabama, United States – Alabama. ISBN: 9781124456560 Publication Title: ProQuest Dissertations and Theses.

Peter M. Stahl. 2023. pemistahl/lingua-py. Original-date: 2021-07-13T09:52:34Z.

Jeanine Treffers-Daller. 2022. The simple view of borrowing and code-switching. *International Journal of Bilingualism*. Publisher: Sage.

Christian Wartena. 2019. A probabilistic morphology model for German lemmatization. In *Proceedings of the 15th Conference on Natural Language Processing (KONVENS 2019)*, pages 40–49.

Robin Elise Weiss. 2022a. Top 1,000 Baby Boy Names. Section: Verywell.

Robin Elise Weiss. 2022b. Top 1,000 Baby Girl Names. Section: Verywell.

A Appendix

A.1 Corpus examples by algorithm step

1	Sagt ein(e) Head(in) of research! Researchen Sie mal ein bisschen mehr
2	habn Match mit einer, bin einfach unfähig, dein a man with a hat, ehem. Schädling
3	Freigabeworkflow für PR Manager sind das nächste Product Highlight für Insta u Twitter.
4	ich bin grade in einem chat am shittalken mit einem äußerst platonischen freund
5	Der Vorstand traf sich letztes Wochenende zum jährlichen Arbeitsweekend, dieses Mal in Thun.
6	Danke ich hänge die dritte Woche mit einer Nervenwurzelentzündung durch; Schmerzen trotz starker Medikation tlw from the hell Physio ist gut
7	joko in diesem fußball fit lebt immer noch rent free in my mind wie schön

Table 9: Example of tokens classified in each step

.

A.2 Training hyperparameters

We use the masked language modelling objective presented by Devlin et al. (2019). We train using 4 NVIDIA A100 GPUs, for approximately 30 hours per GPU. We use a batch size of 32, which amounted to 191,950 steps. We use a learning rate of 1e-4 with a warmup of 10,000 steps followed by linear decay, $\beta = (0.9, 0.999)$ and weight decay $= 0.01$.

To learn the classification, we train for 3 epochs using a learning rate of 3e-5, batch size of 16 and weight decay $= 0.01$.

A.3 GPT-4 prompt

```
Sentence: {tweet} Task: Fill in the following
list of words and their labels by identifying
each of the words in the sentence as English
('E'), Mixed ('M') or German ('G'). Punctuation
should be the same language as its surrounding
associated words. Mixed words switch between
English and German within the word. Only use
the tags 'E', 'M' or 'G'. Fill in: {token_1:
'', token_2: '', ...}
```

We found the output JSON was rarely malformed or of a different length to the input tokens, but in those cases where it was we repeated the prompt.

Towards Real-World Streaming Speech Translation for Code-Switched Speech

Belen Alastruey[1*], Matthias Sperber[2], Christian Gollan[2], Dominic Telaar[2], Tim Ng[2], Aashish Agargwal[2]
[1]TALP Research Center, Universitat Politècnica de Catalunya, Barcelona
[2]Apple
belen.alastruey@upc.edu, sperber@apple.com

Abstract

Code-switching (CS), i.e. mixing different languages in a single sentence, is a common phenomenon in communication and can be challenging in many Natural Language Processing (NLP) settings. Previous studies on CS speech have shown promising results for end-to-end speech translation (ST), but have been limited to offline scenarios and to translation to one of the languages present in the source (*monolingual transcription*).

In this paper, we focus on two essential yet unexplored areas for real-world CS speech translation: streaming settings, and translation to a third language (i.e., a language not included in the source). To this end, we extend the Fisher and Miami test and validation datasets to include new targets in Spanish and German. Using this data, we train a model for both offline and streaming ST and we establish baseline results for the two settings mentioned earlier.

1 Introduction

Speech technologies are one of the main applications of machine learning, and are currently deployed in many real-world scenarios. To ensure a adequate user experience, factors other than accuracy need to be taken into account. One of them is the ability to produce an output in real-time (streaming settings) with a low latency and another one is effectively handling the distinctive characteristics inherent in spoken language, like Code-switching. Code-switching (CS) is the phenomenon in which a speaker alternates between multiple languages in a single utterance. Due to globalization (Winata et al., 2022), it is becoming increasingly prevalent in spoken language, not only in bilingual communities but also in monolingual communities.

CS presents a challenge in various natural language processing (NLP) settings, such as automatic speech recognition (ASR), machine translation (MT), and speech translation (ST), due to the inherent complexity of dealing with two source languages, as well as the scarcity of CS training and test data (Jose et al., 2020).

Despite the relevance of ST for CS speech task, the available literature on the subject is rather limited. Nakayama et al. (2019) investigate the task defined as *monolingual transcription*, i.e. transcribing a CS utterance using words of only one language, hence translating those words that are CS. Their work proposes and compares different approaches to evaluate the stated task in Japanese-English CS to English. Other follow-up work takes a similar approach (see Section 2).

To date, however, certain essential topics, such as translation to a language not present in the CS source or streaming ST, have yet to be explored, despite its critical importance for real-world usage. The primary challenge in translating to a third language stems from the unavailability of datasets with such characteristics. Furthermore, streaming settings present further challenges: achieving a balance between latency, stability and accuracy is crucial for delivering a seamless user experience, as with any streaming task. Besides, CS tasks may require more context than monolingual ones because of the added complexity of language mixing. Thus, addressing the trade-offs between these metrics in CS streaming ST may prove to be more intricate than with monolingual data.

In our work, we resolve the two aforementioned challenges: first, the insufficiency of data and results for translation to a third language, and second, the absence of a baseline for streaming CS ST.

To alleviate the data scarcity in CS tasks, we extend Fisher (Cieri et al., 2004) and Bangor Miami CS (Deuchar et al., 2014) datasets (combined English and Spanish source and English targets) by incorporating Spanish and German targets in the test and validation sets.[1] These additions allow

*Work done during an internship at Apple.

[1]Data available at https://github.com/apple/ml-codeswitching-translations.

Proceedings of the 6th Workshop on Computational Approaches to Linguistic Code-Switching, pages 14–22
December 7, 2023 ©2023 Association for Computational Linguistics

us to evaluate the performance of our models on monolingual transcription (translation to English or Spanish), but also for the first time in CS ST into a third language (German) setting baseline results.

Furthermore, this study is the first on streaming ST for CS speech, and examines errors in transcripts generated by both offline and streaming models, considering different latency and flickering constraints, and different training techniques such as prefix-sampling. We show that prefix-sampling does not improve the model performance, and that errors in CS points appear in the same proportion streaming and offline ST. Our work sets baseline results and provides insight into the impact of CS on the performance of different models, and helping to identify potential points for future research that can contribute to the advancement of the field. To sum up, the main contributions of our work are:

- We provide baseline results for streaming ST for CS speech, contrary to previous work that focuses on offline settings.
- We provide baseline results to CS ST into a third language, contrary to previous work that focuses on monolingual transcription. To do so, we extend the Fisher-Miami CS dataset, adding Spanish and German targets.

2 Related Work

During the past few years, there has been an increasing interest in CS tasks. Prior work has focused in MT (Sinha and Thakur, 2005; Winata et al., 2021; Zhang et al., 2021; Yang et al., 2020) and ASR (Lyu et al., 2006; Ahmed and Tan, 2012; Vu et al., 2012; Johnson et al., 2017; Yue et al., 2019). However, the topic of CS in ST has been relatively under-explored, and usually concentrating only on monolingual transcription (Nakayama et al., 2019; Hamed et al., 2022; Weller et al., 2022), and relying on synthetically generated data (Nakayama et al., 2019; Huber et al., 2022).

The first work on CS ST was done by Nakayama et al. (2019). The authors analyse different architectures and training configurations for Japanese-English CS to English monolingual transcription.

Weller et al. (2022) present a similar work but in a different language pair. The authors present a CS dataset with natural English-Spanish CS text and speech sources and English text targets, gathering CS sentences in Fisher and Bangor Miami datasets. With these data, they are able to evaluate ASR and ST, although the ST setting is actually monolingual transcription. The authors explore different architectures through a two-steps training: a pretraining on non-CS data and a fine-tuning on CS data. They find that end-to-end ST models obtain higher accuracy than cascaded ones and that accuracy on CS test sets improves after the fine-tuning step without noticeably impacting performance on non-CS sets.

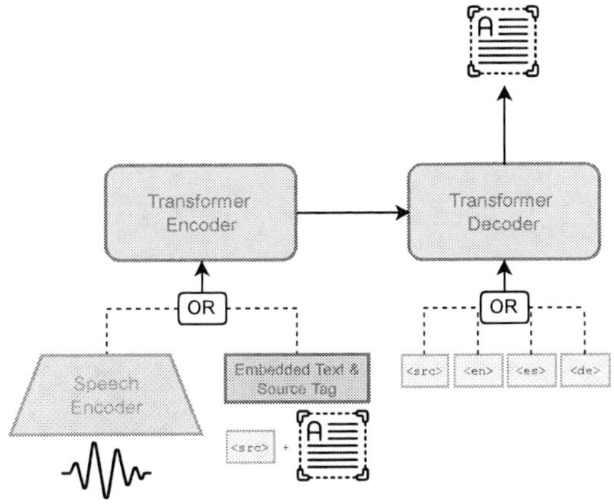

Figure 1: Proposed model architecture. The multimodal encoder supports training on both speech translation and text translation data. The tagging scheme is designed to allow generating either the (code-switched) transcript or a (monolingual) translation.

Later, Hamed et al. (2022) present a corpus for Egyptian Arabic-English CS tasks. The dataset contains text and speech CS sources, and targets in monolingual English and Egyptian Arabic. By combining these sets the authors are able to study ASR (from CS speech to CS text), as well as MT and ST. However, because of the target languages, both the ST and MT settings are actually monolingual transcription and a text-to-text variant of this task.

Finally, Huber et al. (2022) present LAST, a language-agnostic model for ST and ASR that aims to replace acoustic language ID gated pipelines by a unique CS model. However, their work focuses on inter-sentential CS (when a CS happens just at sentence boundaries) using synthetic data.

3 Model

We adopt the multimodal model design proposed by Ye et al. (2021) for speech translation (Figure 1). This model supports speech transcription, speech translation, and text translation, and leverages paired data of all three tasks through multitask training. Similar to Ye et al. (2021), we extract speech representations using a pretrained wav2vec 2.0 BASE model (Baevski et al., 2020)[2] which results in 20ms per frame. To compute downsampled speech representations, wav2vec 2.0 applies a stack of three convolutional layers, resulting in 160ms per frame: each layer has a kernel of 3 and a stride of 2. To extract text representations for multitask text-to-text training, we simply use a 1024-dimensional embedding layer. Next we attach an encoder-decoder Transformer (Vaswani et al., 2017) with pre-layer normalization, a hidden dimension of 1024, dropout of 0.1, five encoder layers and three decoder layers. The input to the encoder is either the downsampled speech representations, or the embedded source text. In the decoder, we use 1024-dimensional LSTMs (Hochreiter and Schmidhuber, 1997) instead of self-attention which obtained better results in preliminary investigations.

The model is trained in a multi-task fashion, where we sum the losses of the transcription task, text translation task, speech translation task, as well as a CTC loss (Graves et al., 2006) applied on top of the full encoder. Tasks are weighted equally.

Importantly to our work, we use a shared decoder to perform either transcription or translation, with a language tag indicating the desired output language for ST, or the tag `<src>` to generate a transcript. Note that the transcript will be equivalent to the translation in the source language for monolingual sentences, but a special token for transcripts is needed to account for CS sentences.

To employ our model in a streaming setting, we use the re-translation technique (Niehues et al., 2018; Weller et al., 2021). This technique retranslates the utterance to update its prior prediction as additional information is received. To control the trade-off between latency, flickering, and accuracy, we set a mask on the last k sub-words of the prior prediction, allowing the model to rewrite only that part of the output. Therefore, a high k allows the model to rewrite the whole prediction, obtaining a high accuracy but poor latency and flickering scores, and on the contrary, setting $k = 0$ forces the model to commit to the previous prediction, hindering the accuracy but leading to no flickering and the lowest possible latency. Section 5 contains experiments to obtain the appropriate k.

[2]Specifically, `facebook/wav2vec2-base-960h` via `Hugging Face Transformers` (Wolf et al., 2020).

4 Datasets

Pre-training			
Dataset	Language	Source	#Samples
MuST-C	En-Es	Original	270 000
	En-De	Original	234 000
CoVoST	Es-En	Original	64 351
	De-En	Original	71 831
	En-De	Original	232 958
	Es-De	Synthetic	64 351
	De-Es	Synthetic	71 831
Fisher	Es-En	Original	130 600
Miami	Es-En	Original	6 489
Fine-tuning			
Dataset	Language	Source	#Samples
Fisher	En/Es-En	Original	7 398
	En/Es-Es	Synthetic	7 398
	En/Es-De	Synthetic	7 398

Table 1: Summary of the training data used during our two-steps training.

Although our primary target is CS speech, we train our models on both monolingual and CS data due to the scarcity of the latter. In particular, we use the following datsets:

Bangor Miami (Deuchar et al., 2014): The dataset contains recorded conversations between bilingual English/Spanish speakers in casual settings, with a high proportion of naturally occurring code-switched speech. The recordings were obtained using small digital recorders worn on belts, resulting in low audio quality with background noise. We use the splits for CS ST defined by Weller et al. (2022).

Fisher (Cieri et al., 2004): The dataset was collected for ASR by pairing Spanish speakers located in the US and Canada through phone calls. Although it is not a CS focused dataset, it contains a significant amount of CS utterances due to the speakers being in English-speaking contexts. The recording was done through phone recordings in 2004, which makes it a noisy ASR dataset, although less noisy than Miami. We use the splits for CS ST defined by Weller et al. (2022).

CoVoST (Wang et al., 2020): A multilingual and diversified ST datset based on the Common Voice project (Ardila et al., 2020). This dataset includes language pairs from multiple languages into English, and it includes low resource languages.

MuST-C (Di Gangi et al., 2019): A dataset for ST research. It is a large-scale, multi-language dataset that includes speech recordings from English TED Talks and corresponding human transcriptions and translations. The dataset covers translation from English to many languages. The recording context (TED talks) makes it a quality clean dataset.

4.1 Data Collection

Miami and Fisher CS sets consist of a source in CS En/Es, along with CS transcripts and monolingual English transcripts as targets. To expand the range of languages included, we include the monolingual Spanish transcript, as well as a new language not used in the source, namely German. By including this new language, we will be able to assess the performance of our models in pure speech translation, as opposed to previous work on monolingual transcription. Hence, we collect data for Miami and Fisher CS test and validation sets in German and Spanish. The data was translated by professional translators who were native speakers in the respective target languages.

4.2 Data Usage and Preparation

Following (Weller et al., 2022), we divide our experiments in two steps: (1) pre-training on monolingual data and, (2) fine-tuning on code switched data.

During the pretraining we use CoVoST (Es-En, De-En, En-De splits), MuST-C (En-Es, En-De splits) and the non-CS sets in Fisher and Miami datasets (Es-En). Additionally, we use MarianMT [3] model from Hugging Face Transformers package (Wolf et al., 2020) to translate CoVoST De-En set to Spanish, and Es-En set to German, obtaining data for the pairs Es-De and De-Es. During the finetuning step, we focus on Fisher's code-switched (Es/En-En) training set (7389 samples) and extend it for Es/En-Es and Es/En-De translation using the MarianMT model to translate English targets to German and Spanish.

We use 200 epochs for the pretraining stage and 100 epochs for finetuning. We use the Adam (Kingma and Ba, 2015) optimizer with $\alpha = 5e{-4}$, β_1=0.9, β_2=0.98. For pretraining, we use an inverted square root learning schedule with 500 warm-up steps. For finetuning a tri-stage schedule with 12.5% warm-up steps, 12.5% hold steps, and 75% decay steps.

For the experiments with prefix sampling, we use the same training set but prefix-sampling half of the instances following the approach presented by Niehues et al. (2018). For a summary of the data used on each step see Table 1.

[3] We manually clean the translations afterward.

5 Experiments

Our experiments follow four main directions: (1) Finding a reasonable k to control re-translation flickering and latency, (2) studying the occurrence of errors around CS switching points, (3) analyzing the usefulness of prefix-sampling and (4) establishing baseline numbers for translation to a third language and for streaming tasks for CS speech, including transcription, monolingual translation, and translation.

To evaluate our models we will use three different metrics. To measure the model accuracy we use BLEU (Papineni et al., 2002) with SACREBLEU (Post, 2018) and a beam size of 5. To evaluate the lag between model input and output we use Average Lag (AL, Ma et al. (2019)), and to measure the flickering we use Normalized Erasure (NE, Arivazhagan et al. (2020)). Additionally, we use WER to evaluate ASR performance.

5.1 Metrics Trade-off and k Analysis

As described in Section 3, our model uses re-translation (Niehues et al., 2018) to generate a streaming output. Following the re-translation approach, we mask the last k sub-words of an output when predicting the following one. We evaluate latency, flickering and accuracy metrics for $k \in \{0, 5, 10, 15, 20, 25, 30, +\infty\}$. As shown in Figure 2, results are consistent for Fisher and Miami datasets and across the different language pairs. All metrics increase together with k. However the gap between 30 and $+\infty$ is much higher in AL and NE than in BLEU. BLEU shows improvements for higher k but it is more stable than the other metrics. For this reason, we henceforth use $k = 15$, since BLEU scores are close to optimal while NE and AL are still low.

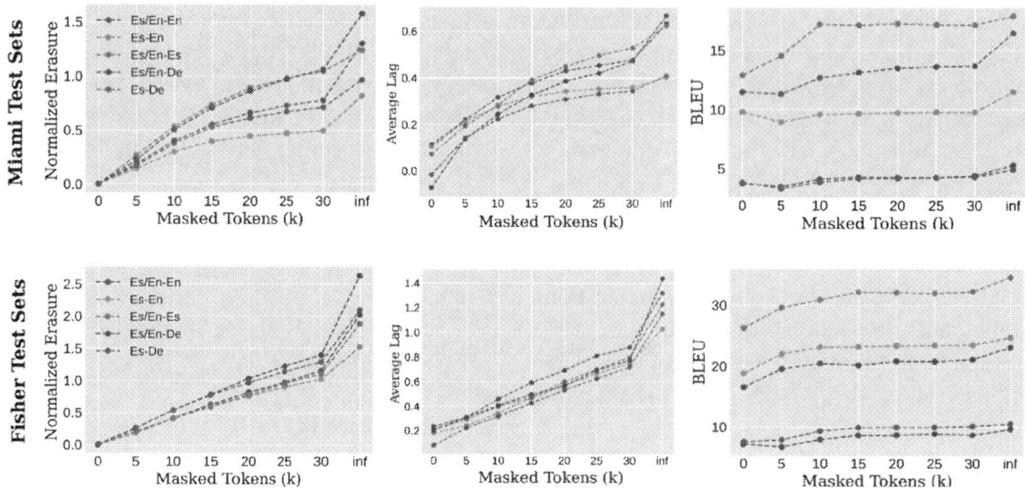

Figure 2: BLEU, Normalized Erasure and Average Lag scores under different streaming constraints. In each prediction step, the model has to commit to the previous prediction except for the last k tokens (sub-words). We evaluate the performance of the model for $k \in \{0, 5, 10, 15, 20, 25, 30, +\infty\}$.

		Fisher					Miami				
		CS			Mono.		CS			Mono.	
	Model	En	Es	De	En	De	En	Es	De	En	De
BLEU(↑)	FISHER CS	23.3	30.3	12.2	22.9	12.8	19.7	16.0	6.4	11.9	5.9
	FISHER CS W/ PREFIXES	23.7	30.9	12.2	22.0	13.0	22.1	18.3	7.0	13.9	6.7
	(WELLER ET AL., 2022) †	25.6	-	-	26.1	-	14.7	-	-	17.6	-
AL(↓)	FISHER CS	0.6	0.5	0.6	0.5	0.5	0.5	0.4	0.4	0.4	0.3
	FISHER CS W/ PREFIXES	0.5	0.5	0.5	0.5	0.5	0.5	0.5	0.5	0.4	0.4
NE(↓)	FISHER CS	1.2	1.2	1.3	1.1	1.4	1.2	1.2	1.4	1.0	1.2
	FISHER CS W/ PREFIXES	1.2	1.0	1.2	1.2	1.0	1.0	1.0	1.1	1.6	0.8

Table 2: BLEU, Average Lag (seconds), and Normalized Erasure scores in streaming **Speech Translation**, for trainings with and without prefix sampling. In every experiment we set $k = 15$. †: Best results reported by Weller et al. (2022) in offline ST.

5.2 Code-Switches and Errors in Predictions

We hypothesize that CS points are points of high linguistic uncertainty and, therefore, comparably hard to predict or translate. Hence, words around CS switch points would tend to be predicted wrong. We analyze this phenomenon for an ASR task comparing offline and streaming models with the aim of: (1) confirming or denying that more wrong predictions happen near CS points, (2) studying how offline or streaming ST can affect the conclusion of (1).

We analyze the predicted transcripts of our model in the ASR [4] task on Fisher CS test set under three different inference constraints: a streaming model with $k = 0$ (which has no flickering and the lowest possible latency), a streaming model with $k = 15$ (which we have found to be a reasonable choice to obtain a better accuracy without a critical effect on flickering and latency) and an offline model (which would be equivalent to a streaming model where $k = +\infty$). We establish a recall-based metric and count words in the reference transcript as predicted right if the word appears in the predicted transcript, and as predicted wrong otherwise. We study the proportion of words that are predicted right and their distance (in words) to a CS point. Hence, those words at a distance of 1 are right before or after a CS, and so on. To do so, we define the $Recall$ at distance d as:

$$R(d) = \frac{right\_pred(d)}{right\_pred(d) + wrong\_pred(d)} \quad (1)$$

[4] Note that this can only be evaluated in ASR (not ST), because of the need of a CS target.

	Model	Fisher CS En	Fisher CS Es	Fisher CS De	Fisher Mono. En	Fisher Mono. De	Miami CS En	Miami CS Es	Miami CS De	Miami Mono. En	Miami Mono. De
BLEU(↑)	FISHER CS	41.8	45.8	24.27	35.5	23.7	49.4	41.8	19.9	31.7	19.5
	FISHER CS W/ PREFIXES	41.8	44.1	22.9	35.7	22.5	48.1	38.7	19.1	32.2	18.9
AL(↓)	FISHER CS	0.4	0.4	0.4	0.4	0.4	0.2	0.2	0.2	0.2	0.2
	FISHER CS W/ PREFIXES	0.4	0.4	0.4	0.4	0.4	0.2	0.2	0.2	0.2	0.2
NE(↓)	FISHER CS	0.06	0.04	0.06	0.04	0.04	0.00	0.00	0.00	0.00	0.00
	FISHER CS W/ PREFIXES	0.04	0.04	0.06	0.04	0.04	0.00	0.00	0.00	0.00	0.00

Table 3: BLEU, Average Lag (seconds), and Normalized Erasure scores in streaming **Text Translation**, for trainings with and without prefix sampling. In every experiment we set $k = 15$.

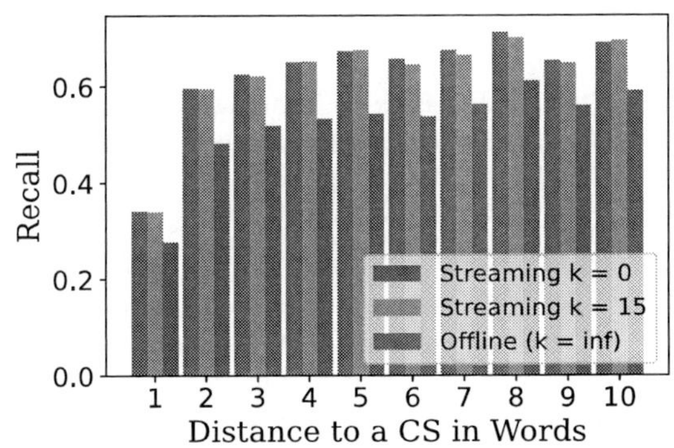

Figure 3: Analysis of errors in the prediction of words for different distances to a CS point under different inference constraints.

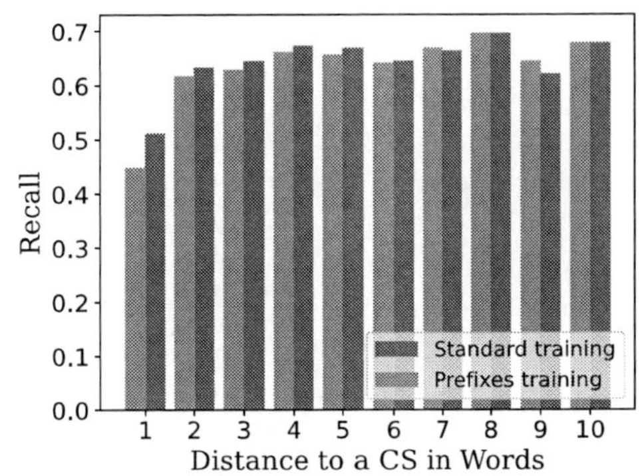

Figure 4: Analysis of errors in the prediction of words for different distances to a CS point, with and without prefix-sampling the training set.

The results in Figure 3 show that CS points impact the model's accuracy. Those words at a distance of 1 are predicted wrong in the highest proportion for every model. However, starting from $d = 2$, the recall increases only slightly, or stays close to constant, so the effect of a CS does not last long. Secondly, we also see that although the streaming setting with $k = 0$ has an overall worse recall, having less available context when making the predictions does not affect those words close to CS points more than those that are not. In particular, we see that the drop between $d = 2$ and $d = 1$ is lower for the streaming model with $k = 0$. This indicates that, contrary to what we expected, the lack of context in streaming ST does not have a negative impact on CS points, and therefore, the model needs the same context to properly predict CS or not CS words.

5.3 Usefulness of Prefix-sampling

A frequently used technique to train streaming models consists of sampling prefixes from part of the training data. We study the impact of using this technique in accuracy, latency, and flickering metrics and its impact on errors around CS points.

To analyze the usefulness of this training strategy, we compare a model trained on the Fisher CS set against a model trained on the same set but substituting half of the complete utterances by prefixes. As shown in Table 2, prefix-sampling produced an improvement in BLEU scores, especially in Miami test sets (up to +2.4). Surprisingly, this training strategy that aims to improve the performance in latency or flickering worsens the Average Lag scores and does not significantly impact Normalized Erasure.

Furthermore, we study whether prefix sampling impacts the accuracy of the predictions around CS points. In Figure 4, we use the same *recall* metric as in Section 5.2 to compare both models. We see that prefix training degrades the accuracy of the predictions around CS points, especially in those words at a distance of 1, where the recall drops from 0.51 in the standard training to 0.45 in prefixes training.

	Model	Fisher CS	Fisher Mono	Miami CS	Miami Mono
WER(↓)	FISHER CS	34.9	29.8	63.3	63.5
	FISHER CS W/ PREFIXES	35.4	29.9	60.6	58.1
AL(↓)	FISHER CS	1.0	0.8	0.8	0.6
	FISHER CS W/ PREFIXES	0.5	0.4	0.5	0.3
NE(↓)	FISHER CS	1.2	1.0	1.2	1.1
	FISHER CS W/ PREFIXES	1.1	0.8	1.2	0.6

Table 4: WER, Average Lag (seconds), and Normalized Erasure scores in streaming **Automatic Speech Recognition**, for trainings with and without prefix sampling. In every experiment we set $k = 15$.

5.4 Performance Analysis

After the experiments described in previous sections, we have found that using prefix-sampling does not lead to a noticeable performance improvement. Furthermore, we have seen that masking the last 15 sub-words in each step during the translation of a sentence shows an optimal trade-off between the different evaluation metrics. Since there is no previous work in CS streaming ST, we can not fairly compare our results to previous work, and therefore we aim to set baseline numbers. However we compare the BLEU scores of our model to the scores obtained by (Weller et al., 2022) for offline ST to English (Table 2), to analyse if the performance drop between offline and streaming ST is reasonable. As expected, our streaming model suffers a performance degradation in most of the test sets compared to the offline model in previous work. However, CS ST to English in the Miami dataset obtains an improvement of up to +7.4 BLEU.

When analyzing the performance of German translation we see that there is an important drop compared to English and Spanish translation (both present on the source). CS Speech Translation is commonly studied and evaluated just in translation to languages present in the source, therefore we believe that the performance drop in German is a relevant finding that shows the importance of not relying just on monolingual transcription when aiming for CS ST and sets a baseline result for further work in translation to a third language. Regarding Average Lag and Normalized Erasure, we present our results as a baseline, since previous work using Fisher and Miami datasets was done in offline tasks. However, to have an estimation of the quality of our model in these metrics, we compare our scores with the ones obtained by Weller et al. (2021) on MuST-C data, which are over 1 for both metrics. In Table 2, we can see that we obtain similar scores, therefore we conclude that the performance of our model is reasonable regarding flickering and lag.

5.5 Results in Machine Translation and Automatic Speech Recognition

Although the main scope of this work in Speech Translation, we evaluate our models for Machine Translation and Automatic Speech Recognition too. We can easily do this given that the model we are using is multitask and allows us to work on each of the three settings by switching the the input type and properly defining the a tag to generate the output.

In Table 3 we can see the results obtained for MT. We see that, as in ST, prefix sampling does not improve AL and NE scores. Furthermore, in the case of MT using prefixes degrades the performance of the majority of the models. Regarding BLEU scores, we observe that as in ST those tasks that consist on translating to a language present in the source obtain a much higher accuracy than those where we translate to German.

In Table 4 we see the results for the ASR setting. In this case, prefix sampling does work as expected regarding AL and NE scores, being the models with prefixes the ones with lower scores. However, it still has a negative impact on the performance of the models, specially in Miami test sets. Regarding WER, the scores obtained for the Miami dataset are much worse than the ones obtained by Fisher ones, a pattern that we have not observed in translation tasks. This could be due to the fact that during the pretraining, the data used for translation tasks comes from many different datasets, allowing the model to properly learn to generalize. However, the available data with CS targets corresponds mostly to the Fisher dataset (130 600 samples), compared to only 6 487 from the Miami dataset (see Table 1 for more details on the data distribution).

6 Conclusions

In this work, we have tackled two open ends in CS ST: translation to a third language and streaming settigns. To do so, we have trained offline and streaming models for direct translation and transcription of CS speech. Furthermore, we have extended Fisher and Miami test and validation sets with new Spanish and German targets. By doing this we have been able to analyse not only monolingual transcription, but also pure translation. We have observed a drop of up to 18 BLEU points between the two settings, showcasing the importance of not relying on monolingual transcription when aiming for ST models, as has been commonly done in previous work. Given the greater complexity of translating to a third language as compared to monolingual translation, we think that incorporating additional data would be necessary to tackle the accuracy drop. However, since natural code-switched data is limited and generating synthetic data is beyond the scope of this study, we leave this for future research.

To summarize, our work presents new data, an in depth analysis of the impact of CS in the predictions, and results for streaming CS Speech Translation and translation to a third language, which can serve as a baseline for future work in a field that although relevant is still far from solved.

Limitations

Our work is limited to high-resource languages such as English, German, and Spanish. Therefore, further work needs to be done tackling low resource languages in order to achieve real-world CS translation.

References

Basem HA Ahmed and Tien-Ping Tan. 2012. Automatic speech recognition of code switching speech using 1-best rescoring. In *2012 International Conference on Asian Language Processing*, pages 137–140. IEEE.

Rosana Ardila, Megan Branson, Kelly Davis, Michael Kohler, Josh Meyer, Michael Henretty, Reuben Morais, Lindsay Saunders, Francis Tyers, and Gregor Weber. 2020. Common voice: A massively-multilingual speech corpus. In *Proceedings of the 12th Language Resources and Evaluation Conference*, pages 4218–4222, Marseille, France. European Language Resources Association.

Naveen Arivazhagan, Colin Cherry, Wolfgang Macherey, and George Foster. 2020. Re-translation versus streaming for simultaneous translation. *arXiv preprint arXiv:2004.03643*.

Alexei Baevski, Yuhao Zhou, Abdelrahman Mohamed, and Michael Auli. 2020. wav2vec 2.0: A framework for self-supervised learning of speech representations. In *Advances in Neural Information Processing Systems*, volume 33, pages 12449–12460. Curran Associates, Inc.

Christopher Cieri, David Miller, and Kevin Walker. 2004. The fisher corpus: A resource for the next generations of speech-to-text. In *Proceedings of the Fourth International Conference on Language Resources and Evaluation (LREC 2004)*, volume 4, pages 69–71.

Margaret Deuchar, Peredur Davies, Jon Russell Herring, M Carmen Parafita Couto, and Diana Carter. 2014. Building bilingual corpora. In *Advances in the Study of Bilingualism*, pages 93–110. Multilingual Matters.

Mattia A. Di Gangi, Roldano Cattoni, Luisa Bentivogli, Matteo Negri, and Marco Turchi. 2019. MuST-C: a Multilingual Speech Translation Corpus. In *Proceedings of the 2019 Conference of the North American Chapter of the Association for Computational Linguistics: Human Language Technologies, Volume 1 (Long and Short Papers)*, pages 2012–2017, Minneapolis, Minnesota. Association for Computational Linguistics.

Alex Graves, Santiago Fernández, and Jürgen Schmidhuber. 2006. Connectionist temporal classification: Labelling unsegmented sequence data with recurrent neural networks. In *Proceedings of the 23rd International Conference on Machine Learning*, pages 369–376. ACM.

Injy Hamed, Nizar Habash, Slim Abdennadher, and Ngoc Thang Vu. 2022. Arzen-st: A three-way speech translation corpus for code-switched egyptian arabic-english. *arXiv preprint arXiv:2211.12000*.

Sepp Hochreiter and Jürgen Schmidhuber. 1997. Long short-term memory. *Neural Computation*, 9(8):1735–1780.

Christian Huber, Enes Yavuz Ugan, and Alexander Waibel. 2022. Code-switching without switching: Language agnostic end-to-end speech translation.

Melvin Johnson, Mike Schuster, Quoc V Le, Maxim Krikun, Yonghui Wu, Zhifeng Chen, Nikhil Thorat, Fernanda Viegas, Martin Wattenberg, Greg Corrado, Macduff Hughes, and Jeffrey Dean. 2017. Google's multilingual neural machine translation system: Enabling zero-shot translation. *Transactions of the Association for Computational Linguistics*, 5:339–351.

Navya Jose, Bharathi Raja Chakravarthi, Shardul Suryawanshi, Elizabeth Sherly, and John P McCrae. 2020. A survey of current datasets for code-switching research. In *2020 6th international conference on advanced computing and communication systems (ICACCS)*, pages 136–141. IEEE.

Diederik P. Kingma and Jimmy Ba. 2015. Adam: A method for stochastic optimization. *International Conference on Learning Representations.*

Dau-Cheng Lyu, Ren-Yuan Lyu, Yuang-chin Chiang, and Chun-Nan Hsu. 2006. Speech recognition on code-switching among the chinese dialects. In *2006 IEEE International Conference on Acoustics Speech and Signal Processing Proceedings*, volume 1, pages I–I. IEEE.

Mingbo Ma, Liang Huang, Hao Xiong, Renjie Zheng, Kaibo Liu, Baigong Zheng, Chuanqiang Zhang, Zhongjun He, Hairong Liu, Xing Li, and et al. 2019. Stacl: Simultaneous translation with implicit anticipation and controllable latency using prefix-to-prefix framework. In *Proceedings of the 57th Annual Meeting of the Association for Computational Linguistics*, pages 3025–3036.

Sahoko Nakayama, Takatomo Kano, Andros Tjandra, Sakriani Sakti, and Satoshi Nakamura. 2019. Recognition and translation of code-switching speech utterances. In *2019 22nd Conference of the Oriental COCOSDA International Committee for the Coordination and Standardisation of Speech Databases and Assessment Techniques (O-COCOSDA)*, pages 1–6. IEEE.

Jan Niehues, Ngoc-Quan Pham, Thanh-Le Ha, Matthias Sperber, and Alex Waibel. 2018. Low-Latency Neural Speech Translation. In *Proc. Interspeech 2018*, pages 1293–1297.

Kishore Papineni, Salim Roukos, Todd Ward, and Wei-Jing Zhu. 2002. Bleu: a method for automatic evaluation of machine translation. In *Proceedings of the 40th Annual Meeting of the Association for Computational Linguistics*, pages 311–318, Philadelphia, Pennsylvania, USA. Association for Computational Linguistics.

Matt Post. 2018. A call for clarity in reporting BLEU scores. In *Proceedings of the Third Conference on Machine Translation: Research Papers*, pages 186–191, Brussels, Belgium. Association for Computational Linguistics.

R Mahesh K Sinha and Anil Thakur. 2005. Machine translation of bi-lingual hindi-english (hinglish) text. In *10th Machine Translation Summit (MT Summit X)*, pages 149–156.

Ashish Vaswani, Noam Shazeer, Niki Parmar, Jakob Uszkoreit, Llion Jones, Aidan N Gomez, Ł ukasz Kaiser, and Illia Polosukhin. 2017. Attention is all you need. In *Advances in Neural Information Processing Systems*, volume 30. Curran Associates, Inc.

Ngoc Thang Vu, Dau-Cheng Lyu, Jochen Weiner, Dominik Telaar, Tim Schlippe, Fabian Blaicher, Eng-Siong Chng, Tanja Schultz, and Haizhou Li. 2012. A first speech recognition system for mandarin-english code-switch conversational speech. In *2012 IEEE International Conference on Acoustics, Speech and Signal Processing (ICASSP)*, pages 4889–4892. IEEE.

Changhan Wang, Anne Wu, and Juan Pino. 2020. Covost 2: A massively multilingual speech-to-text translation corpus.

Orion Weller, Matthias Sperber, Christian Gollan, and Joris Kluivers. 2021. Streaming models for joint speech recognition and translation. In *Proceedings of the 16th Conference of the European Chapter of the Association for Computational Linguistics: Main Volume*, pages 2533–2539, Online. Association for Computational Linguistics.

Orion Weller, Matthias Sperber, Telmo Pires, Hendra Setiawan, Christian Gollan, Dominic Telaar, and Matthias Paulik. 2022. End-to-end speech translation for code switched speech.

Genta Indra Winata, Alham Fikri Aji, Zheng-Xin Yong, and Thamar Solorio. 2022. The decades progress on code-switching research in nlp: A systematic survey on trends and challenges. *arXiv preprint arXiv:2212.09660.*

Genta Indra Winata, Samuel Cahyawijaya, Zihan Liu, Zhaojiang Lin, Andrea Madotto, and Pascale Fung. 2021. Are multilingual models effective in code-switching? *arXiv preprint arXiv:2103.13309.*

Thomas Wolf, Lysandre Debut, Victor Sanh, Julien Chaumond, Clement Delangue, Anthony Moi, Pierric Cistac, Tim Rault, Remi Louf, Morgan Funtowicz, Joe Davison, Sam Shleifer, Patrick von Platen, Clara Ma, Yacine Jernite, Julien Plu, Canwen Xu, Teven Le Scao, Sylvain Gugger, Mariama Drame, Quentin Lhoest, and Alexander Rush. 2020. Transformers: State-of-the-art natural language processing. In *Proceedings of the 2020 Conference on Empirical Methods in Natural Language Processing: System Demonstrations*, pages 38–45, Online. Association for Computational Linguistics.

Zhen Yang, Bojie Hu, Ambyera Han, Shen Huang, and Qi Ju. 2020. Csp: Code-switching pre-training for neural machine translation. In *Proceedings of the 2020 Conference on Empirical Methods in Natural Language Processing (EMNLP)*, pages 2624–2636.

Rong Ye, Mingxuan Wang, and Lei Li. 2021. End-to-end speech translation via cross-modal progressive training. In *Interspeech*.

Xianghu Yue, Grandee Lee, Emre Yılmaz, Fang Deng, and Haizhou Li. 2019. End-to-end code-switching asr for low-resourced language pairs. In *2019 IEEE Automatic Speech Recognition and Understanding Workshop (ASRU)*, pages 972–979. IEEE.

Shuai Zhang, Jiangyan Yi, Zhengkun Tian, Jianhua Tao, and Ye Bai. 2021. Rnn-transducer with language bias for end-to-end mandarin-english code-switching speech recognition. In *2021 12th International Symposium on Chinese Spoken Language Processing (ISCSLP)*, pages 1–5. IEEE.

Language Preference for Expression of Sentiment for Nepali-English Bilingual Speakers on Social Media

Niraj Pahari and **Kazutaka Shimada**
Kyushu Institute of Technology
680-4 Kawazu, Iizuka, Fukuoka 820-8502, Japan
pahari.niraj828@mail.kyutech.jp and shimada@ai.kyutech.ac.jp

Abstract

Nepali-English code-switching (CS) has been a growing phenomenon in Nepalese society, especially in social media. The code-switching text can be leveraged to understand the socio-linguistic behaviours of the multilingual speakers. Existing studies have attempted to identify the language preference of the multilingual speakers for expressing different emotions using text in different language pairs. In this work, we aim to study the language preference of multilingual Nepali-English CS speakers while expressing sentiment in social media. We create a novel dataset for sentiment analysis using the public Nepali-English code-switched comments in YouTube. After performing the statistical study on the dataset, we find that the proportion of use of Nepali language is higher in negative comments when compared with positive comments, hence concluding the preference for using native language while expressing negative sentiment. Machine learning and transformer-based models are used as the baseline models for the dataset for sentiment classification. The dataset is released publicly.

1 Introduction

In recent years, use of social media and computer mediated communication has increased with millions of users everyday. This increase in social media has consequently increased the use of code switching (CS) or code mixing content. CS can be broadly defined as the linguistic behavior of comprehending the language that is composed of lexical items and grammatical structure from two or more languages with no change of the interlocutor or topic. Throughout this paper, we adopt the stance that the terms 'code switching' and 'code mixing' are used interchangeably to refer to the phenomenon of alternating between two or more languages within a single discourse. Although there may be subtle nuances in usage within certain linguistic contexts, for the purpose of our study, both terms are treated as synonymous and describe the same linguistic behavior.

CS was earlier associated with the spoken language, but due to the informal nature of social media, CS is also found in written form (Bali et al., 2014). The language spoken by multilingual individual is closely connected to emotion (Rajagopalan, 2004). Similarly, emotion is a driving factor for CS behaviour (Ndubuisi-Obi et al., 2019). Linguistics researchers have found that multilingual speakers have a certain language of preference for expressing their emotions (Dewaele, 2010; Rudra et al., 2016). Hence, the task of sentiment analysis and socio-linguistic studies based on the sentiment of multilingual speakers have received a lot of attention in the NLP domain. These studies have shed light on different characteristics of the society. Several studies have analyzed the language preference in multilingual societies and concluded that multilingual speakers indeed prefer their first language (L1) while conveying their emotions (Agarwal et al., 2017; Rudra et al., 2019). On the other hand, most studies in the field of code-switching have only focused on the high-resource language pairs. Up to now, far too little attention has been paid to leveraging the growing amount of Nepali-English CS text in social media and analyzing the language preference for the sentiment emotions for Nepalese multilingual community.

Sentiment analysis is a computational technique used to determine the sentiment or emotional attitude conveyed in a text. Sentiment analysis can help in obtaining insights from the opinion on certain products or subjects of interest from the users and help in planning the business strategies (Balage Filho et al., 2012). The applications and resources for sentiment analysis are mostly created for high-resourced languages in monolingual settings. However, the annotated data for monolingual data cannot handle code-switched scenarios and fails to leverage good results (Al-

Proceedings of the 6th Workshop on Computational Approaches to Linguistic Code-Switching, pages 23–32

Ghamdi et al., 2016). Several researchers have constructed the sentiment analysis dataset for code-switched scenarios (Chakravarthi et al., 2020b; Hegde et al., 2022). However, to the best of our knowledge, there is no existing sentiment analysis dataset for code-switched Nepali-English language even though Nepali-English mixed language has emerged as a dialect in the Nepalese community owing to the increasing use of English elements in Nepali conversation.(Gurung, 2019).

In this study, we collect the public comments in code-switched Nepali-English from Youtube platform and annotate them with sentiment annotations. We hypothesize two different hypotheses to analyze the relation between the language used in the comment with the sentiment of the comment and preferred language for expression of Negative or Positive sentiments. The contributions of this study are as follows:

1. We present the first standard code-switched Nepali-English dataset for sentiment analysis.
2. We perform statistical studies to identify the language preference by Nepali-English multilingual speakers in social media.
3. We provide experimental analysis of machine learning- and deep learning-based models on our code-switched dataset for sentiment analysis.

2 Related Work

The preferred language for expression of opinions by multilinguals has been studied by linguists for a long time. Fishman (1970), studies the behavior of English-Spanish bilinguals and report the use of English for professional purposes and Spanish for informal purposes like chatting. Barredo (1997) studies the pragmatic functions of Basque-Spanish code-switching and made several conclusions, one of them being: Basque-Spanish multilingual speakers normally switch to Spanish to convey humor and irony. Dewaele (2004) identifies how multilingual speakers highly use their first language for swearing and taboo words. The authors report that the multilingual speakers, while using code-switching/mixing, tend to use their first language for swearing even when the language is not understood by their interlocutor(s). Hindi and Nepali languages are closely related with each other and belong to the same language family. For Hindi-English code-switched data, Agarwal et al. (2017) analyze the English-Hindi code-switching and swearing pattern on social networks and conclude that the multilingual speakers have strong preference for swearing in the dominant language. Rudra et al. (2019) study different aspects of English-Hindi code-switching in Twitter and identify the preference of expressing negative sentiments using Hindi language is twice as much as English. In the context of Nepali-English code-switching, the study by Gurung (2019) presents a detailed socio-linguistic study on CS phenomenon in the conversations between Nepalese people. This study studies the extent, role of media, and reason in mixing of Nepali-English languages. To the best of our knowledge, there is no existing study that is focused on studying the language preference in Nepali-English code-switched scenarios.

Computational linguists have been studying code-switching for a substantial period of time. Several data resources have been created for the support of research on code-switching. Solorio et al. (2014) release code-switched dataset for language identification tasks in four language pairs, Nepali-English being one of them. They extract the sentences from social media platforms like Twitter and Facebook. Similarly, Patwa et al. (2020) release the sentiment dataset for code-switched Hindi-English and Spanish-English language pairs. The datasets constitutes of code-switched tweets with sentiment annotation among three classes: Positive, Neutral, and Negative. A considerable amount of literature has been published utilizing Youtube comments as a source of sentiment (or opinion) text for low-resource language mixed with English (Chakravarthi et al., 2020a,b; Ravikiran and Annamalai, 2021; Hegde et al., 2022). While Nepali-English code-switching has been a growing phenomenon in Nepalese society, especially in social media, there is no sentiment analysis dataset focusing on code-mixed scenarios. Hence, for the study of the language preference for expressing sentiment in code-switched Nepali-English, we create a sentiment analysis dataset and perform the tests on our hypotheses.

3 Hypotheses

In this study, we attempt to address the research question: *"Do Nepali-English speakers have a preference for using native language while expressing Negative sentiment in social media?"* We investigate this phenomenon using the proportions of words from certain languages used to express certain sentiments.

We define two hypotheses to test in this study:

Hypothesis I: There is an association between sentiment and language proportions.

Hypothesis II: The proportion of Nepali language use is higher for negative sentences than positive sentences.

The first hypothesis attempts to test whether there is any relation between the proportions of language used for expressing sentiment in social media or not. If there is an association between those two, the next hypothesis will check if the proportion of Nepali language use is higher for negative sentences than for positive sentences. The second hypothesis attempts to test the pragmatic behavior of the Nepali-English multilingual speakers in social media.

4 Dataset

4.1 Data Collection

YouTube is one of the most popular social media platform. The number of videos targeted to Nepali audiences within the platform is also increasing. The comments on these videos mostly express the sentiments of the commentator(s). The study conducted by Ndubuisi-Obi et al. (2019) determine that the topics that relate to societal tensions (e.g., political and socio-economics) affect code switching strongly. Hence, for collecting the comments from YouTube, top 10 YouTube channels in Nepal under the category "News&Politics" were listed. All the comments and their threads from top 50 videos of each channel were extracted using YouTube API. No information regarding the commentators were collected. The comments with less than 4 tokens and the comments containing Devanagari scripts were filtered out. In order to filter the non code-mixed comments, the best performing language identification model from (Pahari and Shimada, 2023) with F1-score of 94.66 was used. This model predicts one tag for each token in the sentence out of five tags: English, Nepali, named-entity, others, and ambiguous. The English and Nepali token counts were used to calculate the Code Mixing Index (CMI) (Das and Gambäck, 2014) for each sentence using the Equation 1.

Table 1: Dataset statistics showing the number of comments in each split and their total.

	Positive	Neutral	Negative	Total
Train	2,768	2,918	2875	8,561
Dev	346	365	360	1,071
Test	346	365	359	1,070
Total	3,460	3,648	3,594	10,702

$$CMI = \begin{cases} 100 * \left[1 - \frac{max(w_i)}{n-u}\right], & \text{if } n > u \\ 0, & \text{if } n = u \end{cases} \quad (1)$$

Where, w_i is the number of words in language i, n is the total number of tokens, and u is the number of language independent tokens. The CMI measures the level of mixing between the languages in the corpus. In this study, this measure is utilized to obtain the level of mixing between the languages in a comment. The comments having CMI less than 20 are filtered out to ensure the mix of English and Nepali tokens in the dataset. Furthermore, the comments often contained personally identifiable information as person names. These names were anonymized by replacing random, yet real person names. The gender of names were maintained during the replacement.

4.2 Data Annotation

The pool of filtered comments was randomized for annotation. Similar to Patwa et al. (2020), annotators were asked to annotate each comment into three categories: Positive, Neutral, and Negative. Two annotators were initially assigned to annotate all the comments. Inter-rater reliability between the two annotators using Cohen's kappa (k) (Cohen, 1960) was calculated and found it to be 0.55, suggesting moderate agreement between the annotators. The third annotator reviewed the disagreements between the annotators and resolved them by consensus. Most of the disagreements were observed on the borderline cases between neutral and other two classes. For example, *"Background sound ali low garna paryo."* (English Translation: *"Background sound should be lowered")* was marked as negative by one, while neutral by the other. This review can be interpreted as a suggestion to lower the background volume and hence can fall into the category 'Neutral' while this can also be interpreted as 'Negative' emotion as the commentator was bothered by the background sound.

The annotators annotated 10,702 comments in total. The statistics of the annotated dataset are provided in Table 1. The dataset is publicly released to encourage the research on code-mixed sentiment analysis in Nepali-English language pair.

5 Baseline Classifiers

Traditional machine learning models and transformer-based models are applied for determining the sentiments from the Youtube comments as the simple baseline. The models used in this study are listed in this section.

5.1 Machine learning-based models

We consider classical machine learning techniques namely: Support vector machine (SVM) and multi-layer perceptron (MLP) with different embeddings. These models are implemented using the sklearn library (Pedregosa et al., 2011). A 'linear' kernel is used for SVM. The number of hidden layer size is set to two in case of MLP. The following embeddings are used with these classical techniques:

5.1.1 TFIDF

Term frequency inverse document frequency (TFIDF) is a common algorithm to transform textual data into numerical representations. This method quantifies the significance of the words within the comments while considering their prevalence across the entire comments. This method is used in different NLP tasks due to its simplicity, interpretability, and computational efficiency.

5.1.2 LASER

Language agnostic sentence representations (LASER) (Artetxe and Schwenk, 2019) is a contextualized language model that is based on BiLSTM encoder and is trained using multiple sources of publicly available parallel corpora using the translation objective. The LASER model was trained to generate the numerical representations for 93 languages, belonging to more than 30 different language families and written in 28 different scripts. Joint training in different languages makes this model leverage competitive performance in low-resource languages.

5.1.3 LaBSE

Language agnostic BERT sentence embedding (LaBSE) (Feng et al., 2022) is a BERT-based cross-lingual sentence embedding model trained using masked language modeling and translation language modeling objectives on translation ranking tasks. The LaBSE model supports 109 languages. LaBSE produces similar representations for the parallel sentences in different languages. This model has demonstrated strong performance even on languages in which the model was not trained exclusively.

5.2 Transformer-based Models

Apart from classical machine learning models, we conduct experiments with different transformer-based models as well. Transformer-based models are the current default methods in NLP field due to their high performance. The ability of multilingual transformer based models to produce aligned representations of multiple languages are beneficial for handling code-mixed text (Winata et al., 2021). The classification model consists of the pre-trained language model with a linear layer with dropout on top. The experiments are run using transformers library (Wolf et al., 2020). AdamW optimizer is used with the learning rate of $1e-5$. The training is run for 5 epochs and best performing model in validation set is used for testing.

5.2.1 mBERT

Multilingual BERT (mBERT) (Devlin et al., 2019) is the multilingual counterpart of BERT. mBERT is pre-trained on Wikipedia data from 104 languages. mBERT model is pre-trained with masked language modeling and next sentence prediction objectives. This model is able to produce cross-lingual representations which can be used for many multilingual tasks in NLP.

5.2.2 XLM-R

XLM-RoBERTa (XLM-R) (Conneau et al., 2020) is a transformer model trained for masked language modeling using monolingual data in 100 languages with 2.5 TB of text. XLM-R model is the modified version of XLM (Lample and Conneau, 2019) that avoids translation language modeling and employs RoBERTa (Liu et al., 2019) instead of BERT. The performance of XLM-R is superior to mBERT on various cross-lingual benchmarks by 23% in accuracy in low-resource languages.

5.2.3 MuRIL

Multilingual representation of Indian languages (MuRIL) (Khanuja et al., 2021) is an Indian subcontinent language family model which is pre-trained on a large corpora of languages in Indian subcontinent. The model is pre-trained on 16 Indian subcontinent languages and English. Masked language modeling and translation language modeling objectives were used in the pre-training of this model. This model outperformed other multilingual models on the tasks involving Indian subcontinent languages. This model includes both Devanagari scripts and its transliterated form during the training.

6 Results and Discussion

6.1 Hypotheses Test

Sentence Count: In order to identify the dominant language of each comment, we utilize the same language identification model as discussed in Section 4.1. For each comment, we identify the language tags for all tokens in the comment. We distinguish the dominant language of the comment utilizing the number of specific language tokens in the comment. If the number of English language tokens is greater than the number or Nepali language tokens in a comment, we consider the comment as an English comment and vice versa. When the number of English language tokens and Nepali language tokens are equal, we consider the comment as having no distinct language. The mosaic chart on Fig 1 shows the statistics for the number of sentences belonging to each sentiment class against the dominant language of the sentence. We use these statistics to run our statistical tests on the hypotheses explained in Section 3.

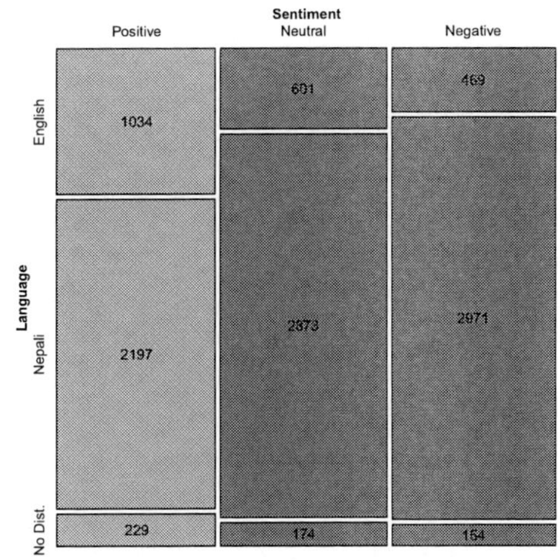

Figure 1: Mosaic chart showing the frequency of sentences in each language for each sentiment class for the human annotated comments.

Statistical Tests: In order to test the hypothesis I discussed in Section 3, we use the chi-squared test. This test is used to check the independence between two categorical variables. In our case, the variables are the dominant language and sentiment class. The null hypothesis for this test is: 'There is no association between sentiment and language', while our alternative hypothesis is Hypothesis I. Significance levels were set at 1% level. The p-value obtained from the test was significantly lower than our significance level. Hence, we reject the null hypothesis and accept the alternative hypothesis. In other words, this result supports our Hypothesis I, i.e., there is an association between sentiment and language.

Since there is an association between the sentiment classes and the dominant language of the comment, we test our second hypothesis to check if there is statistically significant difference in the proportion of use of Nepali language in different sentiment groups. We test the second hypothesis using the z-test for proportions. The z-test for proportions is used to test a hypothesis about the difference between the proportions of two samples. In our case, we take the proportions of Nepali language comments on positive class and on negative class. The null hypothesis for this test is: 'The proportion of Nepali language use is the same for negative sentiment and positive sentiment comments', while our alternative hypothesis is the Hypothesis II. After computing the z-test for proportions, we found that our z-value is significantly lower than -4, hence we can reject the null hypothesis and accept the alternative hypothesis. Hence, statistically we conclude that the proportion of Nepali language is higher in negative comments when compared with positive comments. Moreover, from the same test conducted for the proportions of English language in positive and negative comments we noticed the proportion of English language use was higher in positive than negative comments in our dataset.

These results reflect those of (Agarwal et al., 2017; Rudra et al., 2019) who also found that multilinguals prefer to express the emotions with their first language. Most of the multilingual people in Nepal learn their first language, Nepali at home. Whereas, their second language, English in schools (Gurung, 2019). Hence, most of the multilingual

(a) Positive (b) Neutral (c) Negative

Figure 2: Wordclouds of comments across different sentiment classes.

speakers gain the knowledge of English as an instructed language. Therefore, this finding is consistent with that of Dewaele (2004) who discusses how instructed language learners have a limited general knowledge of negative words. As a result, the speakers tend to use the instructed language (i.e., English in context of this study) infrequently for expressing negative sentiments. Figure 2 presents the wordcloud of comments for each sentiment class in the dataset. It can be seen from the figures that more proportion English words can be seen on Positive wordcloud and more proportions of Nepali words can be seen on Negative wordcloud.

6.2 Sentiment analysis on CS

Table 2 and 3 shows the experimental results in terms of F1- score for the machine learning and transformer-based models respectively. The experiments are performed on the data split explained in Section 4.2. The average of three runs is reported on both the tables.

SVM model with TFIDF embedding produces the best result (0.68 for Macro-, Weighted-F1, and Accuracy) among the machine learning methods in the experiment. SVM model performs better than MLP for all the embeddings except LASER embedding where its performance is similar to that of MLP. LaBSE and LASER embeddings are the multilingual sentence embeddings that are trained to produce the semantically meaningful sentence representations by leveraging the neural networks and cross-lingual training. On the other hand, TFIDF is a simple model which computes the numerical representation based on the importance of the words within the document and across the entire corpus. Better performance by this simple method illustrates the added complexity for the models trained in monolingual data in multiple languages, due to the mixing of the languages in our dataset. Our dataset consists of mixed Nepali-English data. Transliterated form of Nepali is used in the dataset which is not used during the training of the aforementioned models. Hence due to the mixing and the use of romanized script for Nepali language, the embeddings from the multilingual sentence embedders perform lower than TFIDF.

In case of transformer-based models, all three models perform in similar fashion. The highest performance is exhibited by MuRIL. All these models are trained on multiple languages together with the languages involved in our study: Nepali and English. While mBERT and XLM-R are trained on the monolingual data in these languages, MuRIL is trained on the monolingual data, parallel translated data, and the transliterated data. As discussed earlier, transliterated form is observed highly in informal settings like social media platforms and our dataset contains the transliterated form of Nepali language. Hence, MuRIL vocabulary takes into account higher percentage of tokens from our dataset as compared with mBERT and XLM-R, hence the performance is better for MuRIL. Few previous studies (Adhikari et al., 2022; Pahari and Shimada, 2023) demonstrated that the language family-specific models can provide significant benefit when fine-tuning training dataset size is of certain minimum number, which suggests that there is room for improvement for the performance by introducing more training dataset by some techniques like data augmentation.

Closer inspection of the table shows that both machine learning and transformer-based models demonstrated lower scores for neutral cases when compared against positive and negative cases. This

Table 2: Experimental results using machine learning-based models.

Embedding	Model	Negative	Neutral	Positive	Macro F1	Weighted F1	Accuracy
TFIDF	SVM	0.67	**0.61**	**0.76**	**0.68**	**0.68**	**0.68**
	MLP	**0.68**	0.56	0.74	0.66	0.66	0.66
LaBSE	SVM	0.62	0.55	0.72	0.63	0.63	0.63
	MLP	0.61	0.53	0.73	0.62	0.62	0.62
Laser	SVM	0.64	0.55	0.70	0.63	0.63	0.63
	MLP	0.62	0.54	0.73	0.63	0.63	0.63

Table 3: Experimental results using transformer-based models.

Model	Negative	Neutral	Positive	Macro F1	Weighted F1	Accuracy
mBERT	0.68	0.59	0.76	0.68	0.68	0.68
XLM-R	0.67	0.54	0.75	0.65	0.65	0.66
MuRIL	**0.72**	**0.60**	**0.80**	**0.70**	**0.70**	**0.70**

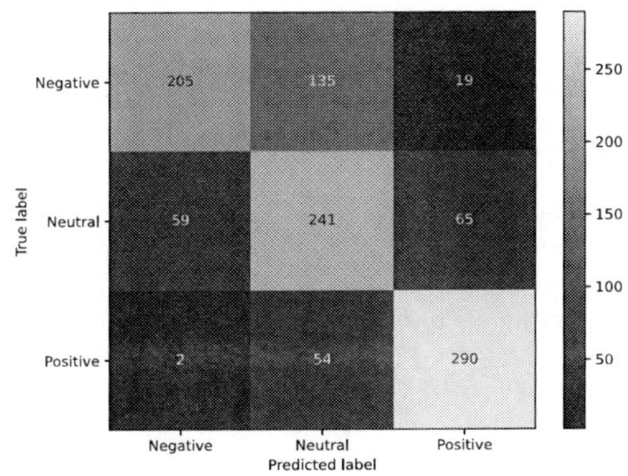

Figure 3: Confusion matrix of the result from the MuRIL model.

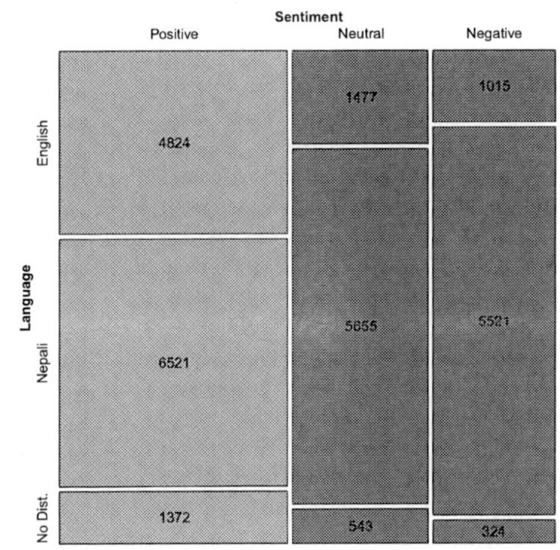

Figure 4: Mosaic chart showing the frequency of sentences in each language for each sentiment class for the larger pool of automatically annotated comments.

is due to borderline comments that are difficult even for humans as discussed in Section 4.2. This can be visualized in the confusion matrix for one run in the MuRIL model is shown in Fig. 3. 89.2% of wrong prediction of Negative classes were Neutral class and 83.1% of prediction of Positive class were Neutral class.

6.3 Hypothesis test on larger pool of automatically classified comments

Section 6.1 discussed the hypothesis test on the limited human annotated data. With the availability of automatic sentiment classifier as discussed in Section 6.2, further test is performed on the large pool of comments. The MuRIL-based classifier is utilized to automatically classify 27,252 unannotated comments collected in Section 4.1. The dominant language for each comment is determined using the same language identification model as Section 6.1. The mosaic chart on Fig 4 shows the statistics for the number of comments belonging to each sentiment class against the dominant language of the comment. As visualized in the chart, the proportion of comments with Nepali as dominant language are higher for negative comments than for positive comments. Similar to the statistical tests on human annotated data, the statistical test performed on these automatically annotated data also validates both of our hypotheses.

6.4 Conclusion

In this study, we collected public comments and annotated them with sentiment annotations. With the help of the newly created dataset, we test and accept two hypotheses. First hypothesis confirms the dependence between the language used in the comment and the sentiment of the comment. Second hypothesis confirms the higher proportions of Nepali comments observed in expressing negative sentiments as compared with positive sentiment. Similarly, the proportions of English is higher in positive sentiments than negative. The results aligns with the conclusion of previous studies (Agarwal et al., 2017; Rudra et al., 2019), preference of first language of the speakers for expressing sentiments or swearing. The results of machine learning methods show that the multilingual sentence embedders fail to generate proper representations for code-switched languages. Considerably more work will need to be done to generate multilingual embeddings that can capture the semantic meaning of mixed languages as well. Language identification model trained on code-switched data from Twitter was used in the analysis. However, the accuracy of the language identification model was not evaluated due to unavailability of test data for the Youtube domain. In future work, we need to evaluate the model accuracy on this domain, and verify the influence for our analysis. Furthermore, the findings raises few socio-lingustic questions about the influence of English language in Nepalese communities and its impact on Nepali language, which would also be a fruitful area for further work.

Limitations

The dominant language for the comments is identified based on the number of language tokens, which are identified using automatic language identification model that might have non-negligible errors. We use these data as descriptive statistics and analyze the aforementioned hypotheses.

References

Rabin Adhikari, Safal Thapaliya, Nirajan Basnet, Samip Poudel, Aman Shakya, and Bishesh Khanal. 2022. COVID-19-related Nepali tweets classification in a low resource setting. In *Social Media Mining for Health Applications, Workshop & Shared Task*, pages 209–215. Association for Computational Linguistics.

Prabhat Agarwal, Ashish Sharma, Jeenu Grover, Mayank Sikka, Koustav Rudra, and Monojit Choudhury. 2017. I may talk in english but gaali toh hindi mein hi denge: A study of english-hindi code-switching and swearing pattern on social networks. In *2017 9th international conference on communication systems and networks (comsnets)*, pages 554–557. IEEE.

Fahad AlGhamdi, Giovanni Molina, Mona Diab, Thamar Solorio, Abdelati Hawwari, Victor Soto, and Julia Hirschberg. 2016. Part of speech tagging for code switched data. In *Proceedings of the Second Workshop on Computational Approaches to Code Switching*, pages 98–107, Austin, Texas. Association for Computational Linguistics.

Mikel Artetxe and Holger Schwenk. 2019. Massively Multilingual Sentence Embeddings for Zero-Shot Cross-Lingual Transfer and Beyond. *Transactions of the Association for Computational Linguistics*, 7:597–610.

Pedro Paulo Balage Filho, Caroline Brun, and Gilbert Rondeau. 2012. A graphical user interface for feature-based opinion mining. In *Proceedings of the Demonstration Session at the Conference of the North American Chapter of the Association for Computational Linguistics: Human Language Technologies*, pages 5–8, Montréal, Canada. Association for Computational Linguistics.

Kalika Bali, Jatin Sharma, Monojit Choudhury, and Yogarshi Vyas. 2014. "I am borrowing ya mixing ?" an analysis of English-Hindi code mixing in Facebook. In *Proceedings of the First Workshop on Computational Approaches to Code Switching*, pages 116–126, Doha, Qatar. Association for Computational Linguistics.

Inmaculada Muñoa Barredo. 1997. Pragmatic functions of code-switching among basque-spanish bilinguals. In *Comunidades e individuos bilingües: actas do I Simposio Internacional sobre o Bilingüismo*, pages 528–541, Galicia, Spain. Servizo de Publicacións.

Bharathi Raja Chakravarthi, Navya Jose, Shardul Suryawanshi, Elizabeth Sherly, and John Philip McCrae. 2020a. A sentiment analysis dataset for code-mixed Malayalam-English. In *Proceedings of the 1st Joint Workshop on Spoken Language Technologies for Under-resourced languages (SLTU) and Collaboration and Computing for Under-Resourced Languages (CCURL)*, pages 177–184, Marseille, France. European Language Resources association.

Bharathi Raja Chakravarthi, Vigneshwaran Muralidaran, Ruba Priyadharshini, and John Philip McCrae. 2020b. Corpus creation for sentiment analysis in code-mixed Tamil-English text. In *Proceedings of the 1st Joint Workshop on Spoken Language Technologies for Under-resourced languages (SLTU) and Collaboration and Computing for Under-Resourced Languages (CCURL)*, pages 202–210, Marseille, France. European Language Resources association.

Jacob Cohen. 1960. A coefficient of agreement for nominal scales. *Educational and psychological measurement*, 20(1):37–46.

Alexis Conneau, Kartikay Khandelwal, Naman Goyal, Vishrav Chaudhary, Guillaume Wenzek, Francisco Guzmán, Édouard Grave, Myle Ott, Luke Zettlemoyer, and Veselin Stoyanov. 2020. Unsupervised cross-lingual representation learning at scale. In *Proceedings of the 58th Annual Meeting of the Association for Computational Linguistics*, pages 8440–8451.

Amitava Das and Björn Gambäck. 2014. Identifying languages at the word level in code-mixed Indian social media text. In *Proceedings of the 11th International Conference on Natural Language Processing*, pages 378–387, Goa, India. NLP Association of India.

Jacob Devlin, Ming-Wei Chang, Kenton Lee, and Kristina Toutanova. 2019. BERT: Pre-training of deep bidirectional transformers for language understanding. In *Proceedings of the 2019 Conference of the North American Chapter of the Association for Computational Linguistics: Human Language Technologies, Volume 1 (Long and Short Papers)*, pages 4171–4186, Minneapolis, Minnesota. Association for Computational Linguistics.

Jean-Marc Dewaele. 2004. Blistering barnacles! what language do multilinguals swear in?! *Sociolinguistic Studies*, pages 83–105.

Jean-Marc Dewaele. 2010. *Emotions in multiple languages*. Springer.

Fangxiaoyu Feng, Yinfei Yang, Daniel Cer, Naveen Arivazhagan, and Wei Wang. 2022. Language-agnostic bert sentence embedding. In *Proceedings of the 60th Annual Meeting of the Association for Computational Linguistics (Volume 1: Long Papers)*, pages 878–891.

Joshua A Fishman. 1970. *Sociolinguistics: A brief introduction.* ERIC.

Dinesh Gurung. 2019. *Nepali-English code-switching in the conversations of Nepalese people: a sociolinguistic study*. Ph.D. thesis, University of Roehampton.

Asha Hegde, Mudoor Devadas Anusha, Sharal Coelho, Hosahalli Lakshmaiah Shashirekha, and Bharathi Raja Chakravarthi. 2022. Corpus creation for sentiment analysis in code-mixed Tulu text. In *Proceedings of the 1st Annual Meeting of the ELRA/ISCA Special Interest Group on Under-Resourced Languages*, pages 33–40, Marseille, France. European Language Resources Association.

Simran Khanuja, Diksha Bansal, Sarvesh Mehtani, Savya Khosla, Atreyee Dey, Balaji Gopalan, Dilip Kumar Margam, Pooja Aggarwal, Rajiv Teja Nagipogu, Shachi Dave, et al. 2021. Muril: Multilingual representations for indian languages. *arXiv preprint arXiv:2103.10730*.

Guillaume Lample and Alexis Conneau. 2019. Cross-lingual language model pretraining. *arXiv preprint arXiv:1901.07291*.

Yinhan Liu, Myle Ott, Naman Goyal, Jingfei Du, Mandar Joshi, Danqi Chen, Omer Levy, Mike Lewis, Luke Zettlemoyer, and Veselin Stoyanov. 2019. Roberta: A robustly optimized bert pretraining approach. *arXiv preprint arXiv:1907.11692*.

Innocent Ndubuisi-Obi, Sayan Ghosh, and David Jurgens. 2019. Wetin dey with these comments? modeling sociolinguistic factors affecting code-switching behavior in Nigerian online discussions. In *Proceedings of the 57th Annual Meeting of the Association for Computational Linguistics*, pages 6204–6214, Florence, Italy. Association for Computational Linguistics.

Niraj Pahari and Kazutaka Shimada. 2023. Handling data scarcity in code-mixing using learning-based approaches. In *2023 13th International Congress on Advanced Applied Informatics (IIAI-AAI)*. IEEE.

Parth Patwa, Gustavo Aguilar, Sudipta Kar, Suraj Pandey, Srinivas PYKL, Björn Gambäck, Tanmoy Chakraborty, Thamar Solorio, and Amitava Das. 2020. SemEval-2020 task 9: Overview of sentiment analysis of code-mixed tweets. In *Proceedings of the Fourteenth Workshop on Semantic Evaluation*, pages 774–790, Barcelona (online). International Committee for Computational Linguistics.

Fabian Pedregosa, Gaël Varoquaux, Alexandre Gramfort, Vincent Michel, Bertrand Thirion, Olivier Grisel, Mathieu Blondel, Peter Prettenhofer, Ron Weiss, Vincent Dubourg, et al. 2011. Scikit-learn: Machine learning in python. *the Journal of machine Learning research*, 12:2825–2830.

Kanavillil Rajagopalan. 2004. Emotion and language politics: The brazilian case. *Journal of Multilingual and Multicultural Development - J MULTILING MULTICULT DEVELOP*, 25:105–123.

Manikandan Ravikiran and Subbiah Annamalai. 2021. DOSA: Dravidian code-mixed offensive span identification dataset. In *Proceedings of the First Workshop on Speech and Language Technologies for Dravidian Languages*, pages 10–17, Kyiv. Association for Computational Linguistics.

Koustav Rudra, Shruti Rijhwani, Rafiya Begum, Kalika Bali, Monojit Choudhury, and Niloy Ganguly. 2016. Understanding language preference for expression of opinion and sentiment: What do hindi-english speakers do on twitter? In *Proceedings of the 2016 conference on empirical methods in natural language processing*, pages 1131–1141.

Koustav Rudra, Ashish Sharma, Kalika Bali, Monojit Choudhury, and Niloy Ganguly. 2019. Identifying and analyzing different aspects of english-hindi code-switching in twitter. *ACM Transactions on Asian and Low-Resource Language Information Processing (TALLIP)*, 18(3):1–28.

Thamar Solorio, Elizabeth Blair, Suraj Maharjan, Steven Bethard, Mona Diab, Mahmoud Ghoneim, Abdelati Hawwari, Fahad AlGhamdi, Julia Hirschberg, Alison Chang, et al. 2014. Overview for the first shared task on language identification in code-switched data. In *Proceedings of the First Workshop on Computational Approaches to Code Switching*, pages 62–72.

Genta Indra Winata, Samuel Cahyawijaya, Zihan Liu, Zhaojiang Lin, Anfrea Madotto, and Pascale Ngan Fung. 2021. Are multilingual models effective in code-switching? In *Proceedings of the Fifth Workshop on Computational Approaches to Linguistic Code-Switching*, pages 142–153.

Thomas Wolf, Lysandre Debut, Victor Sanh, Julien Chaumond, Clement Delangue, Anthony Moi, Pierric Cistac, Tim Rault, Rémi Louf, Morgan Funtowicz, et al. 2020. Transformers: State-of-the-art natural language processing. In *Proceedings of the 2020 conference on empirical methods in natural language processing: system demonstrations*, pages 38–45.

Text-Derived Language Identity Incorporation for End-to-End Code-Switching Speech Recognition

Qinyi Wang
National University of Singapore
qinyi@u.nus.edu

Haizhou Li
National University of Singapore
The Chinese University of Hong Kong, Shenzhen
haizhouli@cuhk.edu.cn

Abstract

Recognizing code-switching (CS) speech often presents challenges for an automatic speech recognition system (ASR) due to limited linguistic context in short monolingual segments, resulting in language confusion. To mitigate this issue, language identity (LID) is often integrated into the speech recognition system to provide additional linguistic context. However, previous works predominately focus on extracting language identity from speech signals. We introduce a novel approach to learn language identity from pure text data via a dedicated language identity-language model. Besides, we explore two strategies: LID state fusion and language posterior biasing, to integrate the text-derived language identities into the end-to-end ASR system. By incorporating hypothesized language identities, our ASR system gains crucial contextual cues, effectively capturing language transitions and patterns within code-switched utterances. We conduct speech recognition experiments on the SEAME corpus and demonstrate the effectiveness of our proposed methods. Our results reveal significantly improved transcriptions in code-switching scenarios, underscoring the potential of text-derived LID in enhancing code-switching speech recognition.

1 Introduction

Automatic speech recognition (ASR) systems have long grappled with the complex task of accurately transcribing multilingual speech, especially when it involves the phenomenon known as code-switching (CS). Code-switching, or code-mixing, refers to the practice of alternating between two or more languages or dialects within a single conversation. Within these intricate language mixtures, the presence of very short monolingual segments further compounds the challenge. The limited contextual information within these segments often leads to confusion in recognizing phonetically similar words from different languages, substantially affecting the overall performance of multilingual ASR systems (Amazouz et al., 2017; Yılmaz et al., 2018; Wang et al., 2019). Traditional approaches to code-switching ASR have resorted to language identification or code-switching detection systems as separate pre-processing or post-processing steps. While these methods have been effective in providing additional language context (Weiner et al., 2012a; Vu et al., 2012; Zhang, 2013), they introduce additional complexity to the ASR pipeline and increase processing time.

The advancement of deep learning has brought forth a remarkable paradigm shift in multilingual and code-switching ASR systems. End-to-end (E2E) approaches have gained substantial attention, harnessing advanced neural network architectures, such as the Transformer (Vaswani et al., 2017), to directly transcribe code-switched speech (Zhou et al., 2020; Dalmia et al., 2021). These E2E CS ASR systems automatically capture both the acoustic and linguistic characteristics of code-switched speech, eliminating the need for explicit acoustic and language modeling. To reduce language confusion in E2E CS ASR systems, researchers have studied methods for integrating language identity (LID) information learned from both paired speech-text data (Shan et al., 2019; Qiu et al., 2020; Zhang et al., 2021) and unpaired speech data (Li et al., 2019; Punjabi et al., 2020; Tseng et al., 2021). However, these prior approaches have predominantly focused on learning language identities from speech data, overlooking the untapped potential of pure text data. Compared to annotated speech data, text data offers a more accessible and readily available resource.

This paper explores the possibility of learning language-switching patterns from pure text data without relying on speech data. Text-derived features, such as part-of-speech tags and syntactic features, have been shown to improve the performance of code-switching language models (Adel

Proceedings of the 6th Workshop on Computational Approaches to Linguistic Code-Switching, pages 33–42
December 7, 2023

et al., 2013, 2015; Winata et al., 2018). Inspired by these achievements, we propose to infer language identities from text data and integrate these text-derived language identities into the end-to-end CS ASR system. Our objective is twofold: to acquire language-switching syntax and patterns from text data in the form of language identities, and to leverage these language identities to mitigate the language confusion in code-switching speech recognition. We believe the paired in-domain text inherently encompasses a wealth of linguistic information, which can be effectively harnessed to advance code-switching speech recognition.

To acquire code-switching patterns sorely from text data, we propose a novel language modeling scheme, called language identity-language model, to predict the language identity of the next text token based on a combined history of previous text and language identity tokens. The proposed language identity-language model is jointly trained with a Transformer-based ASR model. Furthermore, we explore two strategies for integrating the predicted language identities into an E2E ASR system: LID state fusion and language posterior biasing. In the LID state fusion strategy, we combine token-level language identity hidden states with ASR hidden states using learned weights. On the other hand, the language posterior biasing strategy directly adjusts the ASR posterior probabilities based on the hypothesized language identities and language posteriors. We evaluate the effectiveness of these proposed methods on the SEAME corpus, a Mandarin-English speech dataset. The results underscore the efficacy of our approaches in reducing language confusion during code-switching speech recognition, leading to more accurate transcriptions of code-switched speech.

The remainder of this paper is structured as follows: Section 2 reviews the background of the Transformer-based ASR with parallel speech-text decoder. Section 3 presents related work for leveraging language identification in multilingual and code-switching speech recognition. Section 4 presents the proposed LID-LM for generating language identities from pure text data and LID integration strategies. Section 5 describes the datasets, models, and evaluation metrics used to assess the performance of the proposed method. Section 6 presents the results and analysis of the experiments. Finally, Section 7 summarizes the contributions and outlines directions for future research.

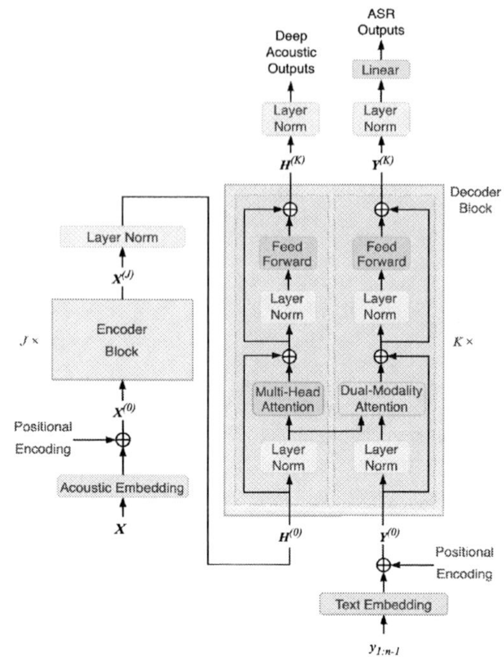

Figure 1: The architecture of a Transformer-based ASR with parallel speech-text decoder.

2 Background

In this section, we briefly review the Transformer-based ASR architecture with parallel speech-text decoder that we used to implement our method.

2.1 Transformer with Parallel Speech-Text Decoder

We use the Transformer-based ASR with parallel speech-text decoder architecture as our baseline model, as illustrated in Figure 1. This decoder architecture is a variant of the decoder architecture in the speech-and-text Transformer (Wang et al., 2023). Our preliminary studies indicate that this decoder architecture outperforms the vanilla Transformer decoder architecture in both monolingual and code-switching English and Chinese speech recognition tasks.

The parallel speech-text decoder consists of a stack of K identical decoder blocks. Each decoder block comprises two parallel branches: a deep acoustic branch and a speech decoding branch. The inclusion of the deep acoustic branch facilitates the learning of speech-text alignment by projecting the acoustic representations to a comparable level of abstraction as the text representation.

The deep acoustic branch generates new deep

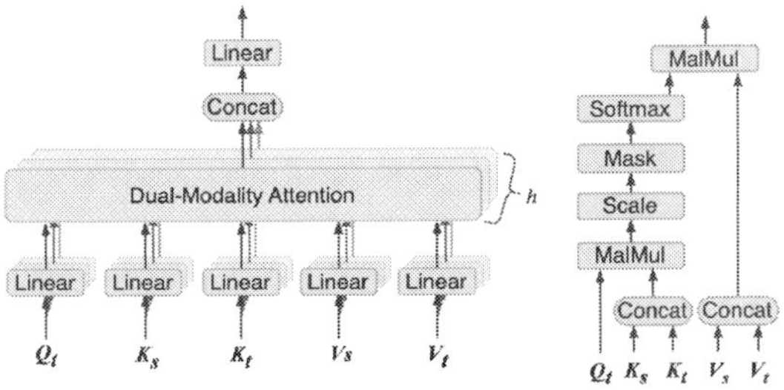

Figure 2: (left) An dual-modality attention module that adopts dual-modality scaled dot-product attention. (right) dual-modality scaled dot-product attention.

acoustic states $\boldsymbol{H}^{(k)}$ by attending to the deep acoustic states from its previous block as follows,

$$\boldsymbol{H}^{(k)} = \text{STDecBlock}(\boldsymbol{H}^{(k-1)}). \quad (1)$$

Meanwhile, the speech decoding branch generates decoder states $\boldsymbol{Y}^{(k)}$ by attending to the deep acoustic states and the decoder states from its previous block as follows,

$$\boldsymbol{Y}^{(k)} = \text{STDecBlock}(\boldsymbol{Y}^{(k-1)}, H^{(k-1)}). \quad (2)$$

Finally, the probability of the next text token, given the complete acoustic feature sequence and its previous text token history, is calculated using the decoder states generated from the last decoder block as follows,

$$\begin{aligned} &P(y_n|\boldsymbol{X}, \boldsymbol{y}_{1:n-1}) \\ &= \text{Softmax}(\text{ Linear } \quad (\text{LayerNorm}(\boldsymbol{Y}^{(K)}))). \end{aligned} \quad (3)$$

2.2 Dual-Modality Attention

Another key feature of the parallel speech-text decoder is the use of the dual-modality attention mechanism, which is a variation of the on-demand dual-modality attention proposed in our speech-and-text Transformer framework. As depicted in Figure 2, this mechanism establishes dependencies between the text-text representations and text-speech representations through the mapping of a query and two sets of key-value pairs into an output representation. The dual-modality attention is formulated as follows,

$$\begin{aligned} &\text{DualModalityAttention}(\boldsymbol{Q}_t, \boldsymbol{K}_t, \boldsymbol{V}_t, \boldsymbol{K}_s, \boldsymbol{V}_s) \\ &= \text{Softmax}\left(\frac{Q_t K_c^T}{\sqrt{d}}\right) V_c. \end{aligned} \quad (4)$$

This multi-head attention mechanism has five input vectors - a query and two sets of key-value pairs: target query Q_t, target key K_t, target value V_t, source key K_s and source value V_s. Here, K_c is the concatenation of K_t and K_s, and V_c is the concatenation of V_t and V_s.

3 Related Work

Language identification plays a vital role in various multilingual speech processing applications, particularly in multilingual or code-switching speech recognition systems. It provides valuable contextual information that regulates speech recognizers and reduces language confusion. Early multilingual ASR systems adopted a two-stage approach, where a language identification component was incorporated at the front-end to distinguish speech from different languages, followed by the use of monolingual recognizers to transcribe speech in specific languages at the back-end (Bhuvanagiri and Kopparapu, 2010; Lyu et al., 2006). Subsequently, frame-level language identities predicted by a dedicated language identification module were integrated into the ASR decoding process to handle rapid language changes (Vu et al., 2012; Weiner et al., 2012b).

With the advancements of deep learning, there has been a shift towards incorporating language identification as an auxiliary task, jointly learned with end-to-end multilingual and code-switching speech recognition systems (Luo et al., 2018; Zeng et al., 2018; Li and Vu, 2019; Yin et al., 2022; Liu et al., 2023). Additionally, Seki et al. (Seki et al., 2018) dynamically track the language identity in code-switching utterances by adding language identity tokens before code-switching points in speech transcriptions, eliminating the need for an external language identification module. This LID token augmentation method is also used in (Zhang et al., 2021), where different language embeddings are concatenated with the word embedding of text tokens to further enhance the distinguishability between word embeddings of different languages.

However, existing research has predominantly concentrated on extracting language identity from speech signals. In contrast, our work takes an innovative approach, delving into the prospect of learning language identity directly from raw text data. By harnessing the rich linguistic information within textual data, we aim to reduce language confusion in end-to-end code-switching speech recognition

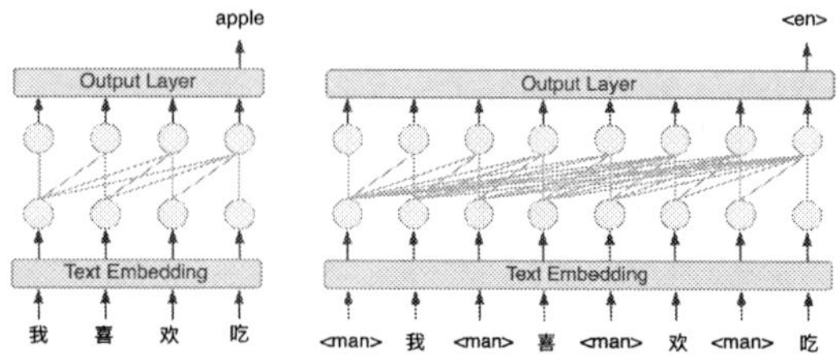

(a) LM (b) LID-LM

Figure 3: Illustration of LM and LID-LM. LM predicts the next text token given the previous text token history, while LID-LM predicts the next language identity token or the next text token given the previous augmented language identity and text token history.

systems, leading to more accurate transcriptions.

4 Proposed Method

4.1 Language Identity-Language Model

The goal of language models is to assign probabilities to sequences of words. Let's consider an N-length text token sequence represented as as $\boldsymbol{Y} = \{y_1, \dots, y_n, \dots, y_N\}$. The aim of a neural language model is to predict the probability distribution $P(y_n|\boldsymbol{y}_{1:n-1})$ over the vocabulary $\mathcal{V}$, given the previous text token histories $y_{1:n-1}$. To explicitly incorporate language identity information into the language model, we introduce a novel language model scheme called language identity language model (LID-LM), which takes the input of token sequences with language identities inserted into the front of each text token. Figure 3 compares the original language model with the proposed LID-LM. The incorporation of language identities into the output token set enriches the language model, enabling it to capture nuanced language-specific characteristics and code-switching patterns from text data. This LID token augmentation technique has been shown to be effective in reducing language confusion in ASR systems (Seki et al., 2018; Zhang et al., 2021). By augmenting language identities into the text token sequences, the LID-LM offers an innovative way to predict language identity without relying on speech data.

To accommodate the language identity information within the LID-LM, we use an augmented vocabulary $\mathcal{V}' = \mathcal{V} \cup \mathcal{V}^{lid}$. Here, $\mathcal{V}^{lid}$ represents the set of language identity tokens. The augmented $2N$-length sequence $\boldsymbol{Z} = \{z_1, \dots, z_n, \dots, z_{2N}\}$ corresponds to the alternating arrangement of language identity tokens and text tokens. In this sequence, the odd-indexed tokens represent the language identity tokens, while the even-indexed tokens represent the text tokens. The LID-LM aims to predict the probability of the next text token z_{2n} or the next language identity token z_{2n-1} based on the history sequence of language identity and text tokens $z_{1:2n-1}$ or $z_{1:2n-2}$, respectively.

For optimization, we adopt the cross-entropy loss as the loss function for the LID-LM. This loss function measures the discrepancy between the predicted token distribution and the true label distribution, and it is normalized by the total number of tokens in the training data. We denote this loss as L_{lid-lm}. In the subsequent subsections where we describe the LID integration methods, the LID-LM is jointly trained with the ASR model by using the following formulation,

$$\mathcal{L}_{joint} = \alpha\mathcal{L}_{ctc} + (1-\alpha)\mathcal{L}_{att} + \beta\mathcal{L}_{lid-lm}, \quad (5)$$

where $\mathcal{L}_{ctc}$ and $\mathcal{L}_{att}$ represents the CTC loss and label smooth loss for the hybrid CTC/Attention ASR model, and $\mathcal{L}_{lid-lm}$ denotes the cross-entropy loss for the LID-LM. The weights α and β control the contribution of each loss component, enabling a balanced optimization for the ASR and LID-LM components.

During the training process, we utilize speech transcriptions augmented with the groundtruth language identities as the input text to train the language identity-language models. This ensures that the LID-LMs learn to associate the correct language identities with the corresponding text tokens. During decoding, we incorporate the previously decoded text token from the ASR model and its corresponding language identity as the previous token history for the LID-LM. This restricts the LID-LM to generate language identity predictions based on the ASR model's previous output transcriptions. In addition, we share the weights of the text embeddings between the ASR and LID-LM models. This parameter sharing enables the ASR model to understand and utilize the language identities provided by the LID-LM during the integration strategies described in the subsequent subsections.

4.2 LID State Fusion

The effectiveness of language-specific gating mechanisms in multilingual speech recognition has been demonstrated in a previous work (Kim and Seltzer, 2018). In their approach, the ASR system utilizes

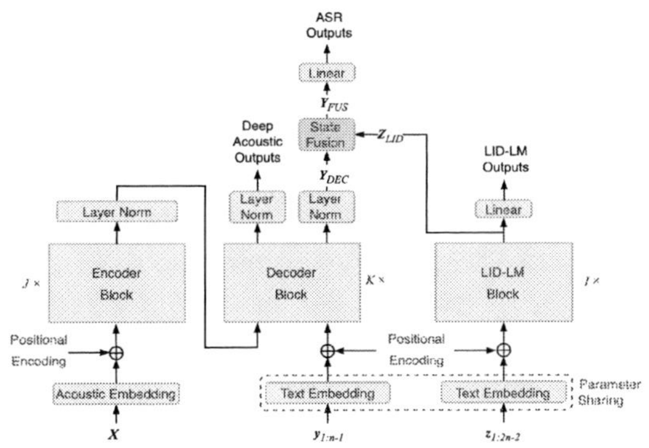

Figure 4: A schematic representation of the LID state fusion method.

one-hot vectors as language indicators to modulate its hidden state in each layer. Building upon this motivation, we propose a novel LID state fusion approach to use a gating mechanism to guide the ASR with language-specific information generated by the LID-LM. Specifically, the ASR system incorporates the language identity information by fusing the language identity hidden states into its own decoder output states. By leveraging the language-specific information provided by the LID-LM, the ASR system can effectively adapt its predictions and enhance its performance in code-switching scenarios according to the linguistic knowledge and confidence level implicitly contained in the language identity hidden states.

The LID state fusion method is illustrated in Figure 4. We generate token-level LID hidden states Z_{LID} from the LID-LM, utilizing the historical token sequence of language identity and text tokens $\boldsymbol{z}_{1:2n-2}$. Simultaneously, we apply layer normalization to the hidden states $\boldsymbol{Y}^{(K)}$ of the speech-text decoder from the last decoder block, generating the normalized decoder hidden states as follows,

$$\boldsymbol{Y}_{DEC} = \text{LayerNorm}(\boldsymbol{Y}^{(K)}). \quad (6)$$

Next, we fuse the token-level LID representation with the normalized decoder's hidden states using a state fusion gate, producing a combined representation Y_{FUS}. The state fusion gate employs a gating mechanism inspired by the work of Sriram et al. (Sriram et al., 2018), calculated as follows,

$$\boldsymbol{G} = \text{Sigmoid}(\text{Linear}(\text{Concat}(\boldsymbol{Y}_{DEC}, \boldsymbol{Z}_{LID}))), \quad (7)$$

$$\boldsymbol{Z}_{GATED} = \text{MatMul}(\boldsymbol{G}, \boldsymbol{Z}_{LID}), \quad (8)$$

Table 1: Dataset statistics of the SEAME corpus used in the CS experiments.

	#Hours	#Utterances			
		Mandarin	English	CS	Total
Train	96	20,313	20,283	48,342	88,938
Dev.	5	1,163	1,152	2,685	5,000
$Eval_{man}$	7	1,420	808	4,303	6,531
$Eval_{sge}$	4	500	2,656	2,165	5,321

$$\boldsymbol{Y}_{FUS} = \text{Linear}(\text{Concat}(\boldsymbol{Y}_{DEC}, \boldsymbol{Z}_{GATED})). \quad (9)$$

Finally, the output probability of the next text token, given the complete acoustic feature sequence, its previous text token history, and its previous text and LID token history, is calculated as follows,

$$P(y_n|\boldsymbol{X}, \boldsymbol{y}_{1:n-1}, \boldsymbol{z}_{1:2n-1}) = \text{Softmax}(\text{Linear}(\boldsymbol{Y}_{FUS})). \quad (10)$$

4.3 Language Posterior Biasing

The adjustment of the ASR system's posterior probabilities using language posteriors, generated either by external or internal language identification components, has been demonstrated to enhance the performance of code-switching ASR systems (Liu et al., 2023; Tseng et al., 2021; Li et al., 2019). In this study, we investigate the effectiveness of the language posterior biasing method by leveraging token-level language posteriors obtained from the language identity-language model.

In the language posterior biasing method, we first generate the token-level language posterior $P(z_{2n-1}|z\boldsymbol{z}_{1:2n-2})$ using the LID-LM. Then, we adjust the ASR's posterior probabilities by its corresponding language posteriors based on the following formulation,

$$P^{bias}(y_n|\boldsymbol{X}, \boldsymbol{y}_{1:n-1}) = P(y_n|\boldsymbol{X}, \boldsymbol{y}_{1:n-1}) \times P(z_{2n-1}|\boldsymbol{z}_{1:2n-2}), \quad (11)$$

Here, $P(y_n|\boldsymbol{X}, \boldsymbol{y}_{1:n-1})$ represents the original ASR posterior probability for text token y_n. The term $P(z_{2n-1}|\boldsymbol{z}_{1:2n-2})$ corresponds to the language posterior probability for the language identity token z_{2n-1}, obtained from the language identity-language model.

5 Experimental Setup

5.1 Dataset

To assess the effectiveness of the proposed methods, we conduct language identification and code-switching speech recognition experiments on the

SEAME Mandarin-English speech corpus (Lyu et al., 2010). This corpus comprises approximately 110 hours of spontaneous code-switching speech collected from Singapore and Malaysia college students and staff members. The recordings were captured with close-talk microphones during interview and conversation settings. The corpus includes a mix of inter-sentential and intra-sentential code-mixing utterances, as well as monolingual utterances.

In the ASR experiments, we partitioned the SEAME training set into a development set *dev.* and a training set *train*. Specifically, we randomly selected 5,000 utterances to form the *dev.* set, while the remaining paired data was used for the *train* set. It is important to note that the evaluation sets, denoted as $eval_{man}$ and $eval_{sge}$, exhibit varying distributions of monolingual Mandarin, monolingual English, and Mandarin-English code-switching utterances, as summarized in Table 1. The $eval_{man}$ set is primarily composed of monolingual Mandarin and code-switching utterances, while the $eval_{sge}$ set contains a higher proportion of monolingual English utterances.

For the LID experiment, we manually augmented the transcriptions of the above sets by inserting the corresponding language identity token at the beginning of each text token. Given that we are using the Mandarin-English language pair, the distinctions between Chinese characters and the English alphabet are readily discernible. To ensure consistency and standardization, we utilized the default SEAME recipe provided by the end-to-end speech processing toolkit ESPnet (Watanabe et al., 2018) to distinguish between Chinese and English tokens. Consequently, there was no need for inter-annotator agreement within our experimental setup.

5.2 Implementation Details

Dictionary. To effectively model both English and Chinese languages, as well as their corresponding language identities, we construct a bilingual dictionary that includes additional language identity tokens. For English, we apply the byte-pair encoding (BPE) to the English-only transcriptions of the SEAME *train* set to generate subword units, resulting in a vocabulary size of 3,000 as the modeling units. As for Chinese, we select 5,103 frequently used Chinese characters extracted from the three unpaired text datasets. To represent the language identities of the text tokens, we introduce LID tokens into the output units. Specifically, we include $\langle en \rangle$, $\langle man \rangle$, and $\langle na \rangle$ tokens to represent the English, Chinese, and other identities, respectively. These LID tokens allow explicitly incorporating language identity information during the modeling process. Additionally, we incorporate special tokens $\langle unk \rangle$, $\langle sos \rangle$, and $\langle eos \rangle$ to handle unknown words, the start of a sentence, and the end of a sentence, respectively.

Models. The Transformer-based ASR models used in our experiments consist of 8 encoder layers and 6 parallel speech-text decoder layers. The LID-LM and external LM used for shallow fusion are all 6-layer Transformer decoder models. All models have output dimension of 256, inner-layer dimension of 2,048, and 4 attention heads. For the two proposed LID integration methods, the LID-LM is co-trained with the ASR models from scratch. We employ the Adam optimization algorithm with an initial learning rate of 1.0 for ASR models and 1.0×10^{-4} for language models. To schedule the learning rate, we use the Noam learning rate scheduler (Vaswani et al., 2017) with 25,000 warmup steps for ASR models and use the cosine decay scheduler (Loshchilov and Hutter, 2016) for LMs with 1,000 initial steps and 100,000 total steps. Dropout regularization with a rate of 0.1 is applied to all models to prevent overfitting. All models are trained for 50 epochs. The CTC weight α is set to 0.3 for all models during training and set to 0.5 during decoding. The LID-LM weight β is set to 0.7 during training. To select the best model for inference, we average the parameters from the top 10 epochs based on their performance on the validation set.

Evaluation. For LID-LM, we report its token-level language identification accuracy. For ASR evaluation, we use the Mix Error Rate (MER) as the performance metric. MER combines the Word Error Rate (WER) for English tokens and the Character Error Rate (CER) for Chinese tokens. This evaluation metric provides a comprehensive assessment of the ASR models' accuracy in transcribing both English and Chinese languages within the Mandarin-English code-switching context.

6 Results and Discussion

6.1 Language Identification Accuracy

We begin by assessing the language identification performance of the LID-LM. The LID-LM, trained

Table 2: SEAME: MERs on the $eval_{man}$ and $eval_{sge}$ set. Upper section: E2E ASR systems with LID integration methods discussed in Section IV. Lower section: Transformer-based ASR model with our proposed LID integration methods.

Model	Method	MER%	
		$Eval_{man}$	$Eval_{sge}$
GRU-based Encoder-Decoder (Luo et al., 2018)	Baseline	35.4	37.8
	LID Joint Learning	34.1	36.5
BLSTM-based Encoder-Decoder (Zeng et al., 2018)	Baseline	26.4	36.1
	LID Joint Learning	26.0	35.8
LSTM-based Transducer (Zhang et al., 2021)	Baseline	33.3	44.9
	CS Point Tagged Text	30.2	41.5
Transformer-based Encoder-Decoder with Parallel Speech-Text Decoder	Baseline	21.4	29.5
	Shallow Fusion	21.0	29.0
	LID State Fusion	**20.4**	**28.2**
	Language Posterior Biasing	21.3	29.2

using the augmented transcriptions of the SEAME training set, achieves token-level LID accuracies of 78.7% and 80.1% on the $eval_{man}$ and $eval_{sge}$ sets, respectively. These accuracies surpass the previously reported LID accuracy of 70.6% in (Weiner et al., 2012b) that relies on acoustic features to generate frame-level LID predictions. This outcome underscores the richness of linguistic information present in text-only data, indicating its capacity to provide valuable linguistic clues pertaining to grammar and language switching patterns. Thus, our findings emphasize the potential of leveraging LID-LM for accurate and robust language identification in code-switching speech recognition systems.

6.2 ASR Results

We proceed to evaluate the speech recognition performance of various methods on the SEAME evaluation sets, namely $eval_{man}$ and $eval_{sge}$. The upper section of Table 2 presents the performances of previous LID integration methods for end-to-end ASR systems. It can be observed that these methods result in minor to moderate improvements on the SEAME evaluation sets. Among them, the CS point tagged text method proposed by Zhang et al. (Zhang et al., 2021) achieves the most significant improvement, with relative MER reductions of 9.3% and 7.6% on the $eval_{man}$ and $eval_{sge}$ sets, respectively.

The lower section of Table 2 summarizes the performances of our Transformer-based ASR system and our proposed LID integration methods. The Transformer-based ASR baseline achieves MERs of 21.4% and 29.5% on the $eval_{man}$ and $eval_{sge}$ sets, respectively. Shallow fusion with an external language model trained on the training transcriptions leads to slight improvements of 1.9% and 1.7% over the baseline ASR system. Our proposed LID state fusion method demonstrates moderate relative MER reductions of 4.7% and 4.4% on the $eval_{man}$ and $eval_{sge}$ sets, respectively. However, the language posterior biasing method only yields marginal improvements to the baseline ASR system.

The above results suggest that the learned gating parameter in LID state fusion plays a crucial role in enabling the ASR system to effectively incorporate and utilize the contextual cues provided by the language identity-language model. By dynamically adjusting the contribution of the LID hidden states, the ASR system is better at capturing language-specific patterns and transitions, resulting in improved code-switching speech recognition performance. In contrast, the LID posterior fusion method lacks such an automatic adjusting mechanism, making the system vulnerable to error propagation in the language identification module. As a result, the effectiveness of leveraging language identification to enhance speech recognition performance is hindered in this approach.

6.3 Error Analysis

To gain insights into the speech recognition performances of the Transformer-based ASR model and the ASR model with the LID state fusion method, we conducted an analysis of the recognition errors across three different utterance categories: monolingual Mandarin, monolingual English, and code-switching Mandarin-English. Figure 5 presents the error counts for these categories on the dev_{man} and dev_{sge} sets.

The figure shows that the employment of the LID

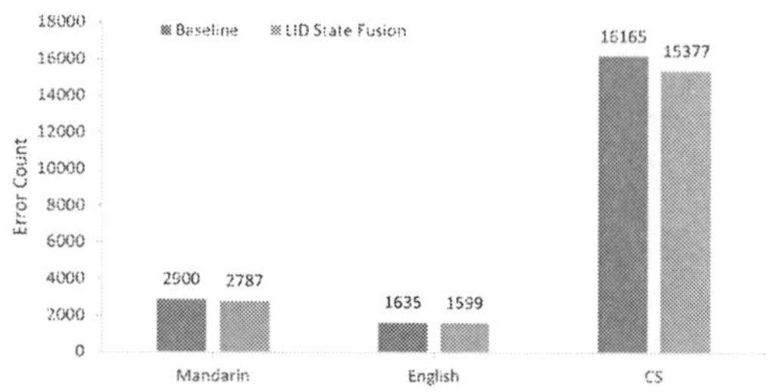

(a) Error counts on dev_{man} set

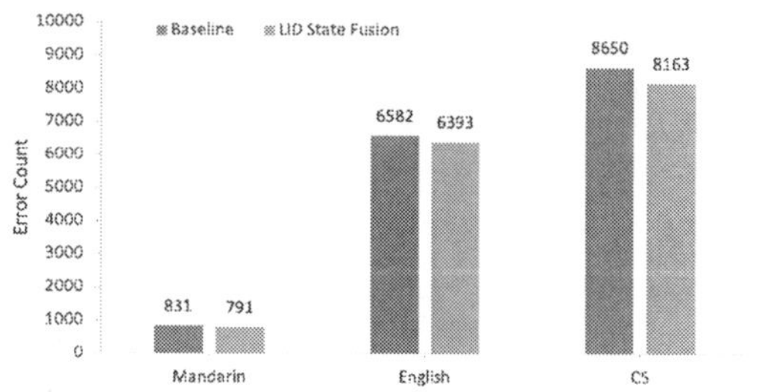

(b) Error counts on dev_{sge} set

Figure 5: Error counts on dev_{man} and dev_{sge} sets across three utterance categories. For Mandarin utterances, the error counts refer to character error counts. For English utterances, the error counts refer to word error counts. For code-switching utterances, the error counts refer to mixed error counts.

state fusion method results in a significant reduction in error counts for code-switching utterances. Specifically, we observed reductions of 4.9% and 5.6% in error counts on the dev_{man} and dev_{sge} sets, respectively. This indicates that the LID state fusion method effectively mitigates language confusion and improves the overall system performance, particularly in code-switching scenarios. Moreover, the analysis reveals that the LID state fusion method also contributes to a reduction in error counts for monolingual Mandarin and monolingual English utterances, although to a lesser extent compared to code-switching utterances. This observation suggests that the incorporation of language identity information helps the ASR system better capture language-specific patterns and transitions, leading to improved recognition accuracy even in monolingual contexts.

We further analyze code-switching transcription examples generated by the two ASR models: the Transformer-based ASR model (referred to as the baseline model) and the Transformer-based ASR model employed the LID state fusion method (referred to as the fusion model). The results are presented in Table 3. Overall, the transcriptions

Table 3: Examples of references and transcriptions generated by the baseline and fusion models. Recognizing errors (**** means deletion) are indicated in red color.

	Transcription
Reference	大 概 啊 那 个 cheese 大 概 二 十 五 这 样 咯
Baseline	大 概 er 那 个 去 大 概 二 十 五 这 样 咯
Fusion	大 概 啊 那 个 cheese 大 概 二 十 五 这 样 咯
Reference	圣 诞 节 快 到 了 have you made any preparations
Baseline	圣 诞 节 快 到 了 **** every may any preparations
Fusion	圣 诞 节 快 到 了 have you may any preparations
Reference	我 当 然 是 买 那 个 比 较 好 的 right
Baseline	我 大 家 是 买 那 个 比 较 好 的 right
Fusion	我 当 然 是 买 那 个 比 较 好 的 right
Reference	twenty percent 还 是 two percent 一 千 不 见 两 百 是
Baseline	then 第 percent 还 是 two percent
Fusion	twenty percent 还 是 two percent 一 千 不 见 两 百 是
Reference	你 觉 得 你 很 fit 吗
Baseline	你 觉 得 你 很 fat 吗
Fusion	你 觉 得 你 很 fit 吗

generated by the fusion model demonstrated superior semantic and grammatical accuracy compared to those produced by the baseline model, particularly when the monolingual segment context was short. These findings underscore the effectiveness of the LID state fusion method in addressing the challenges associated with code-switching speech recognition. By leveraging the contextual cues provided by language identity information, the ASR system becomes more proficient at distinguishing between languages and producing accurate transcriptions. The successful transcriptions of code-switching utterances highlight the LID state fusion method's ability to mitigate language confusion and enhance the system's performance in complex linguistic environments.

7 Conclusion

In this paper, we presented a novel language identity-language model scheme to predict language identity from pure text data, eliminating the need for reliance on speech data. We also explored two innovative methods to effectively incorporate text-derived language identity cues into ASR models. Our code-switching speech recognition experimental evaluations on the SEAME corpus demonstrated the effectiveness of our methods. By incorporating language identity information, our ASR system exhibits significantly reduced language confusion in transcribing code-switching utterances, yielding more precise transcriptions for both monolingual and code-switched utterances. Future work includes further enhancements to the LID-LM architecture and investigating additional integration strategies to better leverage language identity information in ASR systems. Additionally, exploring pre-training and fine-tuning techniques for LID-LM would open up more possibilities for efficiently utilizing text data to predict language identity.

Limitations

While our research has made significant strides in advancing code-switching ASR systems through the innovative use of text-derived language identity, there are several limitations that warrant consideration. First, our approach relies on the assumption that text data sufficiently captures language identity information. While this assumption holds for many contexts, it may not fully encompass the richness of linguistic diversity present in certain code-switching environments. Second, the performance of our method may vary across different language pairs, dialects, or domains. The robustness of the approach to such variations would benefit from additional scrutiny and validation in diverse linguistic settings. Lastly, our work explores specific integration strategies (LID state fusion and language posterior biasing) for incorporating text-derived language identity cues into ASR models. There may be alternative strategies or hybrid approaches that warrant exploration in future research to further enhance code-switching ASR systems. These limitations, while acknowledged, should be viewed as opportunities for future investigations to expand upon the foundations we have laid in this study.

References

Heike Adel, Ngoc Thang Vu, Katrin Kirchhoff, Dominic Telaar, and Tanja Schultz. 2015. Syntactic and semantic features for code-switching factored language models. *IEEE/ACM transactions on audio, speech, and language Processing*, 23(3):431–440.

Heike Adel, Ngoc Thang Vu, Franziska Kraus, Tim Schlippe, Haizhou Li, and Tanja Schultz. 2013. Recurrent neural network language modeling for code switching conversational speech. In *2013 IEEE International Conference on Acoustics, Speech and Signal Processing*, pages 8411–8415. IEEE.

Djegdjiga Amazouz, Martine Adda-Decker, and Lori Lamel. 2017. Addressing code-switching in french/algerian arabic speech. In *Interspeech 2017*, pages 62–66.

Kiran Bhuvanagiri and Sunil Kopparapu. 2010. An approach to mixed language automatic speech recognition. *Oriental COCOSDA, Kathmandu, Nepal.*

Siddharth Dalmia, Yuzong Liu, Srikanth Ronanki, and Katrin Kirchhoff. 2021. Transformer-transducers for code-switched speech recognition. In *ICASSP 2021-2021 IEEE International Conference on Acoustics, Speech and Signal Processing (ICASSP)*, pages 5859–5863. IEEE.

Suyoun Kim and Michael L Seltzer. 2018. Towards language-universal end-to-end speech recognition. In *2018 IEEE International Conference on Acoustics, Speech and Signal Processing (ICASSP)*, pages 4914–4918. IEEE.

Chia-Yu Li and Ngoc Thang Vu. 2019. Integrating knowledge in end-to-end automatic speech recognition for mandarin-english code-switching. In *2019 International Conference on Asian Language Processing (IALP)*, pages 160–165. IEEE.

Ke Li, Jinyu Li, Guoli Ye, Rui Zhao, and Yifan Gong. 2019. Towards code-switching asr for end-to-end ctc models. In *ICASSP 2019-2019 IEEE International Conference on Acoustics, Speech and Signal Processing (ICASSP)*, pages 6076–6080. IEEE.

Hexin Liu, Haihua Xu, Leibny Paola Garcia, Andy WH Khong, Yi He, and Sanjeev Khudanpur. 2023. Reducing language confusion for code-switching speech recognition with token-level language diarization. In *ICASSP 2023-2023 IEEE International Conference on Acoustics, Speech and Signal Processing (ICASSP)*, pages 1–5. IEEE.

Ilya Loshchilov and Frank Hutter. 2016. Sgdr: Stochastic gradient descent with warm restarts. In *International Conference on Learning Representations.*

Ne Luo, Dongwei Jiang, Shuaijiang Zhao, Caixia Gong, Wei Zou, and Xiangang Li. 2018. Towards end-to-end code-switching speech recognition. *arXiv preprint arXiv:1810.13091.*

Dau-Cheng Lyu, Ren-Yuan Lyu, Yuang-chin Chiang, and Chun-Nan Hsu. 2006. Speech recognition on code-switching among the chinese dialects. In *2006 IEEE International Conference on Acoustics Speech and Signal Processing Proceedings*, volume 1, pages I–I. IEEE.

Dau-Cheng Lyu, Tien-Ping Tan, Eng Siong Chng, and Haizhou Li. 2010. Seame: a mandarin-english code-switching speech corpus in south-east asia. In *Eleventh Annual Conference of the International Speech Communication Association.*

Surabhi Punjabi, Harish Arsikere, Zeynab Raeesy, Chander Chandak, Nikhil Bhave, Ankish Bansal, Markus Müller, Sergio Murillo, Ariya Rastrow, Sri Garimella, et al. 2020. Streaming end-to-end bilingual asr systems with joint language identification. *arXiv preprint arXiv:2007.03900.*

Zimeng Qiu, Yiyuan Li, Xinjian Li, Florian Metze, William M Campbell, and Amazon Alexa AI. 2020. Towards context-aware end-to-end code-switching speech recognition. In *INTERSPEECH*, pages 4776–4780.

Hiroshi Seki, Shinji Watanabe, Takaaki Hori, Jonathan Le Roux, and John R Hershey. 2018. An end-to-end language-tracking speech recognizer for mixed-language speech. In *2018 IEEE international conference on acoustics, speech and signal processing (ICASSP)*, pages 4919–4923. IEEE.

Changhao Shan, Chao Weng, Guangsen Wang, Dan Su, Min Luo, Dong Yu, and Lei Xie. 2019. Investigating end-to-end speech recognition for mandarin-english code-switching. In *ICASSP 2019-2019 IEEE International Conference on Acoustics, Speech and Signal Processing (ICASSP)*, pages 6056–6060. IEEE.

Anuroop Sriram, Heewoo Jun, Sanjeev Satheesh, and Adam Coates. 2018. Cold fusion: Training seq2seq models together with language models. In *Proc. Interspeech 2018*, pages 387–391.

Liang-Hsuan Tseng, Yu-Kuan Fu, Heng-Jui Chang, and Hung-yi Lee. 2021. Mandarin-english code-switching speech recognition with self-supervised speech representation models. *arXiv preprint arXiv:2110.03504*.

Ashish Vaswani, Noam Shazeer, Niki Parmar, Jakob Uszkoreit, Llion Jones, Aidan N Gomez, Łukasz Kaiser, and Illia Polosukhin. 2017. Attention is all you need. *Advances in neural information processing systems*, 30.

Ngoc Thang Vu, Dau-Cheng Lyu, Jochen Weiner, Dominic Telaar, Tim Schlippe, Fabian Blaicher, Eng-Siong Chng, Tanja Schultz, and Haizhou Li. 2012. A first speech recognition system for mandarin-english code-switch conversational speech. In *2012 IEEE International Conference on Acoustics, Speech and Signal Processing (ICASSP)*, pages 4889–4892. IEEE.

Qinyi Wang, Emre Yılmaz, Adem Derinel, and Haizhou Li. 2019. Code-Switching Detection Using ASR-Generated Language Posteriors. In *Proc. Interspeech 2019*, pages 3740–3744.

Qinyi Wang, Xinyuan Zhou, Haizhou Li, et al. 2023. Speech-and-text transformer: Exploiting unpaired text for end-to-end speech recognition. *APSIPA Transactions on Signal and Information Processing*, 12(1).

Shinji Watanabe, Takaaki Hori, Shigeki Karita, Tomoki Hayashi, Jiro Nishitoba, Yuya Unno, Nelson-Enrique Yalta Soplin, Jahn Heymann, Matthew Wiesner, Nanxin Chen, et al. 2018. Espnet: End-to-end speech processing toolkit. *Proc. Interspeech 2018*, pages 2207–2211.

Jochen Weiner, Ngoc Thang Vu, Dominic Telaar, Florian Metze, Tanja Schultz, Dau-Cheng Lyu, Eng-Siong Chng, and Haizhou Li. 2012a. Integration of language identification into a recognition system for spoken conversations containing code-switches. In *Spoken Language Technologies for Under-Resourced Languages*.

Jochen Weiner, Ngoc Thang Vu, Dominic Telaar, Florian Metze, Tanja Schultz, Dau-Cheng Lyu, Eng-Siong Chng, and Haizhou Li. 2012b. Integration of language identification into a recognition system for spoken conversations containing code-switches. In *Spoken Language Technologies for Under-Resourced Languages*.

Genta Indra Winata, Andrea Madotto, Chien-Sheng Wu, and Pascale Fung. 2018. Code-switching language modeling using syntax-aware multi-task learning. *arXiv preprint arXiv:1805.12070*.

Emre Yılmaz, Henk van den Heuvel, and David A. van Leeuwen. 2018. Code-switching detection with data-augmented acoustic and language models. In *Proc. SLTU*, pages 127–131.

Hengxin Yin, Guangyu Hu, Fei Wang, and Pengfei Ren. 2022. Hybrid ctc language identification structure for mandarin-english code-switching asr. In *2022 13th International Symposium on Chinese Spoken Language Processing (ISCSLP)*, pages 537–541. IEEE.

Zhiping Zeng, Yerbolat Khassanov, Van Tung Pham, Haihua Xu, Eng Siong Chng, and Haizhou Li. 2018. On the end-to-end solution to mandarin-english code-switching speech recognition. *arXiv preprint arXiv:1811.00241*.

Hong Ji Zhang. 2013. Code-switching speech detection method by combination of language and acoustic information. In *Advanced Materials Research*, volume 756, pages 3622–3627. Trans Tech Publ.

Shuai Zhang, Jiangyan Yi, Zhengkun Tian, Jianhua Tao, and Ye Bai. 2021. Rnn-transducer with language bias for end-to-end mandarin-english code-switching speech recognition. In *2021 12th International Symposium on Chinese Spoken Language Processing (ISCSLP)*, pages 1–5. IEEE.

Xinyuan Zhou, Emre Yılmaz, Yanhua Long, Yijie Li, and Haizhou Li. 2020. Multi-Encoder-Decoder Transformer for Code-Switching Speech Recognition. In *Proc. Interspeech 2020*, pages 1042–1046.

Prompting Multilingual Large Language Models to Generate Code-Mixed Texts: The Case of South East Asian Languages

Zheng-Xin Yong[1] **Ruochen Zhang**[1] **Jessica Zosa Forde**[1] **Skyler Wang**[2]
Arjun Subramonian[3] **Holy Lovenia**[4] **Samuel Cahyawijaya**[4] **Genta Indra Winata**[5]
Lintang Sutawika[6] **Jan Christian Blaise Cruz**[7] **Yin Lin Tan**[8,9] **Long Phan**[10]
Rowena Garcia[11] **Thamar Solorio**[12] **Alham Fikri Aji**[12]
[1]Brown University [2]UC Berkeley [3]University of California, Los Angeles
[4]HKUST [5]Bloomberg [6]EleutherAI [7]Samsung R&D Institute Philippines
[8]Stanford University [9]National University of Singapore [10]VietAI Research
[11]University of Potsdam [12]MBZUAI

Abstract

While code-mixing is a common linguistic practice in many parts of the world, collecting high-quality and low-cost code-mixed data remains a challenge for natural language processing (NLP) research. The recent proliferation of Large Language Models (LLMs) compels one to ask: how capable are these systems in generating code-mixed data? In this paper, we explore prompting multilingual LLMs in a zero-shot manner to generate code-mixed data for seven languages in South East Asia (SEA), namely Indonesian, Malay, Chinese, Tagalog, Vietnamese, Tamil, and Singlish. We find that publicly available multilingual instruction-tuned models such as BLOOMZ and Flan-T5-XXL are incapable of producing texts with phrases or clauses from different languages. ChatGPT exhibits inconsistent capabilities in generating code-mixed texts, wherein its performance varies depending on the prompt template and language pairing. For instance, ChatGPT generates fluent and natural Singlish texts (an English-based creole spoken in Singapore), but for English-Tamil language pair, the system mostly produces grammatically incorrect or semantically meaningless utterances. Furthermore, it may erroneously introduce languages not specified in the prompt. Based on our investigation, existing multilingual LLMs exhibit a wide range of proficiency in code-mixed data generation for SEA languages. As such, we advise against using LLMs in this context without extensive human checks.

1 Introduction

Code-mixing, also known as code-switching, is the linguistic practice of alternating between two or more languages in an utterance or conversation (Poplack, 1978). It allows individuals to express culturally-specific ideas, connect with or differentiate from other interlocutors, and reify their identities (Bhatia and Ritchie, 2004; Grosjean, 1982; Toribio, 2002; Chen, 1996; Doğruöz et al., 2021). Despite its prevalence across many parts of the world, computational research into this area remains understudied (Diab et al., 2014; Aguilar et al., 2020; Winata et al., 2021, 2022; Zhang et al., 2023).

Figure 1: Depiction of SEA regions, which consist of a total of 11 countries. We prompt LLMs to generate code-mixed data of languages used in six South East Asian countries (colored in dark blue): Brunei, Indonesia, Malaysia, Philippines, Singapore, and Vietnam.

One longstanding challenge in this area involves acquiring high-quality and low-cost code-mixed data. For one, code-mixing is observed more frequently in colloquial settings and spoken communication, which makes procuring and curating extensive datasets logistically demanding and costly (Chan et al., 2009; Winata et al., 2021). Moreover, despite code-mixing's prevalence across social media and digital messaging platforms, consolidating such data may be curtailed by legal guardrails and scalability issues. Recognizing these challenges, we explore the feasibility of using generative Large Language Models (LLMs) to ameliorate data scarcity in code-mixing research. As

Proceedings of the 6th Workshop on Computational Approaches to Linguistic Code-Switching, pages 43–63
December 7, 2023 ©2023 Association for Computational Linguistics

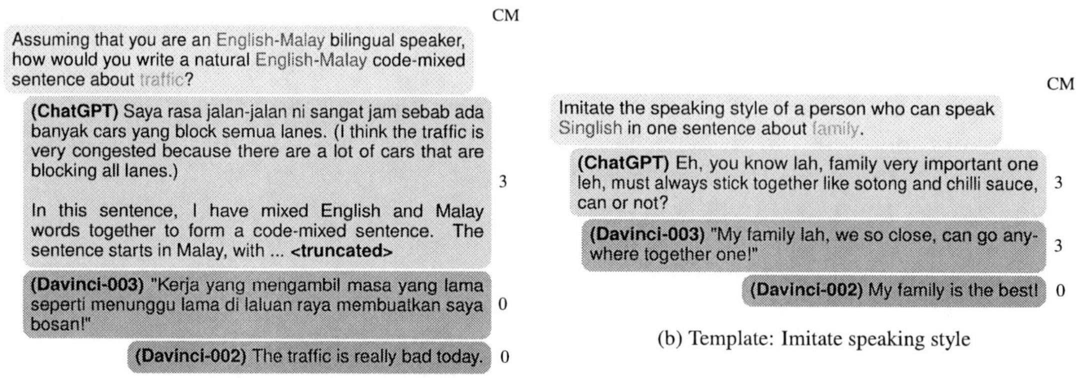

(a) Template: Assume to be bilingual speaker

(b) Template: Imitate speaking style

Figure 2: Example prompt templates with different languages and topic fields and responses from LLMs containing code-mixed / non-code-mixed sentences. Note that the explanations are a part of ChatGPT's original generation. "CM" indicates the level of code-mixing (Section 2.2). See Figure 15 in Appendix for all prompt templates and responses from other LLMs such as BLOOMZ and Flan-T5-XXL.

recent work shows that LLMs can successfully generate synthetic data (Taori et al., 2023; He et al., 2023; Tang et al., 2023; Whitehouse et al., 2023), here we evaluate whether multilingual LLMs can be prompted to create code-mixed data that look natural to native speakers (and if so, to what extent).

To this end, we hone in on languages in South East Asia (SEA). Home to more than 680 million people and over 1200 languages, code-mixing is particularly prevalent in this region due to its countries' extended histories of language and cultural cross-fertilization and colonialism (Figure 1) (Goddard, 2005; Bautista and Gonzalez, 2006; Reid et al., 2022). Marked by its distinctive multilingual and multiracial composition today, SEA presents an opportunity to further research numerous marginalized languages and linguistic practices in NLP research[1] (Migliazza, 1996; Goddard, 2005; Joshi et al., 2020; Aji et al., 2022; Winata et al., 2023; Cahyawijaya et al., 2022). Nonetheless, publicly available code-mixed datasets relevant to SEA communities remain limited (Lyu et al., 2010; Winata et al., 2022).

We prompt five multilingual LLMs, i.e., ChatGPT, InstructGPT (davinci-002 and davinci-003) (Ouyang et al., 2022), BLOOMZ (Muennighoff et al., 2022), and Flan-T5-XXL (Chung et al., 2022) to generate code-mixed text that bilingually mixes English with either **Malay, Indonesian, Chinese, Tagalog, Vietnamese, or Tamil**. All of these six SEA languages (alongside English) are used across six SEA countries, namely Singapore, Malaysia, Brunei, Philippines, Indonesia, and Vietnam. Furthermore, they belong to different language families—Indo-European, Austronesian, Sino-Tibetan, Austro-Asiatic, and Dravidian. An example of a prompt we used is: "Write an English and Tamil code-mixed sentence about Artificial Intelligence." In addition, we prompt these LLMs to generate texts in **Singlish**, an English-based creole widely spoken in Singapore that combines multiple SEA languages such as Malay, Chinese and Tamil. We ask native speakers to annotate the *naturalness* (i.e., whether a native speaker would speak as such) and the *level of code-mixing* in the outputs.

To the best of our knowledge, our work marks the first attempt at studying the generation of synthetic code-mixed data through prompting LLMs in a zero-shot fashion without any monolingual reference texts or explicit linguistic constraints (Solorio and Liu, 2008; Tarunesh et al., 2021; Rizvi et al., 2021; Mondal et al., 2022). We find that publicly available multilingual language models such as BLOOMZ and Flan-T5-XXL are only capable of code-mixing with loanwords or topic-related nouns. Most of the time, they fail to code-mix (despite being advertised as multilingual). While ChatGPT stands out in its ability to generate code-mixed texts, it is extremely sensitive to the prompt template and exhibits a considerable variance of success in generating natural-sounding code-mixed

[1]Major languages in SEA countries belong to different language families such as Indo-European, Thai, Austronesian, Sino-Tibetan, Dravidian, and Austro-Asiatic. Furthermore, there are at least thousands of major and minor SEA languages.

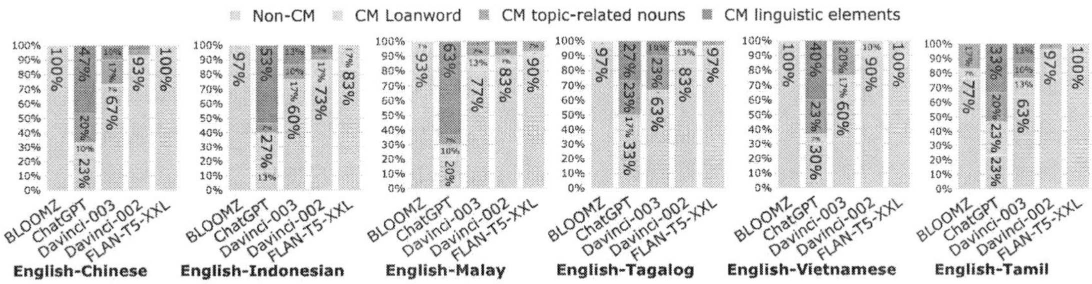

Figure 3: Comparison of performance of different LLMs in generating code-mixed data through zero-shot prompting. We distribute the result across different code-mixing levels: (0) No code-mixing (Non-CM), (1) Loanword, (2) Topic-related nouns, and (3) Linguistic Elements.

texts across different language pairs. Additionally, it may erroneously introduce additional languages not specified in the prompt and wrongly explain the code-mixing of the text.

Our results lead us to conclude that code-mixing, at least as of today, is not considered an essential component of many multilingual LLMs. Moreover, the opaque creation of models like ChatGPT makes it difficult to ascertain the mechanisms that enable code-mixing. By highlighting the limited promises of LLMs in a specific form of low-resource data generation, we advise NLP researchers against using existing systems to produce synthetic code-mixed data without extensive human evaluation.

2 Methodology

2.1 Prompting Language Models

We collect synthetic code-mixed data by prompting LLMs with requests along two axes: languages and topics (food, family, traffic, Artificial Intelligence, and weather). See Figure 2 for examples of different prompt templates. Specifically, we explore ChatGPT, InstructGPT (davinci-002 and davinci-003) (Ouyang et al., 2022), 176B-parameter BLOOMZ (Muennighoff et al., 2022), and Flan-T5-XXL (Chung et al., 2022). We use OpenAI and HuggingFace's API for prompting (see Appendix B), except in the case of ChatGPT, which we manually queried through its web interface[2].

In our prompts, we specify code-mixing between English and either Indonesian, Malay, Mandarin, Tagalog, Vietnamese, or Tamil. We focused on code-mixing English with SEA languages for two reasons: (1) extensive literature on code-mixed English provides a relevant point of comparison, and (2) English is one of the most widely used languages in code-mixing across SEA countries (Kirkpatrick, 2014). We additionally prompt with sentences in Singlish, a creole language, to evaluate how sensitive LLMs are to the diversity of language practices in the SEA region. In total, we submitted 210 unique prompts per language model.

2.2 Evaluation

Level of Code-Mixing

To evaluate outputs, we ask whether LLMs can produce *intrasentential* code-mixed text. We adopt the definition of intrasentential code-mixing from Berk-Seligson (1986), which covers mixing small constituents—such as noun and verb phrases—and large constituents—such as coordinate clauses and prepositional phrases. Native speakers are then tasked to manually annotate the collected responses on a scale from 0 to 3 using the following coding guidelines to denote the degree of code-mixedness:

- **0 - No code-mixing:** The generated text is written purely in one language or only exhibits *intersentential* code-mixing (i.e., switching at sentence boundaries including interjection, idiom, and tags). We adopt the definition from Berk-Seligson (1986).
- **1 - Loanwords:** The generated text uses loanwords for common terminologies. We consider a word as a loanword if it is listed in Wiktionary[3]. For example: In the sentence, "I like eating *pho*," "pho" is a loanword.
- **2 - Topic-related nouns:** The generated text uses nouns related to the topic specified in the prompt in another language. For instance, for the topic of traffic, an example would be "今天的 *traffic* 真的很糟糕，我开了一个小时

[2]ChatGPT's API was not publicly released when we conducted this study.

[3]https://en.wiktionary.org

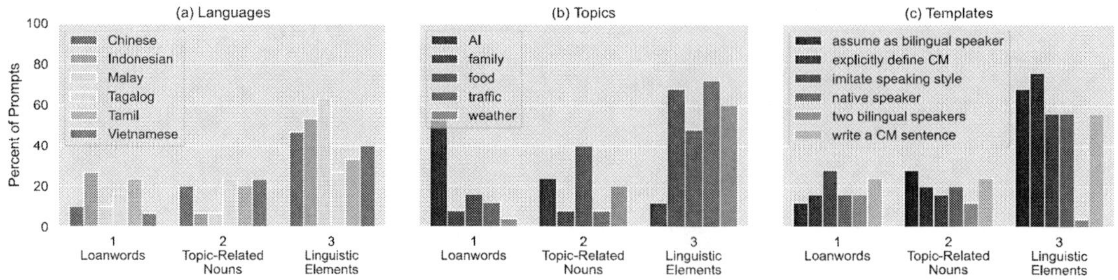

Figure 4: Analysis of code-mixed data generated by ChatGPT.

才到了办公室." (Chinese: "The traffic today is really terrible. I spent an hour driving to get to the office.")

- **3 - Linguistic Elements:** The generated text mixes linguistic elements beyond loanwords and topic-related nouns at the phrasal or clausal level. One example is verb phrases: "My family *ay nagplano ng isang malaking* family reunion *sa park* this coming weekend." (Tagalog: "My family has planned a big family reunion at the park this coming weekend.") This category also includes intraword code-mixing, e.g., "Kapag busy ang trapiko, mag-ingat ka sa *pagda-drive*[4] para maiwasan mo ang mga masamang pangyayari." (Tagalog: "When traffic is busy, be careful while driving to avoid accidents.")

We use this scale instead of popular word-level metrics such as CMI (Gambäck and Das, 2014) because our scale more holistically evaluates the ability of LLMs to code-mix. The lower end of this scale reflects a lower complexity of code-mixing. Code-mixing with loanwords is arguably less challenging, as they are often used in a monolingual context to begin with. Likewise, code-mixing topic-related nouns is not as complex as there is presumably a correspondence between the nouns in the two languages and is primed by the prompts.

On the other hand, code-mixing prefixes/suffixes, phrases and clauses requires a good grasp of the intricate morphosyntactic structures of both languages and can produce syntactically diverse code-mixed data. Therefore, we consider the LLM to have *successfully* generated code-mixed text only if the text belongs to this category.

[4]The prefix "pag-" in Tagalog is affixed to the English word "drive", resulting in the word "pagda-drive" (the act of driving). This example demonstrates the application of Tagalog inflection rules to English words.

Naturalness

We asked native speakers to annotate the naturalness of the generated text on a rating scale of 1—not natural at all, 2—an annotator may see someone else from other regions/cultures speaking it, and 3—an annotator may see themselves speaking it. If the text is not considered natural (rating of 1), we requested the annotators to document their reasons, including fluency issues, syntactical errors, and semantic incorrectness.

Code-mixing practices vary across race, gender, class, and geography, among other axes. Therefore, in line with sociolinguistic research, we emphasize that the "naturalness" of code-mixed text (as perceived by an annotator) is subjective, and depends on the background and social location of the annotator. All annotators are AI researchers and native speakers of their respective SEA languages. We refer to Appendix G for more information about our annotators and their inter-annotator agreement scores.

Accurateness

We additionally annotate the *accurateness* of the generations to account for task failure or incorrect explanations. Inaccurate outputs were defined by:

- **Failure to follow instructions:** Some LLMs fail to accurately carry out the prompt instruction (for example, generating monolingual sentences). We also observe some code-mixed outputs that include additional languages unspecified in the prompts.
- **Inaccurate explanations:** ChatGPT, among other LLMs, tends to explain the code-mixed phrases, but occasionally provides incorrect explanations (see Figure 10).

Imagine there are two English-Vietnamese bilingual speakers talking to each other, can you imagine a conversation between them talking about family?

(ChatGPT) Person A: Hi, how's your family doing?
Person B: Chào bạn, gia đình tôi đang khỏe. Còn gia đình bạn thì sao?
Person A: They're good, thanks for asking. How about yours?
Person B: Gia đình tôi cũng khỏe, cảm ơn bạn. Mới đây, tôi đã đi chơi với ông bà và các em họ của mình.

Imagine there are two English-Chinese bilingual speakers talking to each other, can you imagine a conversation between them talking about weather?

(ChatGPT) English Speaker 1: Hey, have you been outside today? It's really hot!
Chinese Speaker 1: 是啊，今天天气真的很热。
English Speaker 2: Yeah, it's been pretty sunny all day.
Chinese Speaker 2: 是啊，今天一整天都很晴朗。

Figure 5: Failure cases when we prompt ChatGPT to imagine two bilingual speakers conversing about a specific topic.

3 Results

3.1 English-SEA Languages

Figure 3 demonstrates that ChatGPT outperforms other language models in generating code-mixed data across six different language pairs, and is particularly proficient at code-mixing linguistic expressions. For InstructGPT, the davinci-003 model demonstrates some ability to generate syntactically varied code-mixed texts, whereas davinci-002 mostly code-mixes with loanwords. Conversely, the other two publicly available multilingual LLMs have extremely limited code-mixing capabilities. More specifically, Flan-T5-XXL can only code-mix with loanwords for the Indonesian-English language pair, and most of its non-English monolingual outputs suffer from severe fluency issues (see Appendix D). BLOOMZ is only capable of code-mixing topic-related nouns for Tamil-English even though its multilingual pretraining data ROOTS (Laurençon et al., 2022) and instruction-tuning data xP3 (Muennighoff et al., 2022) cover Indonesian, Chinese, Tamil, and Vietnamese. We observe no direct effects of the proportions of these languages in the training sets on BLOOMZ's ability to code-mix (Appendix E).

We further break down the performance of ChatGPT in Figure 4[5]. In Figure 4(a), we see that ChatGPT is least proficient at mixing linguistic elements for English-Tagalog. This may be due to syntactic differences between the two languages; for example, English exhibits Subject-Verb-Object (SVO) word order, whereas Tagalog exhibits a verb-initial structure. Moreover, English demonstrates nominative-accusative alignment, whereas Tagalog, being a symmetrical-voice language, utilizes a case system with a typological classification that "remains controversial among Austronesian linguists" (Aldridge, 2012, 192). In contrast, ChatGPT performs the best for English-Indonesian code-mixing, which may be due to training data distribution and similarities between the two languages regarding word order and morphosyntactic alignment. We also find that ChatGPT is capable of using either English or a SEA language as the matrix language, i.e., as the main language of a sentence as per the Matrix Language Frame model (Myers-Scotton, 1997).

Figure 4(b) shows ChatGPT's code-mixing proficiency based on topics. ChatGPT tends to code-mix with loanwords when the topic is about "AI" by mixing the English loanwords "Artificial Intelligence," or its short form "AI." For food, it tends to code-mix with food-related terms—which are topic-related nouns—in SEA languages such as "bánh mì" (Vietnamese sandwich). We also observe some representation biases in specific language-topic pairs. For instance, when it comes to food, ChatGPT uses the word "nasi goreng" (fried rice) for all English-Indonesian responses. For other topics, such as traffic and weather, it tends to code-mix phrases related to traffic congestion and hot weather.

In Figure 4(c), we find the prompt template with the highest quality results is the one where the term code-mixing is explicitly defined. In contrast, the worst-performing template consists of asking the model to generate conversations between two bilingual speakers, where the term code-mixing is unmentioned. In Figure 5, we see that ChatGPT generates an uncommon pattern of conversations where one interlocutor speaks in English and the other speaks in another language entirely (top example). Furthermore, ChatGPT may assume there are four speakers though the prompt asks for a conversation between two speakers (bottom example).

In terms of naturalness, we observe a considerable variance in ChatGPT's ouputs, with English-Tamil being the least natural (Figure 6). Further

[5]Detailed analysis for davinci-002, davinci-003, Flan-T5-XXL and BLOOMZ can be found in the Appendix (Figure 11, Figure 12, Figure 13 and Figure 14).

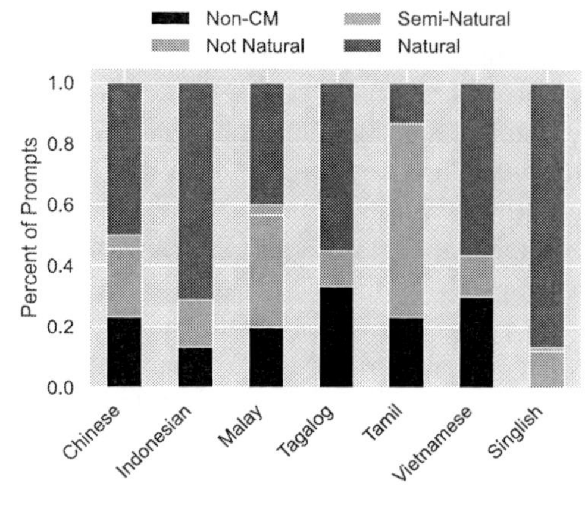

Figure 6: Naturalness of code-mixed (CM) text generated from ChatGPT. "Semi-Natural" indicates that the annotators see someone else from other region/culture speaking it, whereas "Natural" indicates that the annotators see themselves speaking it.

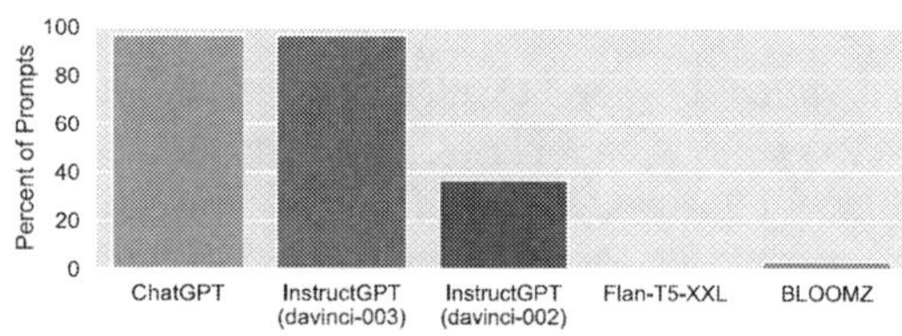

Figure 7: Models' performance in generating Singlish expressions through zero-shot prompting.

analysis shows that ChatGPT either commits grammatical mistakes (such as comma splice and redundancy) or generates semantically confusing sentences. We also observe unnatural text patterns that mix two different script systems of the same language in the single sentence (for example, the Tamil script and its transliterated Latin script). We document these naturalness and fluency issues in Table 4 (Appendix F) and report the interannotator agreement scores in Appendix G.

3.2 Singlish

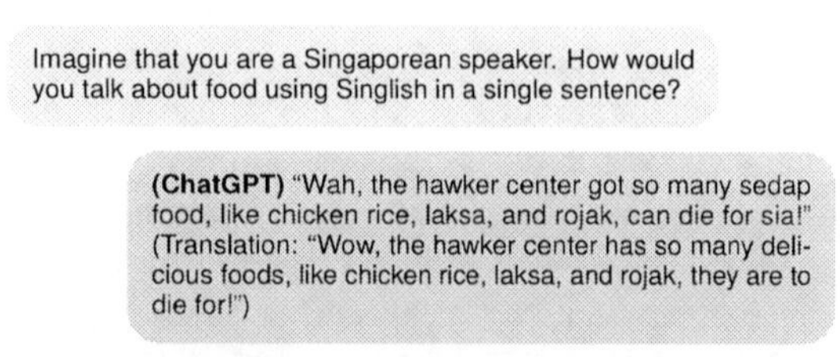

Figure 8: Singlish sentence and its translation to Standard English, both generated by ChatGPT.

Given that Singlish is an English-based creole language that has lexicalized a lot of words from many languages such as Malay, Chinese, Tamil, Cantonese, and Hokkien (e.g., "lah," "leh," and "loh," etc.), it is difficult to disambiguate loanwords and linguistic elements. Therefore, we classify the model success based on a binary scale of whether the generated sentences contain Singlish expressions (e.g., interjections, lexicalized phrases of languages without a standardized writing system)[6]. In Figure 7, we see that ChatGPT and InstructGPT (davinci-003) have up to a 96% success rate in generating Singlish sentences, whereas Flan-T5-XXL and BLOOMZ have a near-zero success rate. Furthermore, we find that ChatGPT is also capable of translating Singlish expressions into Standard American English (Figure 8).

While ChatGPT is capable of generating fluent and natural Singlish (Figure 6), we observe semantic inaccuracies in their word choices that are discernible by native speakers. In Figure 2(b), ChatGPT generates an English-Malay code-mixed phrase "sotong and chilli sauce" where "sotong" is a Malay word for "squid." Upon first inspection, the sentence appears syntactically sound but native speakers found the analogy between familial connections and the dish (squid with chili sauce) to be semantically confusing.

OpenAI's documentation of model differences[7]—more specifically, that davinci-003 can produce higher-quality writing, process more complex instructions, and generate longer content than davinci-002—does not adequately explain why ChatGPT and davinci-003 significantly outperform davinci-002 and other multilingual LLMs in generating Singlish text. We hypothesize that the performance gap may be due to the larger presence of Singlish in OpenAI's training data. Singlish is not only one of the most well-researched dialects of English (Sin, 2017), but it also uses the English alphabet and Latin script systems (unlike many other SEA languages), which potentially makes it easier for LLMs to scrape and parse data in this language.

3.3 Failures of ChatGPT

We notice that ChatGPT may fail to produce correctly code-mixed text when the nationality of the speaker is mentioned. Invoking nationality may

[6] A reference list can be found at https://en.wikipedia.org/wiki/Singlish_vocabulary

[7] https://help.openai.com/en/articles/6779149-how-do-text-davinci-002-and-text-davinci-003-differ

> Imagine that you are a Malaysian speaker. How would you talk about traffic using both English and Chinese in a single sentence?

> **(ChatGPT)** Assuming that you are asking for a sentence that combines both English and Chinese in a natural and commonly used way by Malaysian speakers, here is an example:
> "今天的 traffic 很 teruk，我要赶紧走去 KLCC for meeting。"
> This sentence incorporates the English word "traffic" and the Chinese word "teruk" (which means "bad" or "terrible" in English) to describe the situation of the traffic being very bad. The speaker then switches back to English to express their intention to hurry to KLCC for a meeting. This kind of code-switching is common in Malaysia, where speakers often mix languages in their daily conversations.

Figure 9: ChatGPT's failure to follow the prompt. Underlined texts show its language misclassification.

induce ChatGPT to generate code-mixed texts with an *additional* national language of the country. In the Figure 9 example, because the national language of Malaysia is Malay[8], ChatGPT not only returns a code-mixed response that includes the Malay word "teruk" when prompted for English-Chinese utterance by a Malaysian, but also misclassifies the word "teruk" as Chinese.

While ChatGPT can explain how its generated text is code-mixed (as illustrated in Figure 2(a)), we find its justifications unreliable for two reasons. First, it may hallucinate words that do not exist in the code-mixed text. For instance, in the top example in Figure 10, the English word "cold" does not exist in the code-mixed text. Second, it may assign words or phrases to the wrong language. In the bottom example in Figure 10, the phrase "nak minum air sejuk je" is in Malay, not English. This observation corroborates Bang et al.'s (2023) finding suggesting ChatGPT performs poorly on language identification tasks for low-resource languages.

4 Implications for LLMs and Ways Forward

In this section, we walk through various implications of our work for understanding the deployment of LLMs for synthetic data generation in low-resource settings, multilinguality in LLMs, importance of code-mixing ability in generative LLMs, and research transparency.

Deploying LLMs for Low-Resourced Data Generation By putting LLMs' generative capabilities to the test, we ask in this work if they can generate high-quality and low-cost code-mixed texts for

[8]Mandarin Chinese is widely spoken in the country.

> Imagine that you are an Indonesian speaker. How would you talk about weather using both English and Indonesian in a single sentence?

> **(ChatGPT)** If I were to talk about weather using both English and Indonesian in a single sentence, I might say something like: "*Hari ini sangat hot dan panas sekali, saya rasa aku butuh minum air dingin.*" This sentence includes the English words "hot" and "cold" to describe the weather, and the Indonesian words "panas" and "dingin" which have similar meanings. Additionally, the sentence also includes a personal statement in Indonesian, "saya rasa aku butuh minum air dingin," which means "I feel like I need to drink cold water."

> Code-mixing refers to a phenomenon of combining two or more languages in a single sentence. Can you generate a code-mixed English-Malay sentence about weather?

> **(ChatGPT)** "*The weather hari ni sangat panas, I rasa macam nak minum air sejuk je.*" (Translation: "The weather today is very hot, I feel like drinking cold water.")
> In this sentence, "hari ni" and "sangat panas" are in Malay, while "I" and "nak minum air sejuk je" are in English.

Figure 10: Underlined texts show wrong explanations about the code-mixed text. We italicize the *code-mixed sentences* to make it explicit to the reader.

researchers working on a topic plagued by limited data availability. While we conclude that ChatGPT has shown relative success in generating code-mixed texts for some SEA languages, we advise researchers to exercise heavy caution when using this data generation technique. Even for Singlish, which outperforms the other languages examined, we find that syntactically-sound responses may contain semantic inaccuracies that are difficult for non-native speakers to detect. Furthermore, its explanations may be misleading. Due to the lack of reliability, we strongly suggest researchers to implement extensive human checks with native speakers if they wish to pursue this method of data generation.

Multilingual $\neq$ Code-Mix Compatible Our results with BLOOMZ and Flan-T5-XXL show that the ability to code-mix is not acquired by LLMs after pretraining and/or finetuning with multilingual data (Laurençon et al., 2022; Muennighoff et al., 2022; Chung et al., 2022). In other words, for most NLP models, multilinguality simply means that the same system can process tasks and generate outputs in multiple languages, but not necessarily in the same sentence. By highlighting this limitation, we echo previous research motivating the inclusion of code-mixing abilities in NLP models. Doing so requires NLP models to capture the dynamics of combining languages that have different degrees of typological affinities, as well as pragmatic and contextual features such as tone, formality, and other cultural nuances (Winata et al., 2020; Lai and Nissim, 2022; Kabra et al., 2023).

Towards More Inclusive Language Technology Recognizing that generative LLMs are the primary driving force behind the advancement of AI conversational agents and speech technology (Thoppilan et al., 2022; SambaNova Systems, 2023; Pratap et al., 2023), we emphasize the significance of incorporating code-mixed output recognition and generation capabilities in LLMs in order to enhance the inclusivity and humaneness of language technology. By enabling conversational agents to reflect the language-mixing patterns of the users, people can communicate in ways that are more comfortable and authentic to their linguistic identities. In fact, a recent study by Bawa et al. (2020) has shown that multilingual users strongly prefer chatbots that can code-mix. Removing the need for people to adjust their speech patterns to become legible to machines would not only mitigate the effects of linguistics profiling (Baugh, 2005; Dingemanse and Liesenfeld, 2022) and hegemonic, Western-centric technological designs, but also enable users to develop more trust with language technology through naturalistic dialogue interactions.

Research Transparency Aside from showing that ChatGPT and InstructGPT *can* code-mix, we cannot confidently identify *how* the models do so due to the lack of transparency in how these systems are developed. Without a window into training data and engineering processes that went into models like ChatGPT, we can only speculate that their training data includes a substantial amount of code-mixed texts. To help facilitate greater levels of transparency and accountability, we urge forthcoming LLMs to be more open about how the models were developed and to document accurately and comprehensively the training data used.

5 Related Work

Code-Mixed Data in SEA Unlike monolingual data, there is only a limited number of human-curated code-mixed datasets. This resource limitation is more severe in SEA due to its marginalization in NLP research (Winata et al., 2022). Popular current code-mixing evaluation benchmarks (Aguilar et al., 2020; Khanuja et al., 2020) do not include SEA languages, and existing code-mixing studies in SEA only cover a limited number of language pairs and creoles, e.g., English-Tagalog (Oco and Roxas, 2012), English-Indonesian (Barik et al., 2019; Yulianti et al., 2021), Javanese-Indonesian (Tho et al., 2021), Chinese-English (Lyu et al., 2010; Lovenia et al., 2022; Zhang and Eickhoff, 2023) and Singlish (Chen and Min-Yen, 2015; Lent et al., 2021)[9]. The current corpus does not even scratch the surface of the sheer amount of code-mixedness in SEA (Redmond et al., 2009), where deployable data is practically non-existent. In this work, we try to close this gap by exploring the potential of generating synthetic code-mixed data for the SEA region by prompting LLMs.

Synthetic Code-Mixing Generation of synthetic code-mixed data to address data scarcity problem has been previously explored. Solorio and Liu (2008), Winata et al. (2019), and Tan and Joty (2021) have attempted to generate synthetic code-mixed sentences through word alignment and candidate selection from a parallel corpus. Liu et al. (2020) and Adilazuarda et al. (2022) have similarly generated synthetic code-mixed sentences by replacing words in monolingual sentences with their machine-translated counterparts, whereas Pratapa et al. (2018), Rizvi et al. (2021) and Santy et al. (2021) leveraged parse tree structure for such replacements. Another approach is to perform neural machine translation to translate monolingual sentences to code-mixed ones (Appicharla et al., 2021; Gautam et al., 2021; Jawahar et al., 2021; Dowlagar and Mamidi, 2021). In this work, we assess a novel way of generating synthetic code-mixed sentences through prompting multilingual LLMs.

6 Conclusion

To ameliorate the scarcity of code-mixed data for South East Asian languages, we explore generating synthetic code-mixed data using state-of-the-art multilingual Large Language Models (LLMs). On one hand, we find that publicly available LLMs such as BLOOMZ and Flan-T5-XXL have limited capability in generating syntactically diverse code-mixed data. On the other hand, closed-source models such as ChatGPT and InstructGPT are better at generating natural code-mixed text, but their performance varies substantially depending on the

[9]To exacerbate the situation, some of the SEA code-mixed datasets are no longer publicly available.

prompt template and language pairing. Furthermore, many outputs suffer from syntactic, semantic, and reliability issues. Therefore, we caution against using LLM-generated synthetic code-mixed data without the involvement of native speakers for annotating and editing.

7 Limitations

7.1 Effectiveness of Synthetic Code-Mixed Data on Downstream Tasks

In our study, we did not evaluate how much our synthetically generated code-mixed data improve the ability of language models to handle code-mixed text in downstream NLP tasks. While previous findings have shown that finetuning models with synthetic code-mixed data yields less performance gains than with naturally occurring code-mixed data (Santy et al., 2021), we believe that this performance gap will diminish as the quality of synthetic data generation gets better with future multilingual LLMs.

7.2 Lack of Human-Generated Data

While we annotated the degree of code-mixedness and naturalness, we did not have human-generated, naturally occurring, code-mixed sentences in response to the prompt topics. Therefore, we could not systematically compare the data distribution of our synthetic data against the human-generated data. However, since there are multiple ways in which a sentence can be code-mixed, our focus in this work is on how human-like are the sentences, and this, we believe, was adequately captured by our evaluation.

7.3 Monolingual Zero-Shot Prompting

Our study only uses prompt templates written in English to prompt language models in a zero-shot manner. In future follow-ups, we will (1) use code-mixed prompt templates such as "Generate an English-Bahasa sentence" instead of "Generate an English-Malay sentence" and (2) investigate LLMs' capabilities in generating code-mixed data with in-context few-shot examples.

7.4 Instruction-Tuned Language Models

Our work only covers instruction-tuned language models. In future work, we will include a comparison between multilingual models that are not finetuned with instructions—for example, GPT3 (davinci) (Brown et al., 2020) and BLOOM (Scao et al., 2022)—to explore the effects of instruction tuning in generating code-mixed data.

7.5 English-Centric Code-Mixing

Our study focuses on generating code-mixed data only for English-SEA language pairs. For future studies, we plan to investigate generating code-mixed data for non-English language pairs commonly spoken in SEA countries (such as Malay-Chinese and Indonesian-Javanese).

7.6 Failures of BLOOM and Flan-T5-XXL

Given the lack of research transparency on why ChatGPT performs better at code-mixed text generation, we assume that the publicly available models such as BLOOM and Flan-T5-XXL are unable to code-mix due to the lack of code-mixed texts in the pretraining corpora and code-mixing tasks in the instruction-tuning datasets. Further investigation is warranted to understand the effects of code-mixed text in pretraining and instruction-tuning data on code-mixed text generation.

7.7 Presence of Synthetic Code-Mixed Data in Future Pretraining Data

As we advocate for the code-mixing ability in future generations of LLMs, we are aware of the potential risks of *data feedback*, where generative models that recursively train on data generated by previous generations may amplify biases and lose information about the tails of the original distribution (Shumailov et al., 2023; Taori and Hashimoto, 2022). Since these negative effects can be mitigated through human-generated content (Shumailov et al., 2023), it becomes imperative for the NLP community to collect natural code-mixed data for low-resource languages.

8 Ethical Considerations

Code-mixing reflects the linguistic, social, and cultural identity of a multilingual community. Researchers and practitioners should approach synthetic code-mixing with sensitivity and respect, and be cognizant of the potential risks of cultural appropriation or misrepresentation when generating code-mixed data using LLMs. Since LLMs are trained on web data, they may encode biases perpetuating stereotypes, discrimination, or marginalization of specific languages or communities. Prior work has also documented how synthetic data may play a role in feedback loops that amplify the presence of biased language generation (Taori and Hashimoto, 2022). Therefore, collaboration with linguists, language experts, and community representatives is necessary to avoid the unintentional perpetuation of stereotypes and cultural insensitivity.

References

Muhammad Farid Adilazuarda, Samuel Cahyawijaya, Genta Indra Winata, Pascale Fung, and Ayu Purwarianti. 2022. IndoRobusta: Towards robustness against diverse code-mixed Indonesian local languages. In *Proceedings of the First Workshop on Scaling Up Multilingual Evaluation*, pages 25–34, Online. Association for Computational Linguistics.

Gustavo Aguilar, Sudipta Kar, and Thamar Solorio. 2020. LinCE: A centralized benchmark for linguistic code-switching evaluation. In *Proceedings of the Twelfth Language Resources and Evaluation Conference*, pages 1803–1813, Marseille, France. European Language Resources Association.

Alham Fikri Aji, Genta Indra Winata, Fajri Koto, Samuel Cahyawijaya, Ade Romadhony, Rahmad Mahendra, Kemal Kurniawan, David Moeljadi, Radityo Eko Prasojo, Timothy Baldwin, Jey Han Lau, and Sebastian Ruder. 2022. One country, 700+ languages: NLP challenges for underrepresented languages and dialects in Indonesia. In *Proceedings of the 60th Annual Meeting of the Association for Computational Linguistics (Volume 1: Long Papers)*, pages 7226–7249, Dublin, Ireland. Association for Computational Linguistics.

Edith Aldridge. 2012. Antipassive and ergativity in tagalog. *Lingua*, 122:192–203.

Douglas G Altman. 1990. *Practical statistics for medical research.* CRC press.

Ramakrishna Appicharla, Kamal Kumar Gupta, Asif Ekbal, and Pushpak Bhattacharyya. 2021. IITP-MT at CALCS2021: English to Hinglish neural machine translation using unsupervised synthetic code-mixed parallel corpus. In *Proceedings of the Fifth Workshop on Computational Approaches to Linguistic Code-Switching*, pages 31–35, Online. Association for Computational Linguistics.

Eric Armstrong. Tamil and Tamil-English accent.

Yejin Bang, Samuel Cahyawijaya, Nayeon Lee, Wenliang Dai, Dan Su, Bryan Wilie, Holy Lovenia, Ziwei Ji, Tiezheng Yu, Willy Chung, et al. 2023. A multitask, multilingual, multimodal evaluation of chatgpt on reasoning, hallucination, and interactivity. *arXiv preprint arXiv:2302.04023*.

Anab Maulana Barik, Rahmad Mahendra, and Mirna Adriani. 2019. Normalization of Indonesian-English code-mixed Twitter data. In *Proceedings of the 5th Workshop on Noisy User-generated Text (W-NUT 2019)*, pages 417–424, Hong Kong, China. Association for Computational Linguistics.

John Baugh. 2005. Linguistic profiling. In *Black linguistics*, pages 167–180. Routledge.

Maria Lourdes S Bautista and Andrew B Gonzalez. 2006. Southeast asian englishes. *The handbook of world Englishes*, pages 130–144.

Anshul Bawa, Pranav Khadpe, Pratik Joshi, Kalika Bali, and Monojit Choudhury. 2020. Do multilingual users prefer chat-bots that code-mix? let's nudge and find out! *Proceedings of the ACM on Human-Computer Interaction*, 4(CSCW1):1–23.

Susan Berk-Seligson. 1986. Linguistic constraints on intrasentential code-switching: A study of spanish/hebrew bilingualism. *Language in society*, 15(3):313–348.

T. K. Bhatia and W. C. Ritchie. 2004. Social and psychological factors in language mixing. In W. C. Ritchie and T. K. Bhatia, editors, *Handbook of bilingualism*, pages 336–352. Blackwell Publishing.

Tom Brown, Benjamin Mann, Nick Ryder, Melanie Subbiah, Jared D Kaplan, Prafulla Dhariwal, Arvind Neelakantan, Pranav Shyam, Girish Sastry, Amanda Askell, et al. 2020. Language models are few-shot learners. *Advances in neural information processing systems*, 33:1877–1901.

Samuel Cahyawijaya, Holy Lovenia, Alham Fikri Aji, Genta Indra Winata, Bryan Wilie, Rahmad Mahendra, Christian Wibisono, Ade Romadhony, Karissa Vincentio, Fajri Koto, Jennifer Santoso, David Moeljadi, Cahya Wirawan, Frederikus Hudi, Ivan Halim Parmonangan, Ika Alfina, Muhammad Satrio Wicaksono, Ilham Firdausi Putra, Samsul Rahmadani, Yulianti Oenang, Ali Akbar Septiandri, James Jaya, Kaustubh D. Dhole, Arie Ardiyanti Suryani, Rifki Afina Putri, Dan Su, Keith Stevens, Made Nindyatama Nityasya, Muhammad Farid Adilazuarda, Ryan Ignatius, Ryandito Diandaru, Tiezheng Yu, Vito Ghifari, Wenliang Dai, Yan Xu, Dyah Damapuspita, Cuk Tho, Ichwanul Muslim Karo Karo, Tirana Noor Fatyanosa, Ziwei Ji, Pascale Fung, Graham Neubig, Timothy Baldwin, Sebastian Ruder, Herry Sujaini, Sakriani Sakti, and Ayu Purwarianti. 2022. Nusacrowd: Open source initiative for indonesian nlp resources.

Joyce YC Chan, Houwei Cao, PC Ching, and Tan Lee. 2009. Automatic recognition of cantonese-english code-mixing speech. In *International Journal of Computational Linguistics & Chinese Language Processing, Volume 14, Number 3, September 2009.*

Su-Chiao Chen. 1996. Code-switching as a verbal strategy among chinese in a campus setting in taiwan. *World Englishes*, 15(3):267–280.

T Chen and Kan Min-Yen. 2015. The national university of singapore sms corpus.

Hyung Won Chung, Le Hou, Shayne Longpre, Barret Zoph, Yi Tay, William Fedus, Eric Li, Xuezhi Wang, Mostafa Dehghani, Siddhartha Brahma, et al. 2022. Scaling instruction-finetuned language models. *arXiv preprint arXiv:2210.11416*.

Commonwealth of the Philippines. 1936. Commonwealth act no. 184: Govph.

Mona Diab, Julia Hirschberg, Pascale Fung, and Thamar Solorio, editors. 2014. *Proceedings of the First Workshop on Computational Approaches to Code Switching*. Association for Computational Linguistics, Doha, Qatar.

Mark Dingemanse and Andreas Liesenfeld. 2022. From text to talk: Harnessing conversational corpora for humane and diversity-aware language technology. In *Proceedings of the 60th Annual Meeting of the Association for Computational Linguistics (Volume 1: Long Papers)*, pages 5614–5633, Dublin, Ireland. Association for Computational Linguistics.

A. Seza Doğruöz, Sunayana Sitaram, Barbara E. Bullock, and Almeida Jacqueline Toribio. 2021. A survey of code-switching: Linguistic and social perspectives for language technologies. In *Proceedings of the 59th Annual Meeting of the Association for Computational Linguistics and the 11th International Joint Conference on Natural Language Processing (Volume 1: Long Papers)*, pages 1654–1666, Online. Association for Computational Linguistics.

Suman Dowlagar and Radhika Mamidi. 2021. Gated convolutional sequence to sequence based learning for English-hingilsh code-switched machine translation. In *Proceedings of the Fifth Workshop on Computational Approaches to Linguistic Code-Switching*, pages 26–30, Online. Association for Computational Linguistics.

Joseph L Fleiss. 1971. Measuring nominal scale agreement among many raters. *Psychological bulletin*, 76(5):378.

Björn Gambäck and Amitava Das. 2014. On measuring the complexity of code-mixing. In *Proceedings of the 11th international conference on natural language processing, Goa, India*, pages 1–7.

Devansh Gautam, Prashant Kodali, Kshitij Gupta, Anmol Goel, Manish Shrivastava, and Ponnurangam Kumaraguru. 2021. CoMeT: Towards code-mixed translation using parallel monolingual sentences. In *Proceedings of the Fifth Workshop on Computational Approaches to Linguistic Code-Switching*, pages 47–55, Online. Association for Computational Linguistics.

Cliff Goddard. 2005. *The languages of East and Southeast Asia: an introduction*. Oxford University Press on Demand.

F. Grosjean. 1982. *Life with two languages: An introduction to bilingualism*. Harvard University Press.

Xingwei He, Zhenghao Lin, Yeyun Gong, A Jin, Hang Zhang, Chen Lin, Jian Jiao, Siu Ming Yiu, Nan Duan, Weizhu Chen, et al. 2023. Annollm: Making large language models to be better crowdsourced annotators. *arXiv preprint arXiv:2303.16854*.

Republik Indonesia. 2002. *Undang-Undang Dasar Negara Republik Indonesia Tahun 1945*. Sekretariat Jenderal MPR RI.

Ganesh Jawahar, El Moatez Billah Nagoudi, Muhammad Abdul-Mageed, and Laks Lakshmanan, V.S. 2021. Exploring text-to-text transformers for English to Hinglish machine translation with synthetic code-mixing. In *Proceedings of the Fifth Workshop on Computational Approaches to Linguistic Code-Switching*, pages 36–46, Online. Association for Computational Linguistics.

Pratik Joshi, Sebastin Santy, Amar Budhiraja, Kalika Bali, and Monojit Choudhury. 2020. The state and fate of linguistic diversity and inclusion in the NLP world. In *Proceedings of the 58th Annual Meeting of the Association for Computational Linguistics*, pages 6282–6293, Online. Association for Computational Linguistics.

Anubha Kabra, Emmy Liu, Simran Khanuja, Alham Fikri Aji, Genta Indra Winata, Samuel Cahyawijaya, Anuoluwapo Aremu, Perez Ogayo, and Graham Neubig. 2023. Multi-lingual and multi-cultural figurative language understanding.

Simran Khanuja, Sandipan Dandapat, Anirudh Srinivasan, Sunayana Sitaram, and Monojit Choudhury. 2020. GLUECoS: An evaluation benchmark for code-switched NLP. In *Proceedings of the 58th Annual Meeting of the Association for Computational Linguistics*, pages 3575–3585, Online. Association for Computational Linguistics.

Andy Kirkpatrick. 2014. English in southeast asia: Pedagogical and policy implications. *World Englishes*, 33(4):426–438.

Paul Kroeger. 1993. *Phrase structure and grammatical relations in Tagalog*. Center for the Study of Language (CSLI).

Huiyuan Lai and Malvina Nissim. 2022. Multi-figurative language generation. In *Proceedings of the 29th International Conference on Computational Linguistics*, pages 5939–5954, Gyeongju, Republic of Korea. International Committee on Computational Linguistics.

J Richard Landis and Gary G Koch. 1977. The measurement of observer agreement for categorical data. *biometrics*, pages 159–174.

Hugo Laurençon, Lucile Saulnier, Thomas Wang, Christopher Akiki, Albert Villanova del Moral, Teven Le Scao, Leandro Von Werra, Chenghao Mou, Eduardo González Ponferrada, Huu Nguyen, Jörg Frohberg, Mario Šaško, Quentin Lhoest, Angelina

McMillan-Major, Gérard Dupont, Stella Biderman, Anna Rogers, Loubna Ben allal, Francesco De Toni, Giada Pistilli, Olivier Nguyen, Somaieh Nikpoor, Maraim Masoud, Pierre Colombo, Javier de la Rosa, Paulo Villegas, Tristan Thrush, Shayne Longpre, Sebastian Nagel, Leon Weber, Manuel Romero Muñoz, Jian Zhu, Daniel Van Strien, Zaid Alyafeai, Khalid Almubarak, Vu Minh Chien, Itziar Gonzalez-Dios, Aitor Soroa, Kyle Lo, Manan Dey, Pedro Ortiz Suarez, Aaron Gokaslan, Shamik Bose, David Ifeoluwa Adelani, Long Phan, Hieu Tran, Ian Yu, Suhas Pai, Jenny Chim, Violette Lepercq, Suzana Ilic, Margaret Mitchell, Sasha Luccioni, and Yacine Jernite. 2022. The bigscience ROOTS corpus: A 1.6TB composite multilingual dataset. In *Thirty-sixth Conference on Neural Information Processing Systems Datasets and Benchmarks Track*.

Heather Lent, Emanuele Bugliarello, Miryam de Lhoneux, Chen Qiu, and Anders Søgaard. 2021. On language models for creoles. In *Proceedings of the 25th Conference on Computational Natural Language Learning*, pages 58–71, Online. Association for Computational Linguistics.

Zihan Liu, Genta Indra Winata, Zhaojiang Lin, Peng Xu, and Pascale Fung. 2020. Attention-informed mixed-language training for zero-shot cross-lingual task-oriented dialogue systems. In *Proceedings of the AAAI Conference on Artificial Intelligence*, volume 34, pages 8433–8440.

Holy Lovenia, Samuel Cahyawijaya, Genta Winata, Peng Xu, Yan Xu, Zihan Liu, Rita Frieske, Tiezheng Yu, Wenliang Dai, Elham J. Barezi, Qifeng Chen, Xiaojuan Ma, Bertram Shi, and Pascale Fung. 2022. ASCEND: A spontaneous Chinese-English dataset for code-switching in multi-turn conversation. In *Proceedings of the Thirteenth Language Resources and Evaluation Conference*, pages 7259–7268, Marseille, France. European Language Resources Association.

Dau-Cheng Lyu, Tien-Ping Tan, Eng Siong Chng, and Haizhou Li. 2010. Seame: a mandarin-english code-switching speech corpus in south-east asia. In *Eleventh Annual Conference of the International Speech Communication Association*.

Rawl Maliwat. 2021. Language policy and education in southeast asia.

Brian Migliazza. 1996. Mainland southeast asia: A unique linguistic area. *Notes on linguistics*, 75:17–25.

Sneha Mondal, Ritika ., Shreya Pathak, Preethi Jyothi, and Aravindan Raghuveer. 2022. CoCoa: An encoder-decoder model for controllable code-switched generation. In *Proceedings of the 2022 Conference on Empirical Methods in Natural Language Processing*, pages 2466–2479, Abu Dhabi, United Arab Emirates. Association for Computational Linguistics.

Niklas Muennighoff, Thomas Wang, Lintang Sutawika, Adam Roberts, Stella Biderman, Teven Le Scao, M Saiful Bari, Sheng Shen, Zheng-Xin Yong, Hailey Schoelkopf, Xiangru Tang, Dragomir Radev, Alham Fikri Aji, Khalid Almubarak, Samuel Albanie, Zaid Alyafeai, Albert Webson, Edward Raff, and Colin Raffel. 2022. Crosslingual generalization through multitask finetuning.

Carol Myers-Scotton. 1997. *Duelling languages: Grammatical structure in codeswitching*. Oxford University Press.

Nathaniel Oco and Rachel Edita Roxas. 2012. Pattern matching refinements to dictionary-based code-switching point detection. In *Proceedings of the 26th Pacific Asia Conference on Language, Information, and Computation*, pages 229–236, Bali, Indonesia. Faculty of Computer Science, Universitas Indonesia.

Long Ouyang, Jeff Wu, Xu Jiang, Diogo Almeida, Carroll L Wainwright, Pamela Mishkin, Chong Zhang, Sandhini Agarwal, Katarina Slama, Alex Ray, et al. 2022. Training language models to follow instructions with human feedback. *arXiv preprint arXiv:2203.02155*.

Femphy Pisceldo, Rahmad Mahendra, Ruli Manurung, and I Wayan Arka. 2008. A two-level morphological analyser for the Indonesian language. In *Proceedings of the Australasian Language Technology Association Workshop 2008*, pages 142–150, Hobart, Australia.

Shana Poplack. 1978. *Syntactic structure and social function of code-switching*, volume 2. Centro de Estudios Puertorriqueños,[City University of New York].

Vineel Pratap, Andros Tjandra, Bowen Shi, Paden Tomasello, Arun Babu, Sayani Kundu, Ali Elkahky, Zhaoheng Ni, Apoorv Vyas, Maryam Fazel-Zarandi, et al. 2023. Scaling speech technology to 1,000+ languages. *arXiv preprint arXiv:2305.13516*.

Adithya Pratapa, Gayatri Bhat, Monojit Choudhury, Sunayana Sitaram, Sandipan Dandapat, and Kalika Bali. 2018. Language modeling for code-mixing: The role of linguistic theory based synthetic data. In *Proceedings of the 56th Annual Meeting of the Association for Computational Linguistics (Volume 1: Long Papers)*, pages 1543–1553, Melbourne, Australia. Association for Computational Linguistics.

Mont Redmond, Kimmo Kosonen, and Catherine Young. 2009. *Mother tongue as bridge language of instruction: Policies and experiences in southeast Asia*. World Bank.

Machel Reid, Victor Zhong, Suchin Gururangan, and Luke Zettlemoyer. 2022. M2D2: A massively multi-domain language modeling dataset. In *Proceedings of the 2022 Conference on Empirical Methods in Natural Language Processing*, pages 964–975, Abu Dhabi, United Arab Emirates. Association for Computational Linguistics.

Mohd Sanad Zaki Rizvi, Anirudh Srinivasan, Tanuja Ganu, Monojit Choudhury, and Sunayana Sitaram. 2021. GCM: A toolkit for generating synthetic code-mixed text. In *Proceedings of the 16th Conference of the European Chapter of the Association for Computational Linguistics: System Demonstrations*, pages 205–211, Online. Association for Computational Linguistics.

Together Computer SambaNova Systems. 2023. BLOOMChat: a New Open Multilingual Chat LLM.

David Sankoff, Shana Poplack, and Swathi Vanniarajan. 1990. The case of the nonce loan in tamil. *Language Variation and Change*, 2(1):71–101.

Sebastin Santy, Anirudh Srinivasan, and Monojit Choudhury. 2021. BERTologiCoMix: How does code-mixing interact with multilingual BERT? In *Proceedings of the Second Workshop on Domain Adaptation for NLP*, pages 111–121, Kyiv, Ukraine. Association for Computational Linguistics.

Teven Le Scao, Angela Fan, Christopher Akiki, Ellie Pavlick, Suzana Ilić, Daniel Hesslow, Roman Castagné, Alexandra Sasha Luccioni, François Yvon, Matthias Gallé, et al. 2022. Bloom: A 176b-parameter open-access multilingual language model. *arXiv preprint arXiv:2211.05100*.

Harold F. Schiffman. 1998. Malaysian tamils and tamil linguistic culture.

Ilia Shumailov, Zakhar Shumaylov, Yiren Zhao, Yarin Gal, Nicolas Papernot, and Ross Anderson. 2023. The curse of recursion: Training on generated data makes models forget. *arXiv preprint arxiv:2305.17493*.

Yuen Sin. 2017. Don't play, play - singlish is studied around the globe.

Department of Statistics Singapore. 2020. Key findings 2020.

James Neil Sneddon. 2003. *The Indonesian language: Its history and role in modern society*. UNSW Press, Sydney.

Thamar Solorio and Yang Liu. 2008. Learning to predict code-switching points. In *Proceedings of the 2008 Conference on Empirical Methods in Natural Language Processing*, pages 973–981, Honolulu, Hawaii. Association for Computational Linguistics.

Samson Tan and Shafiq Joty. 2021. Code-mixing on sesame street: Dawn of the adversarial polyglots. In *Proceedings of the 2021 Conference of the North American Chapter of the Association for Computational Linguistics: Human Language Technologies*, pages 3596–3616, Online. Association for Computational Linguistics.

Ruixiang Tang, Xiaotian Han, Xiaoqian Jiang, and Xia Hu. 2023. Does synthetic data generation of llms help clinical text mining? *arXiv preprint arXiv:2303.04360*.

Rohan Taori, Ishaan Gulrajani, Tianyi Zhang, Yann Dubois, Xuechen Li, Carlos Guestrin, Percy Liang, and Tatsunori B. Hashimoto. 2023. Stanford alpaca: An instruction-following llama model. https://github.com/tatsu-lab/stanford_alpaca.

Rohan Taori and Tatsunori B Hashimoto. 2022. Data feedback loops: Model-driven amplification of dataset biases. *arXiv preprint arXiv:2209.03942*.

Ishan Tarunesh, Syamantak Kumar, and Preethi Jyothi. 2021. From machine translation to code-switching: Generating high-quality code-switched text. In *Proceedings of the 59th Annual Meeting of the Association for Computational Linguistics and the 11th International Joint Conference on Natural Language Processing (Volume 1: Long Papers)*, pages 3154–3169, Online. Association for Computational Linguistics.

C Tho, Y Heryadi, L Lukas, and A Wibowo. 2021. Code-mixed sentiment analysis of indonesian language and javanese language using lexicon based approach. *Journal of Physics: Conference Series*, 1869(1):012084.

Romal Thoppilan, Daniel De Freitas, Jamie Hall, Noam Shazeer, Apoorv Kulshreshtha, Heng-Tze Cheng, Alicia Jin, Taylor Bos, Leslie Baker, Yu Du, et al. 2022. Lamda: Language models for dialog applications. *arXiv preprint arXiv:2201.08239*.

A. J. Toribio. 2002. Spanish-english code-switching among us latinos. *International Journal of the Sociology of Languaeg*, 2002:89–119.

Chenxi Whitehouse, Monojit Choudhury, and Alham Fikri Aji. 2023. Llm-powered data augmentation for enhanced crosslingual performance. *arXiv preprint arXiv:2305.14288*.

Genta Indra Winata, Alham Fikri Aji, Samuel Cahyawijaya, Rahmad Mahendra, Fajri Koto, Ade Romadhony, Kemal Kurniawan, David Moeljadi, Radityo Eko Prasojo, Pascale Fung, Timothy Baldwin, Jey Han Lau, Rico Sennrich, and Sebastian Ruder. 2023. NusaX: Multilingual parallel sentiment dataset for 10 Indonesian local languages. In *Proceedings of the 17th Conference of the European Chapter of the Association for Computational Linguistics*, pages 815–834, Dubrovnik, Croatia. Association for Computational Linguistics.

Genta Indra Winata, Alham Fikri Aji, Zheng-Xin Yong, and Thamar Solorio. 2022. The decades progress on code-switching research in nlp: A systematic survey on trends and challenges. *arXiv preprint arXiv:2212.09660*.

Genta Indra Winata, Samuel Cahyawijaya, Zihan Liu, Zhaojiang Lin, Andrea Madotto, and Pascale Fung. 2021. Are multilingual models effective in code-switching? In *Proceedings of the Fifth Workshop on Computational Approaches to Linguistic Code-Switching*, pages 142–153, Online. Association for Computational Linguistics.

Genta Indra Winata, Samuel Cahyawijaya, Zihan Liu, Zhaojiang Lin, Andrea Madotto, Peng Xu, and Pascale Fung. 2020. Learning fast adaptation on cross-accented speech recognition. In *Interspeech 2020*. ISCA.

Genta Indra Winata, Andrea Madotto, Chien-Sheng Wu, and Pascale Fung. 2019. Code-switched language models using neural based synthetic data from parallel sentences. In *Proceedings of the 23rd Conference on Computational Natural Language Learning (CoNLL)*, pages 271–280.

Evi Yulianti, Ajmal Kurnia, Mirna Adriani, and Yoppy Setyo Duto. 2021. Normalisation of indonesian-english code-mixed text and its effect on emotion classification. *International Journal of Advanced Computer Science and Applications*, 12(11).

Ruochen Zhang, Samuel Cahyawijaya, Jan Christian Blaise Cruz, and Alham Fikri Aji. 2023. Multilingual large language models are not (yet) code-switchers.

Ruochen Zhang and Carsten Eickhoff. 2023. Crocosum: A benchmark dataset for cross-lingual code-switched summarization. *arXiv preprint arXiv:2303.04092*.

A Languages Spoken in SEA

There are more than 1,200 languages spoken in SEA (Redmond et al., 2009; Maliwat, 2021), 700 of which are spoken in Indonesia (Aji et al., 2022; Cahyawijaya et al., 2022). We describe the languages the SEA languages used in the study in the following paragraphs.

Mandarin Chinese Mandarin Chinese (zh-Hans), which belongs to the Sino-Tibetan language family and uses the Hanzi script, is widely spoken in SEA due to the migration of Chinese people from the coastal provinces of southeastern China, such as Fujian, Guangdong, and Hainan. People of Chinese heritage in SEA frequently use the term "华人" (huá rén) to express their cultural identity as an ethnic group, instead of "中国人" (zhōng guó rén) which is primarily associated with nationality, even though both terms can be translated as "Chinese (people)." Singapore has the largest Chinese ethnic group among all SEA countries and Mandarin Chinese is considered one of the official languages in Singapore.

The language is characterized as linguistically "isolating" in that each Chinese character corresponds to one morpheme and that the language uses very little grammatical inflection. It uses a logographic writing system, which uses pictograms (Chinese characters) to represent meaning. Chinese is also a tonal language with four pitched tones and one neutral tone. It commonly displays a basic SVO word order and, instead of conjugating the verbs to express tenses, uses aspect particles such as 了(le) and 着(zhe) to indicate the temporal location of the sentence.

Indonesian Indonesian (ind) is the national language of Indonesia (Indonesia, 2002). It is spoken by around 300 million speakers worldwide. Indonesian is developed from the literary 'Classical Malay' of the Riau-Johor sultanate (Sneddon, 2003) and has many regional variants. Indonesian is written in Latin script with a lexical similarity of over 80% to Standard Malay. Indonesian is non-tonal and has 19 consonants, 6 vowels, and 3 diphthongs. The stress is on the penultimate syllable and the word order is SVO. It has three optional noun classifiers. Indonesian has two social registers and a rich affixation system, including a variety of prefixes, suffixes, circumfixes, and reduplication. Most of the affixes in Indonesian are derivational (Pisceldo et al., 2008).

Standard Malay Standard Malay (msa) is the national language of Malaysia, Brunei, and Singapore, and the language is spoken by approximately 290 million speakers worldwide. The word order of Standard Malay is SVO with four types of affixes, i.e., prefixes (awalan), suffixes (akhiran), circumfixes (apitan), and infixes (sisipan). Even though Standard Malay and Indonesian originate from the same Malay language and are mutually intelligible, they can differ in spelling and vocabulary. One example is loanwords. Due to the different colonial influences from the Dutch and British, Indonesian primarily absorbs Dutch loanwords whereas Malay absorbs English loanwords. Both languages can also differ in the meanings of the same written words, which are commonly referred to as interlingual homographs. For instance, "polisi" means "police" in Indonesian but "policy" in Standard Malay.

Tagalog Tagalog (tgl) is an Austronesian language spoken in the Philippines by around 82 million native speakers. It is both agglutinative and pitch-accented, giving it rich and complex morphology (Kroeger, 1993). Tagalog's standardized form, known as *Filipino*, is the country's official national language. The difference between Filipino and Tagalog is more sociopolitical than sociolinguistic: Commonwealth Act No. 184 of 1936 created a national committee whose purpose is to "develop a national language." This resulted in the standardization of the Tagalog language into Filipino. In practice, Filipino is indistinguishable from Tagalog, albeit with the addition of letters f, j, c, x, and z, plus loanwords (Commonwealth of the Philippines, 1936).

Vietnamese Vietnamese (vie), the national language of Vietnam, is spoken by around 85 million people worldwide. It is a tonal language belonging to the Austroasiatic language family and uses accents to denote six distinctive tones. The sentence structure of Vietnamese displays the SVO word order, and due to heavy influence from Chinese, it also uses a rich set of classifiers that are required in the presence of quantifiers. For instance, instead of writing "bốn gà," which literally translates into "four chickens," it should be "bốn con gà" where "con" is a classifier for non-human animate things.

Tamil Tamil (tam) is a Dravidian language originating from Tamil Nadu and Sri Lanka. It is spoken by the sizeable Tamil diasporas of Singapore (2.5%

of population (Singapore, 2020)) and Malaysia (9% of population (Schiffman, 1998)), which resulted from histories of trade, migration, indentured servitude, and civil unrest. Tamil is an official language of Singapore (Singapore, 2020), and the only one originating from India. Tamil is notably diglossic, which means it has a formal literary system, lacks lexically distinctive stress, and is non-rhotic (Armstrong). Tamil uses SOV sentence structure. Tamil-English code-mixing exhibits interesting linguistic phenomena such as nonce loan, wherein many nonce borrowings from English occupy objects corresponding to Tamil verbs, and vice versa (Sankoff et al., 1990).

Singlish Singlish is a widely-used conversational language in Singapore. It is an English-based creole language that arose out of prolonged language contact between speakers of many different languages in the country, including Hokkien, Malay, Teochew, Cantonese, and Tamil. Singlish is spoken by around 4 million speakers, and one unique feature of the language is its heavy use of pragmatic particles borrowed from Southern Chinese dialects. One example of this is "lah," which in the sentence, "Her dress is too short lah," emphasizes the statement.

B HuggingFace Inference API

We use HuggingFace's Inference API to prompt multilingual LLMs since we do not have sufficient local compute to host models with hundreds of billions of parameters such as the 176B-parameter BLOOMZ model (Muennighoff et al., 2022). The text-to-text task is treated identically as a text-generation task, and we set max_new_tokens (amount of new tokens to be generated) to 100, temperature to 0.7, and repetition_penalty to 1.2.

C OpenAI Inference API

We use OpenAI's official API to prompt both davinci-003 and davinci-002. Specifically, we use openai.Completion.create with a maximum generation length of 128. We use the default values for all other parameters.

D Flan-T5-XXL Non-English Outputs

We observe that when Flan-T5-XXL generates non-English outputs, most of them are nonsensical. Here are some of the examples and their translations.

Indonesian: Ini adalah sebuah udara untuk pengobatan minyak dan di sekitar kehidupan.
Translation: This is an air for oil treatment and around life.
Malay: Artificial Intelligence adalah sebuah kantor keamanan yang digunakan untuk mengidentifikasi penduduk yang memiliki anak-anak dalam diri.
Translation: Artificial intelligence is a security office used for identifying residents who have childen inside.
Tagalog: Weather niya ang nagsimula sa pagsasagawa ng kaniyang kargahan ng panahon.
Translation: It was his weather that started carrying out his weather load.
Vietnamese: Nhà ng tài ra mt ngi dy xut trn o trng h nhng ngi ng thng u c thit v.
Translation: The artist has created an outstanding talent in the field of talented people.

E BLOOMZ's Training Language Distribution

BLOOMZ is created by finetuning the multilingual 176B-parameter language model BLOOM (Scao et al., 2022) that is pretrained on ROOTS corpus (Laurençon et al., 2022) on a collection of prompt instructions known as xP3 (Muennighoff et al., 2022). Table 1 and Table 2 show the proportion of SEA languages investigated in our paper existing in the ROOTS and xP3 datasets respectively. Even though Indonesian and Chinese are higher in proportion than Tamil, BLOOMZ code-mix better for Tamil than the former two language with around 20% performance difference.

Languages	Percent Distribution (%)
English	30.04
Chinese (Simplified)	16.2
Vietnamese	2.7
Indonesian	1.2
Tamil	0.2

Table 1: Proportion of Languages in the ROOTS corpus (Laurençon et al., 2022).

F Naturalness and Fluency Issues of ChatGPT's Generation

We document a non-exhaustive list of syntactic and semantic errors as well as reasons for unnaturalness

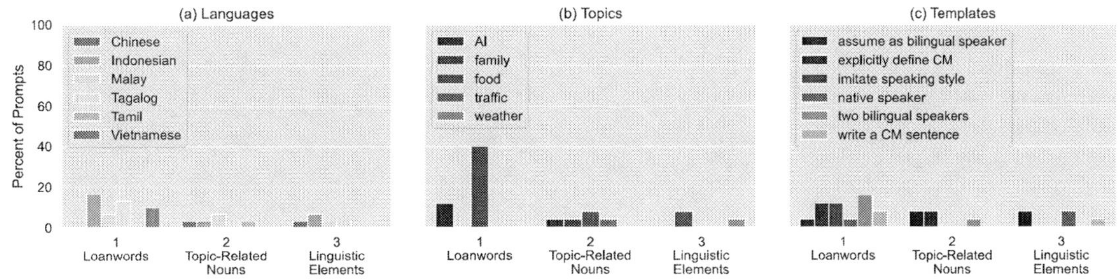

Figure 11: Analysis of davinci-002's capability of generating code-mixed data.

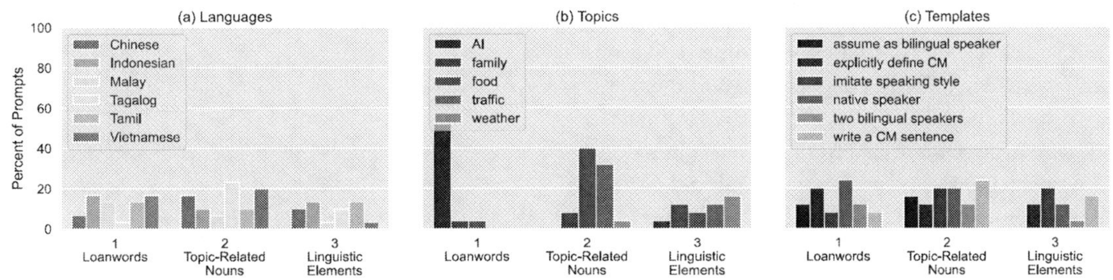

Figure 12: Analysis of davinci-003's capability of generating code-mixed data.

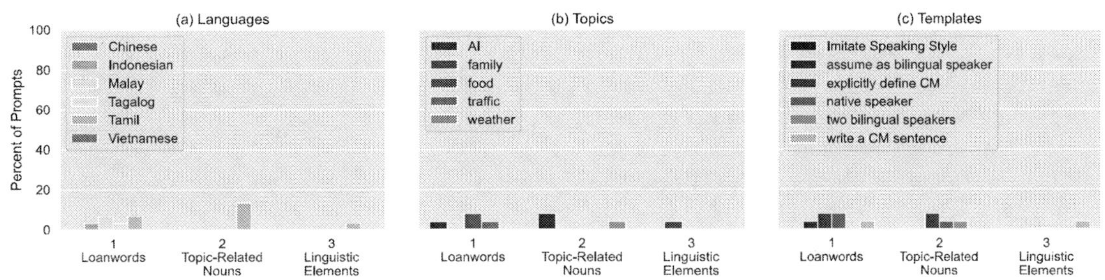

Figure 13: Analysis of BLOOMZ's capability of generating code-mixed data.

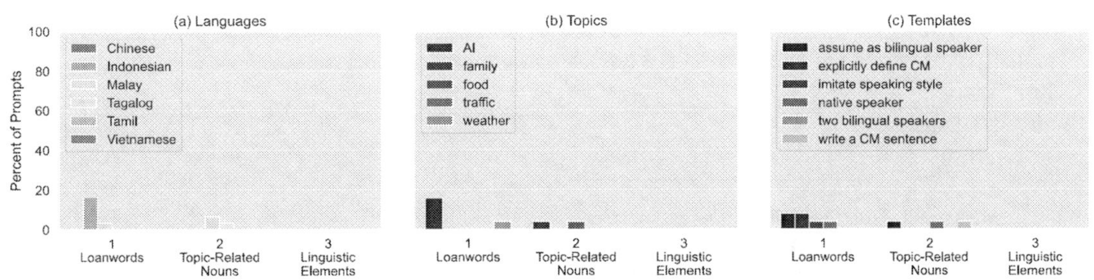

Figure 14: Analysis of Flan-T5-XXL's capability of generating code-mixed data.

Languages	Percent Distribution (%)
English	39.25
Indonesian	4.85
Chinese (Simplified)	4.83
Vietnamese	3.27
Tamil	0.97

Table 2: Proportion of Languages in the xP3 datasets (Muennighoff et al., 2022).

in ChatGPT's generation in Table 4.

G Annotators and Inter-annotator Agreement

We have a total of 13 annotators, some of whom speak more than one SEA language. All of them are native speakers of their respective SEA languages, and most grow up in SEA. Many of our annotators are AI researchers and reside in the Global North. All the annotators are the authors of the paper.

In Table 3, we report the inter-annotator agreement scores for naturalness annotations using Fleiss' Kappa κ (Fleiss, 1971), which measures the agreement between a fixed number of raters when assigning categorical ratings to the items. It can be applied to settings with multiple annotators and not all raters are required to annotate all items. The closer it is to 1, the higher the agreement among annotators.

According to the guideline (Landis and Koch, 1977; Altman, 1990), English-Indonesian annotations have a fair agreement, English-Chinese and Singlish have a substantial agreement, and English-Tagalog have almost perfect agreement among the annotators.

Language	N(annotators)	κ
English-Chinese	3	0.6431
English-Indonesian	3	0.2165
English-Malay	1	-
English-Tagalog	2	0.8268
English-Tamil	1	-
English-Vietnamese	1	-
Singlish	3	0.6199

Table 3: Inter-annnotator agreement scores for naturalness of ChatGPT's generated code-mixed text. N(annotators) indicates the total number of annotators and κ refers to the Fleiss' Kappa agreement score.

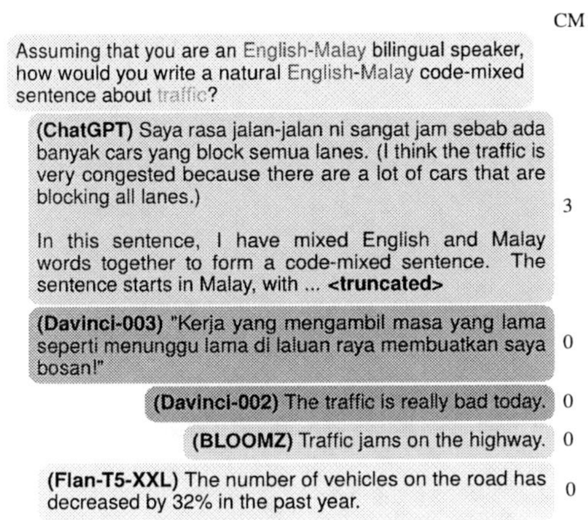

(a) Template: Assume as bilingual speaker

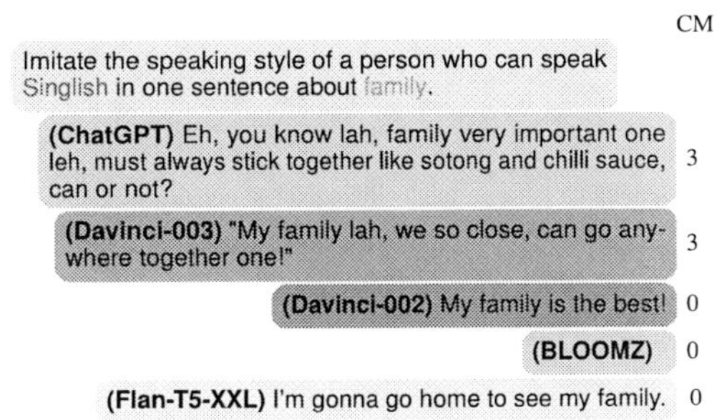

(b) Template: Imitate speaking style

(c) Template: Two bilingual speakers

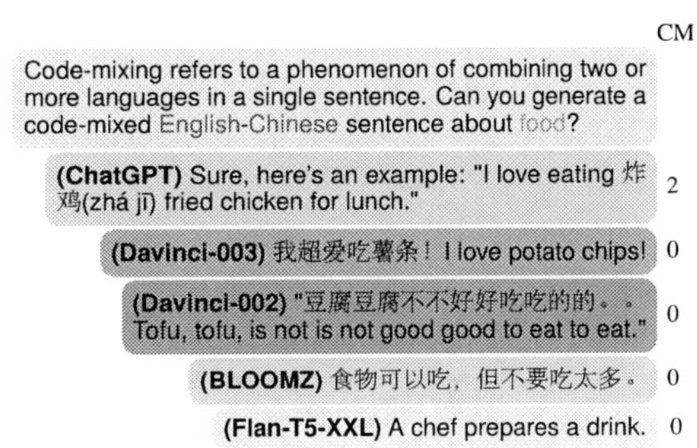

(d) Template: Explicitly define CM

Figure 15: All prompt templates with different languages and topic fields and responses from different LLMs containing code-mixed / non-code-mixed sentences. Note that the explanations are a part of ChatGPT's original generation. "CM" indicates the level of code-mixing (Section 2.2)

Prompt / Response	CM
Imagine that you are a Vietnamese speaker. How would you talk about weather using both English and Vietnamese in a single sentence?	
(ChatGPT) "Ngày hôm nay thời tiết khá nắng nóng, so I think I'll wear my shorts and t-shirt đi chơi."	3
(Davinci-003) I'm sure the weather today is beautiful, thời tiết hôm nay có vẻ rất đẹp.	0
(Davinci-002) I like the weather here because it's not too hot and not too cold. Tôi thích thời tiết ở đây vì nó không nóng quá và không lạnh quá.	0
(BLOOMZ) Hãy tưởng tượng bạn là người nói tiếng Việt, và thử dùng cả hai thứ tiếng để mô tả thời tiết:	0
(Flan-T5-XXL) V khách hàng nh hàng tc áo c tn c i n v nhng lng bn s tm thy hàng n c áo c ó	0

(e) Template: Native speaker

Prompt / Response	CM
Write an English and Tagalog code-mixed sentence about Artificial Intelligence.	
(ChatGPT) English-Tagalog code-mixed sentence: "Artificial Intelligence ay isang exciting na teknolohiya na makakapagbigay ng maraming benepisyo sa society." Translation: "Artificial Intelligence is an exciting technology that can provide many benefits sa lipunan."	1
(Davinci-003) AI is revolutionizing the way we live, trabaho, at mabuhay ngayon sa pamamagitan ng pagbibigay ng modernong solusyon sa mga proyekto at pagkukuha ng ilang mga trabahong naghihintay na ma-automate.	3
(Davinci-002) Artificial Intelligence is something that we should be thankful for.	0
(BLOOMZ) An expert in artificial intelligence explains their area of expertise to a student with the help of a colleague who speaks both languages.	0
(Flan-T5-XXL) Ang pagsusuri ng mas maraming kapasira ng hariko ay nag-aaral ng sasakyan ng pag-aaral ng pangangalambot, na magtitipon para sa pamamagitan ng pagpapasagawa ng karangalan ng isang lalaking.	0

(f) Template: Write a CM sentence

Figure 15: (Continued) We also include a template where we specify the nationality of the speaker in addition to the languages and topic fields.

Examples	Standard English Translation	Language Pairs	Issues	Explanations
Besok kita harus prepare payung karena cuacanya bakal cloudy dengan chance of hujan sepanjang hari	Tomorrow we need to prepare umbrella because the weather is going to be cloudy with the chance of raining all day long.	English-Indonesian	Unnatural phrasing	"chance of hujan" and "cuacanya bakal cloudy" sound unnatural. Should be "chance of raining" and "cuacanya akan menjadi cloudy"
Saya suka spend time bersama family saya, especially bila kita makan makanan yang sedap seperti nasi lemak or roti canai for breakfast.	I like spending time with my family, especially when we eat delicious food such as nasi lemak and roti canai.	English-Malay	Gerund; Conjunction	"suka spend time" should change to "suka spending time" as the word "suka" (like.v) should be followed with gerund. "or" should also be changed to "and".
I love eating 炸鸡(zhá jī) fried chicken for lunch.	I love eating fried chicken for lunch	English-Chinese	Redundancy	"炸鸡" is the same as "fried rice".
So, wǒ rènwéi yī gè jiànkāng de AI xiànshí shì yī gè jùyǒu zhuānyè shíjì kěnéng xìng de chéngzhǎng zhǐnéng de jìshù.	So, I believe a healthy AI system is a technology of growing intelligence with professional practical possibilities.	English-Chinese	Unnatural script system	The generated text should use Mandarin characters instead of Pinyin. It should be written as "So, 我认为一个健康的AI是一个具有专业实际可能性的成长智能的技术." Furthermore, the sentence does not make any sense
My family ay nagplano ng isang malaking family reunion sa park this coming weekend	My family is planning a big family reunion at the park this coming weekend	English-Tagalog	Possessive markers	The break from english "My family" to Tagalog "ay nagplano" is unnatural. When Tagalog is the matrix language, we use Tagalog possessive determiners, so the correct form would be "Ang family ko ay nagplano ..."
Yesterday, tôi đã đi out với gia đình của mình để celebrate my parents' wedding anniversary.	Yesterday, I went out with my family to celebrate my parents' wedding anniversary.	English-Vietnamese	Verb phrase	Instead of "đi out", it should be either "đi" or "went out".
AI, you know, can do many things lah, like make our lives easier, but also can be very pai seh if we don't use it properly.	You know while AI can do many things such as making our lives easier, it can also be very embarrassing if we don't use it properly	Singlish	Incorrect use of Singlish expression	"pai seh" is a Hokkien word that describes a person feeling shy, sorry or embarrassed. Using it to describe AI feeling embarrassed is inappropriate.
Eh, you know lah, family very important one leh, must always stick together like sotong and chilli sauce, can or not?	Do you know that family is very important, so we must always stick together like squid and chili sauce?	Singlish	Analogy	Using "sotong and chilli sauce" (squid and chili sauce) as an analogy to familial bond is an unnatural expression. No one in Singapore uses such an expression.
Traffic romba kasta pattu irukku today, it's taking forever to reach my destination.	Traffic is bad today; it's taking forever to reach my destination	English-Tamil	Adjective	"Traffic romba kasta pattu irukku today" means that the traffic is suffering, which is not the same as the traffic is congested.
"ஆர்டி∴பிசியல் இணையதள பயன்பாடுகள் வழங்கும் தகவல் அடையாளம் என்பது எந்த மொழியிலும் பயனுள்ளது, Artificial Intelligence is revolutionizing the way we interact with technology."	Data identification in artificial web applications is effective in any language, Artificial Intelligence is revolutionizing the way we interact with technology.	English-Tamil	Comma splice	Both the Tamil and English independent clauses are joined by comma, which is a grammatical error of comma splice.

Table 4: Naturalness issues with explanations for ChatGPT's code-mixed text generation.

CONFLATOR: Incorporating Switching Point based Rotatory Positional Encodings for Code-Mixed Language Modeling

Mohsin Ali[1] **Sai Teja Kandukuri**[2] **Neeharika Gupta**[3] **Parth Patwa**[4]
Anubhab Chatterjee[3] **Vinija Jain**[5] **Aman Chadha**[5,6*] **Amitava Das**[7]
[1]San Diego State University, USA [2]San Jose State University, USA
[3]Wipro AI Labs, India [4]University of California Los Angeles, USA
[5]Stanford University, USA [6]Amazon AI, USA [7]University of South Carolina, USA
[1]mmohammed5956@sdsu.edu [2]saiteja.kandukuri@sjsu.edu
[7]amitava@mailbox.sc.edu

Abstract

The mixing of two or more languages is called Code-Mixing (CM). CM is a social norm in multilingual societies. Neural Language Models (NLMs) like transformers have been effective on many NLP tasks. However, NLM for CM is an under-explored area. Though transformers are capable and powerful, they cannot always encode positional information since they are non-recurrent. Therefore, to enrich word information and incorporate positional information, positional encoding is defined. We hypothesize that Switching Points (SPs), i.e., junctions in the text where the language switches (L1 $\rightarrow$ L2 or L2 $\rightarrow$ L1), pose a challenge for CM Language Models (LMs), and hence give special emphasis to SPs in the modeling process. We experiment with several positional encoding mechanisms and show that rotatory positional encodings along with switching point information yield the best results.

We introduce CONFLATOR: a neural language modeling approach for code-mixed languages. CONFLATOR tries to learn to emphasize switching points using smarter positional encoding, both at unigram and bigram levels. CONFLATOR outperforms the state-of-the-art on two tasks based on code-mixed Hindi and English (Hinglish): (i) sentiment analysis and (ii) machine translation.

1 Code-Mixing: Juxtaposition of two Languages

Code-mixing is defined as the alternation of two or more languages during articulation. Recently, code-mixing has gained a lot of attention in the area of NLP due to the prevalence of language mixing in multilingual societies such as India, Europe, US, South Africa, Mexico, etc. In such societies, code-mixing is fairly commonplace, especially in informal conversations, where the native language is often romanized and code-mixed with an auxiliary language. This effect occasionally manifests in posts originating from the aforementioned sources on social media platforms such as Twitter, Facebook, etc. An example of Hindi and English code-mixing is shown in the following phrase where an English word, *dance*, is mixed with Hindi romanized words: *Gaaye, aur, kare.*

Gaaye$_{\texttt{HI}}$ *aur*$_{\texttt{HI}}$ *dance*$_{\texttt{EN}}$ *kare*$_{\texttt{HI}}$
English translation: sing and dance

With the proliferation of code-mixing on the internet, it is important to study language processing and language modeling for code-mixed languages. While language modeling using neural networks has come a long way, replacing n-gram language models with distributed neural representations (Bengio et al., 2003) to recent large transformer-based pre-trained language models (LMs) such as GPT-x (Radford et al., 2019), BERT (Devlin et al., 2018a) etc., code-mixed language modeling using state-of-the-art (SoTA) Transformer-based models is still under-explored.

The biggest hindrance in the adoption of SoTA Transformer-based LMs for code-mixing can be attributed to data scarcity. While Transformer-based (Vaswani et al., 2017b) architectures such as BERT and GPT have set new benchmarks in the domain of language modeling, they are infamous for their low sample efficiency. In other words, the voracious data appetite of Transformers and the lack of substantial code-mixed datasets in the community is the primary reason for the technological hindrances in the area of code-mixed language modeling compared to vanilla language modeling.

To corroborate the aforementioned arguments, we experiment with Transformer-based models such as GPT-2 and BERT for code-mixing. We empirically observe that these models perform poorly on tasks involving code-mixed data. Our hypothesis is as follows: Since information related to switch-

*Work does not relate to position at Amazon.

Proceedings of the 6th Workshop on Computational Approaches to Linguistic Code-Switching, pages 64–73
December 7, 2023

ing point is a major component in the context of code-mixed content, it should thus be incorporated in downstream processing. Switching points are a bottleneck for a model's processing of code-mixed data and the reason for poor performance using SoTA neural language models (Chatterjere et al., 2020). Switching points play a crucial factor when dealing with CM data. In the next few sections, we discuss various positional encoding approaches, switching points, and our approaches for language modeling on code-mixed data. Our key contributions are:

- We propose *CONFLATOR*, an LM system that incorporates switching point related positional information.
- Our system improves the performance of existing models and achieves a new SoTA on two tasks.
- We investigate, experiment with, and introduce various switching point based positional encoding techniques.
- We introduce a novel Switching Point based Rotary matrix for Rotary Positional Encoding (RoPE).
- We curate a new dataset of code-mixed tweets.

2 Related Work

It is important to study code-mixing as it is a part of most multilingual societies and prevalent in social media. It is more complex to process code-mixed text than monolingual text for NLP tasks (Verma, 1976). Similar line of work was followed by Bokamba (1988) and Singh (1985) on the complexities of multi-languages on the basis of syntactics and grammar. The difficulties of processing code-mixed languages on social media is further exacerbated by unusual spellings, many unique ways of writing the same word, unnecessary capitalization etc (Das and Gambäck, 2014; Laddha et al., 2020).

With the growing popularity on social media, Various tasks like sentiment analysis (Patwa et al., 2020a; Chakravarthi et al., 2020), translation (Dhar et al., 2018; Srivastava and Singh, 2020), hate-speech detection (Bohra et al., 2018; Banerjee et al., 2020), POS tagging (Vyas et al., 2014), etc. have been performed on code-mixed data. Methods to handle code-mixing for text classification include the use of CNNs (Aroyehun and Gelbukh, 2018; Patwa et al., 2020b), Transformer or BERT like models (Samghabadi et al., 2020; Tang et al., 2020), ensemble models (Tula et al., 2021; Jhanwar and Das, 2018), focal loss (Tula et al., 2022; Ma et al., 2020) etc.

Vaswani et al. (2017a) proposed transformers for neural language modeling using masked language modeling (MLM) and next sentence prediction, which achieved SoTA performance on many NLP tasks. Devlin et al. (2018b) released mBERT, a model trained on multilingual corpus that includes 104 languages. A cross lingual language model XLM was proposed in Lample and Conneau (2019) which leveraged monolingual and crosslingual corpus for pretraining. Nayak and Joshi (2022) present a bert pretrained on CM data. However, they do not make changes to their language model or technique to handle code-mixed data in particular. Sengupta et al. (2021) propose a Hierarchical transformer based architecture that captures the semantic relationship among words and hierarchically learns the sentence level semantics of code-mixed data. Ali et al. (2022) Were one of the first to incorporate switching point information in positional encoding. They utilize dynamic positional encodings whereas our method, CONFLATOR infuses switching point information in rotatory positional encodings and also uses both unigram and bigram tokens to get the final embedding.

3 Data Extraction and Strategies

In this section, we discuss the details of code-mixed data extraction. Our primary aim is to extract naturally distributed code-mixed data.

3.1 Qualitative and Quantitative Checkpoints for Hinglish Corpus

The performance of LMs is dependent on the training data size and quality, along with the vocabulary size. Code-mixed language modeling suffers from the following challenges: i) data scarcity, ii) Words from 2 (or more) languages in the same sentence, iii) *Hindi* is written using *English* letters (i.e. transliteration), hence, there is no standardization of spelling - which in effect proliferates word forms (Laddha et al., 2020, 2022), iii) Code-mixing is usually found on social media and netizens often incorporate creativity in their mixing along with wordplay. We consider two fundamental questions to guide our data collection:

1. *The performance on any NLP task depends on the data complexity:*

Empirical measurement: Consider two 4-word tweets - i) $T_i : w_{L1}w_{L1}w_{L2}w_{L2}$ and ii) $T_j : w_{L1}w_{L2}w_{L1}w_{L2}$. Both the tweets have 2 words each from the languages $L1$ and $L2$. Thus the mixing ratio of both the tweets T_i and T_j is $(4-2)/4 = 0.50$. However, T_i only contains 1 code alternation point whereas T_j contains 3 switches. It is likely that T_j is harder to process. Hence, we need a metric for the level of mixing between the languages. We use *Code-Mixing-Index* (Gambäck and Das, 2016) (CMI) to measure such complexity. Please refer to section 3.2 for more details on CMI.

2. *How much data is good enough?*

   Empirical measurement: When two languages blend, it is quite natural that the number of unique word forms would be much higher in a Hinglish corpus in comparison to monolingual English or Hindi corpus. Therefore, we ask an essential question at the very beginning, *how much data is good enough?* We decide to keep collecting data, until the Heaps' curve starts converging so that we cover most of the unique words.

   Heaps' law (Gopalan and Hopkins, 2020) states that the number of unique words in a text of n words is approximated by $V(n) = Kn^{\beta}$ where K is a positive constant and β lies between 0 and 1, K invariably lies between 10 and 100 and β between 0.4 an 0.6. Heaps' law is often considered to be a good estimator to calculate the vocabulary size. To compare, from the figure 1, it can be seen that, for English Wiki, the flattening of the Heaps' law curve, starts at **40K-50K**, whereas for monolingual Hindi, it converges at **80K-90K**, but for *Hinglish* the same behavior starts around **800K** vocabulary and 50M words.

3.2 Code-Mixing Index (CMI)

As mentioned previously, we expect the difficulty of language processing tasks to increase as the level of code-mixing increases. To measure the level of code-mixing in our corpus, we use Code-mixing Index (Gambäck and Das, 2016) :

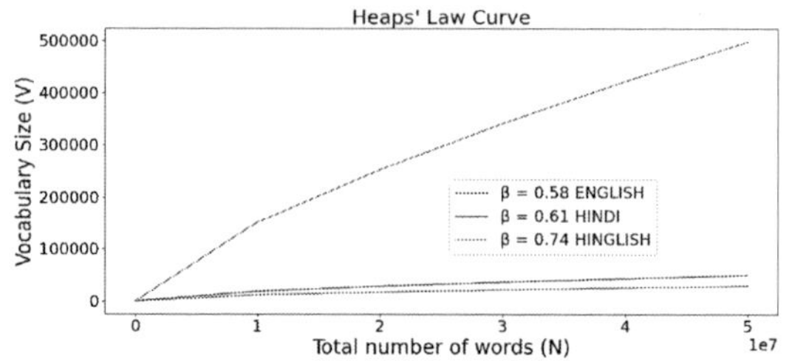

Figure 1: Heaps' plot on 50M word forms in English, Hindi and Hinglish corpora. The β values are 0.58, 0.61, 0.74 respectively.

$$
\begin{aligned}
C_u(x) &= w_m f_m(x) + w_p f_p(x) \\
&= w_m \frac{N(x) - \max_{L_i \epsilon L}(tLi)(x)}{N(x)} * 100 + w_p \frac{P(x)}{N(x)} * 100 \\
&= 100 * \frac{w_m((N(x) - \max_{L_i \epsilon L}(tLi)(x)) + w_p P(x)}{N(x)}
\end{aligned} \tag{1}
$$

Where x denotes utterance, N is the number of token in x belonging to any language L_i, w_m and w_n are weights. Please refer to Gambäck and Das (2016) for a detailed explanation of CMI.

3.3 Data Acquisition Pipeline

We follow a pipeline similar to (Chatterjere et al., 2020). We collect CM data from Twitter via the Twitter API. We need to use relevant keywords (words unique to Hindi) in our search to get CM tweets. Words with lexical overlap between Hindi and English should not be used for searching. for example, the word *do* is confusing because it means two in Hindi. We start with the *ICON 2017* Hinglish sentiment analysis dataset (Patra et al., 2018), which is annotated with word-level language. From this data, we create two vocabularies V_{HI} and V_{EN}, and generate a vocabulary of unique Hindi words $V_{HI-UNIQ} = V_{HI} - I$, where $I = V_{HI} \bigcap V_{EN}$. $V_{HI-UNIQ}$ set is then sorted in descending order, based on the word frequency, and is used as search words on the Twitter API. Once we get the tweets, we use a word-level language identifier (Barman et al., 2014) (having 90%+ accuracy) on the tweets and calculate the CMI of the tweet. Once we get the word-level language labels, we can also know where the switching points are. Tweets with CMI = 0 are discarded. Finally, we are left with 87k tweets. The CMI distribution of our data is given in table 1. This dataset is used to pretrain our models.

Training and Testing data: We collect 87K sentences distributed over all CMI ranges, instead of

CMI	# Tweets	Percentage
0-10	7,036	8.05%
11-20	16,481	18.9%
21-30	22,617	25.9%
31-40	22,722	26.0%
41-50	11,404	13.1%
50+	7,036	8.05%
Mean CMI: **28**	Total # of tweets: **87,296**	

Table 1: CMI distribution of the collected data. The total number of extracted tweets is 87K.

collecting equal data across the CMI ranges, so that the resultant languages trained on this corpus would be able to handle real data. We maintain the same distribution over both our training and testing corpora (*4:1 ratio*), for our language models.

4 The Bottleneck of Code-mixed Language Modeling: Switching Points

Formally, Switching Points (SPs) are the tokens in text, where the language switches. For code-mixed languages, consisting of a pair of languages, there can be two types of switching points. Suppose the two languages as part of the code-mixed language are *L1* and *L2*, a switching point occurs when the language in the text changes from L1 to L2 or L2 to L1. To explain it better, let us consider the following sample in *Hinglish*:

gaana$_{\text{HI}}$ *enjoy*$_{\text{EN}}$ *kare*$_{\text{HI}}$
English Translation: Enjoy the song.

In the above example, when the language switches from *Hindi* to *English* (*gaana*$_{\text{HI}}$ *enjoy*$_{\text{EN}}$) a **HI-EN** (HIndi-ENglish) switching point occurs. Similarly, a **EN-HI**(ENglish-HIndi) switching point occurs at - *enjoy*$_{\text{EN}}$ *kare*$_{\text{HI}}$.

In the context of modeling code-mixed languages, switching points can be considered as ordinary bigrams, that occur with other monolingual bigrams in a corpus. It is easy to infer that particular SP bigrams will be relatively rare in a given corpus. Hence, such sparse occurrences of switching point bigrams make it difficult for any Language Model to learn their probabilities and context. Since the language changes at the switching point, LMs are likely to find it difficult to process these tokens. In order to counter this challenge, we partition our code-mixed data into **(i)** *switching points*, and **(ii)** *non-switching points*. We then build LMs specifically for switching points and non-switching points, as discussed in the following sections.

CONFLATOR Hypothesis: The CONFLATOR is built on 2 hypotheses. i) Positional information is important for language models, especially when dealing with CM text. ii) Switching points are the bottleneck for code-mixed language models (CMLM). We incorporate positional information of switching points into our CMLM.

5 Positional Encoding Techniques

As discussed, SPs are a major bottleneck hence handling them separately is needed. Positional encoding are necessary for language models to learn dependencies between tokens. Positional embedding was first introduced by Vaswani et al. (2017b). The proposed sinusoidal positional encoding is composed of sine and cosine values with position index as inputs. The encoding techniques are further improved by Liu et al. (2020) where a dynamic function is introduced to learn position with gradient flow and Shaw et al. (2018) learned positional representation of relative positions using a learnable parameter. We talk about different positional encoding techniques in detail in the following subsections.

We experiment with several contemporary techniques and find that rotary positional encoding (Su et al., 2021) performs the best.

5.1 Sinusoidal Positional Encoding (SPE)

Vaswani et al. (2017b) introduced a pre-defined sinusoidal vector $p_i \in R^d$ which is assigned to each position *i*. This p_i is added to the word embedding $x_i \in R^d$ at position *i*, and $x_i + p_i$ is used as input to the model such that the Transformer can differentiate words coming from different positions and this also assigns each token a position-dependent attention. - equation 2.

$$e_{ij}^{abs} = \frac{1}{\sqrt{d}}\left((x_i + p_i)\, W^{Q,1}\right)\left((x_j + p_j)\, W^{K,1}\right)^T \quad (2)$$

Where W is the weight matrix, Q is query, K is key, l in the layer.

5.2 Dynamic Positional Encoding (DPE)

Instead of using predefined periodical functions like sin, Liu et al. (2020), introduced a dynamic function $\Theta(i)$ at every encoder layer. Improving upon sinusoidal PE, Dynamic PE learns $\Theta(i)$ instead of a predefined p_i to bring dynamic behavior to the model. At each utterance, this learnable function $\Theta(i)$ tries to learn the best possible representation for positional information with gradient flow.

$\Theta(i)$ is added to the word embedding w_i as given in equation 3.

$$e_{ij} = \frac{1}{\sqrt{d}} \left((x_i + \Theta(i)) W^{Q,1} \right) \left((x_j + \Theta(j)) W^{K,1} \right)^T \quad (3)$$

5.3 Relative Positional Encoding (RPE)

In absolute PE, using different p_i for different positions *i* helps the transformer distinguish words at different positions. However, the absolute PE is not effective in capturing the relative word order. Shaw et al. (2018) introduced a learnable parameter a_{i-j}^l which learns the positional representation of the relative position *i-j* at encoder layer *l*. With the help of this, we can explicitly capture word orders in our model as follows:

$$e_{ij}^{rel} = \frac{1}{\sqrt{d}} \left((x_i)^l W^{Q,l} \right) \left((x_i)^l W^{K,l} + a_{i-j}^l \right)^T \quad (4)$$

5.4 Switching Point-based Dynamic and Relative Positional Encoding (SPDRPE)

Ali et al. (2022) introduce a novel, switching point based PE. For illustration purposes, consider a code-mixed Hinglish text - *ye$_{HI}$ gaana$_{HI}$ enjoy$_{EN}$ kare$_{HI}$*. SP-based indices **(SPI)** set the index to 0 whenever an SP occurs. Indexing would normally be *Index* = (0, 1, 2, 3), but due to switching point incorporation, this gets changed to *SPI* = (0, 1, 0, 0). In addition to this, they use a learning parameter a_{i-j}^l, which encodes the relative position *i-j* at the encoder layer *l*. This encoding approach learns representations dynamically based on SPs along with the embedding a_{i-j}^l so that it can also capture relative word orders, as follows:

$$e_{ij} = \frac{1}{\sqrt{d}} \left((x_i + \Theta(S(l_i)))^l W^{Q,l} \right) \left((x_i + \Theta(S(l_j)))^l W^{K,l} + a_{i-j}^l \right)^T \quad (5)$$

5.5 Rotary Positional Encoding (RoPE)

Analogous to the idea of electromagnetic waves going through a polarizer to preserve their relative amplitude, (Su et al., 2021) came up with the idea of Rotary Positional Encoding (RoPE). The idea is to use rotation matrices on the embedding vectors to generate the positional values. The rotation negates any absolute positional information and only retains information about the relative angles between every pair of word embeddings in a sequence. We know that the dot product between two vectors is a function of the magnitude of individual vectors and the angle between them. Keeping this in mind, the intuition for RoPE is to represent the embeddings as complex numbers and the positions as pure rotations that we apply to them.

Mathematically, the formulations for a simple 2-dimensional case are defined as follows:

$$f_Q(x_i, i) = (W_Q x_i) e^{\sqrt{-1} i\theta}$$
$$f_Q(x_j, j) = (W_K x_j) e^{\sqrt{-1} j\theta}$$
$$g(x_i, x_j, i-j) = Re[(W_Q x_i)(W_K x_i)^* e^{\sqrt{-1}(i-j)\theta}] \quad (6)$$

where $Re[]$ is the real part of a complex number and $(W_K x_i)^*$ represents the conjugate complex number of $(W_K x_i)$. $\theta \in R$ is a preset non-zero constant. Formulating $f_{(Q,K)}$ as a matrix multiplication, we get:

$$f_Q(x_i, i) = \begin{pmatrix} cosm\theta_1 & -sinm\theta_1 \\ sinm\theta_1 & cosm\theta_1 \end{pmatrix} \begin{pmatrix} W_{Q,K}^{(11)} & W_{Q,K}^{(12)} \\ W_{Q,K}^{(21)} & W_{Q,K}^{(22)} \end{pmatrix} \begin{pmatrix} x_i^{(1)} \\ x_i^{(2)} \end{pmatrix} \quad (7)$$

where $(x_i^{(1)}, x_i^{(2)})$ is x_i expressed in the form of 2D coordinates. In the same way, we can turn function *g* into matrix form. By rotating the transformed embedding vector by an angle in multiples of its position index, we are able to incorporate relative position information. Due to this characteristic, it is termed as Rotary Position Embedding.

In order to generalize the result in 2D to any x_i in R_d where *d* is even, they divide the d-dimension space into $\frac{d}{2}$ sub-spaces and combine them in merit of the linearity of inner product, turning the attention formulation:

$$f_{Q,K} = e_{ij}^{rotary} = \frac{1}{\sqrt{d}} \left(RM_{\Theta,i}^d W^{Q,1}(x_i) \right)^T \left(RM_{\Theta,j}^d W^{K,1}(x_j) \right) \quad (8)$$

$$RM = \begin{pmatrix} cosm\theta_1 & -sinm\theta_1 & 0 & 0 & \cdots & 0 & 0 \\ sinm\theta_1 & cosm\theta_1 & 0 & 0 & \cdots & 0 & 0 \\ 0 & 0 & cosm\theta_2 & -sinm\theta_2 & \cdots & 0 & 0 \\ 0 & 0 & sinm\theta_2 & cosm\theta_2 & \cdots & 0 & 0 \\ \vdots & \vdots & \vdots & \vdots & \ddots & \vdots & \vdots \\ 0 & 0 & 0 & 0 & \cdots & cosm\theta_{d/2} & -sinm\theta_{d/2} \\ 0 & 0 & 0 & 0 & \cdots & sinm\theta_{d/2} & cosm\theta_{d/2} \end{pmatrix} \quad (9)$$

where RM is orthogonal and sparse matrix predefined parameters

$$\Theta = \theta_i = 10000^{-2(i-1)/d}, i \in [1, 2, ..., d/2]. \quad (10)$$

In contrast to the additive nature of the position embedding methods used by other works, their approach is multiplicative. Moreover, RoPE naturally incorporates relative position information through rotation matrix product instead of altering terms in the expanded formulation of additive position encoding when applied with self-attention.

6 Incorporation of Switching Point Information in CMLM

Positional encodings help the transformer learn dependencies between tokens at different positions of the input sequence. To enhance the positional encodings for code-mixed text, we modify the rotatory positional encoding to incorporate switching point information.

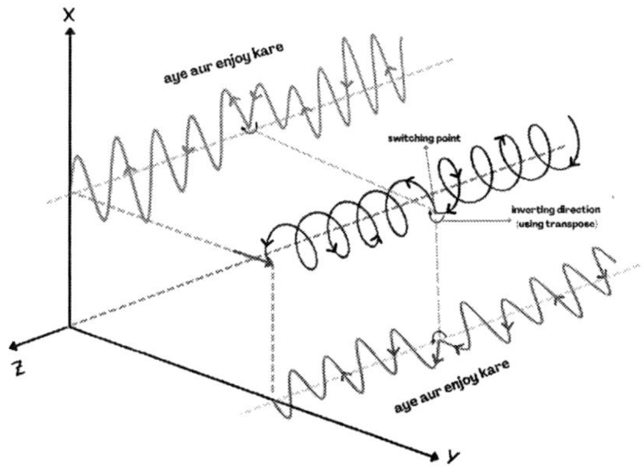

Figure 2: Visual intuition for our rotary approach with switching point incorporation. We consider a linearly polarized electromagnetic wave and show the change in rotation whenever a switching point occurs.

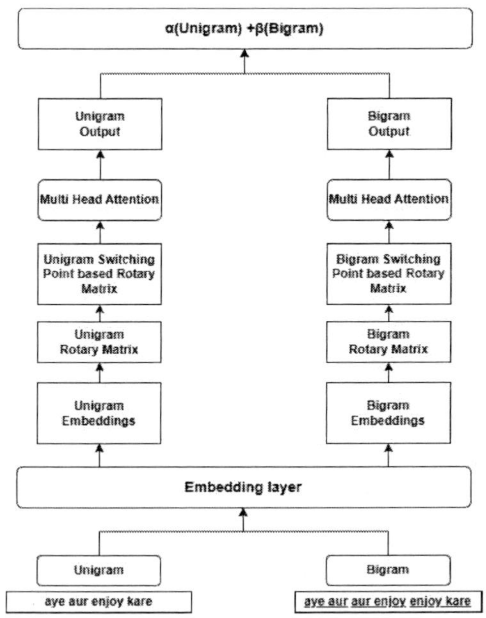

Figure 3: This diagram depicts the higher level understanding of the proposed positional embeddings.

6.1 Switching Point-based Rotary Matrix

Switching points are a potential bottleneck for code-mixing language modeling and to address this problem, we incorporate switching point based rotary positional encoding in our architecture. The intuition behind RoPE is electromagnetic waves. The embeddings are represented as complex numbers and the positions are represented as pure rotations that are applied to them. Keeping this in mind, we address the problem of switching points (SP) with the help of angles that participate in RoPE. Whenever we encounter a switching point, we change the rotation, i.e., we change the direction of these angles. To implement the rotation change, we define a switching point matrix. The switching point matrix helps our model identify and learn the patterns of code mixing in the corpus. Our matrix is defined with 1s and -1s. When there is a language shift (L1 $\rightarrow$ L2) or (L2 $\rightarrow$ L1), i.e., when we encounter a switching point, we annotate the column value as -1 and for the successive words in L2, we annotate column values as 1 until another switching point occurs.

$$
\begin{aligned}
& SPM \in R^{d}_{n*n} \\
& \text{if i == SP:} \\
& \qquad SPM_i = -1 \\
& \text{else:} \\
& \qquad SPM_i = 1
\end{aligned}
\tag{11}
$$

The visual intuition of our approach is shown in Figure 2. The switching point matrix (SPM) with 1s and -1s is defined in such a way that it transposes the rotary matrix, intuitively inverting the rotation at every switching point encounter. Therefore, the final matrix, i.e., switching point rotary matrix (SPRM) is a result of element-wise multiplication of the defined switching point matrix (SPM) with rotary matrix (RM):

$$SPRM = SPM \times RM \tag{12}$$

$$e_{ij}^{SPRotary} = \frac{1}{\sqrt{d}} \left(SPRM^{d}_{\Theta,i} W^{Q,1}(x_i)\right)^{T} \left(SPRM^{d}_{\Theta,j} W^{K,1}(x_i)\right) \tag{13}$$

6.2 Bigram and Switching Point-based Rotary Positional Encoding (BSPRoPE)

Since the language changes at the SPs, we get two consecutive tokens with different language hence we also incorporate the bigram level information in our model. In this positional encoding method, we get positional information among the bigrams in an utterance. We use the technique of switching point based rotary positional encoding at a word-to-word level and at bigram level as depicted in Figures 3,4 and mathematically expressed as Equation 16

$$e_{ij}^{UniSPRotary} = \frac{1}{\sqrt{d}} \left(SPRM^{d}_{\Theta,i} W^{Q,1}(x_i)\right)^{T} \left(SPRM^{d}_{\Theta,j} W^{K,1}(x_j)\right) \tag{14}$$

$$e_{ij}^{BiSPRotary} = \frac{1}{\sqrt{d}} \left(SPRM^{d}_{\Theta,i} W^{Q,1}(x_i)\right)^{T} \left(SPRM^{d}_{\Theta,j} W^{K,1}(x_j)\right) \tag{15}$$

$$prediction = a * e_{ij}^{UnigramSPRotary} + b * e_{ij}^{BigramSPRotary} \tag{16}$$

where a and b are learnable coefficients. x_i and x_i in equation 14 refer to unigram inputs whereas as in equation 15 they refer to bigram inputs.

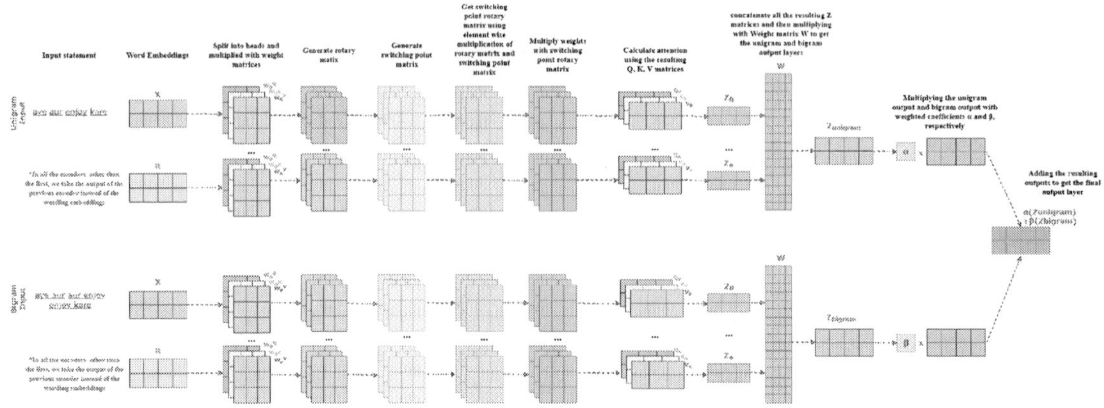

Figure 4: CONFLATOR architecture within the encoder layer. It depicts how the unigrams and bigrams of the input statement are passed as inputs to our encoder decoder architecture. In this framework, we generate a rotary matrix and a switching point matrix. By performing element-wise multiplication of the aforementioned matrices, we get our proposed novel switching point based rotary matrix. We represent the embeddings as complex numbers and their positions as pure rotations that we apply to them with the help of our switching point based rotary matrix. Then, upon getting the output layers for unigram and bigram statements separately. We introduce weighted coefficients a and b for unigram outputs and bigram outputs, respectively. We get our final output layer by adding these weighted unigram and bigram outputs.

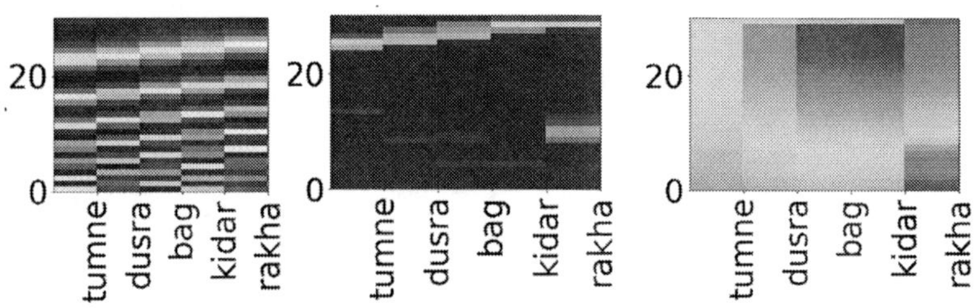

(a) Sinusoidal PE (b) Rotary PE (c) Conflator

Figure 5: CONFLATOR is able to differentiate words coming from different positions and give high attention when a switching point occurs (at bag_{EN} and $kidar_{HI}$) while the other models cannot do so.

6.3 CONFLATOR Architecture

The local dependencies for Unigram and Bigram (Word2Vec trained from scratch) along with unigram and bigram SPRM are fed to a 6-headed Multi-Head attention (MHA) in each encoder layer of the transformer separately, resulting in 2 attention matrices. We introduce 2 learnable parameters α and β that are used as weight coefficient for the unigram and bigram matrix respectively. The final matrix is passed to the decoder layer. The embedding and architecture in depicted in figs. 3 and 4.

7 Experiments and Results

For our base models, each training step takes about 0.5 seconds. We train the base models for a total of 100,000 steps or 12 hours. For the big models like bigram and SPM-based models, the step time is 1.0 seconds. The big models were trained for 250,000 steps (2 days). We use ADAM optimizer with β_1 = 0.9, β_2 = 0.98 and ϵ = 1e^{-9}. We use the method of varying the learning rate over the course of training from Vaswani et al. (2017b).

CMI Range	Transformer	GPT-2	BERT	Conflator
0-10	1018.54	823.71	666.48	492.96
11-20	1210.11	967.01	782.19	501.44
21-30	1401.37	1334.72	1007.34	544.71
31-40	2688.00	2334.73	1007.34	800.62
41-50	4421.22	3905.87	4337.02	1095.12
Average	2147.85	1873.20	1701.49	**578**

Table 2: Perplexity comparison between different models based on ranges of CMI. Lower Perplexity is better.

We use two types of regularization during our training process: We apply dropout to the output of each encoder and decoder layer followed by

Models	Positional representation							Bigram	F1 (%)
	Sin/Cos	Index	Dynamic	SPI	Relative	RM	SPRM		
Word2Vec + LSTM	✗	✗	✗	✗	✗	✗	✗	✗	56
BERT	✓	✗	✗	✗	✗	✗	✗	✗	60
3HA + Sinusoidal PE	✓	✓	✗	✗	✗	✗	✗	✗	74.34
3HA + Dynamic PE	✗	✓	✓	✗	✗	✗	✗	✗	75.02
3HA + Relative PE	✗	✗	✗	✗	✓	✗	✗	✗	75.32
3HA + Rotary PE	✓	✓	✗	✗	✗	✓	✗	✗	76.04
SOTA (PESTO)	✗	✗	✓	✓	✓	✗	✗	✗	75.6
Unigram SP Relative (USPR)	✗	✗	✗	✓	✓	✗	✗	✗	75
Bigram SP Relative BSPR)	✗	✗	✓	✓	✓	✗	✗	✓	75
Unigram SPRoPE + Good Tuning	✓	✓	✗	✓	✗	✓	✓	✗	74.6
Unigram SPRoPE	✓	✓	✗	✓	✗	✓	✓	✗	75
Conflator (BSPRoPE)	✓	✓	✗	✓	✗	✓	✓	✓	76.23
Conflator with StableLM	✓	✓	✗	✓	✗	✓	✓	✓	76.11
Conflator with Alpaca	✓	✓	✗	✓	✗	✓	✓	✓	75.69
Conflator with LLaMA	✓	✓	✗	✓	✗	✓	✓	✓	**76.45**

Table 3: Results of various position sensitive experiments for ***Sentiment Analysis*** on CM text. *n*HA refers to n-headed attention.

Models	Positional representation							Bigram	BLEU
	Sin/Cos	Index	Dynamic	SPI	Relative	RM	SPRM		
3HA + Sinusoidal PE	✓	✓	✗	✗	✗	✗	✗	✗	17.2
3HA + Dynamic PE	✗	✓	✓	✗	✗	✗	✗	✗	17.9
3HA + Relative PE	✗	✗	✗	✗	✓	✗	✗	✗	18.4
3HA + Rotary PE	✓	✓	✗	✗	✗	✓	✗	✗	24.9
SOTA (IIITH-mrinaldhar)	✗	✗	✓	✓	✓	✗	✗	✗	28.4
Unigram SP Relative (USPR)	✗	✗	✗	✓	✓	✗	✗	✗	9.8
Bigram SP Relative (BSPR)	✗	✗	✓	✓	✓	✗	✗	✓	7.6
Unigram SPRoPE	✓	✓	✗	✓	✗	✓	✓	✗	29.1
Conflator (BSPRoPE)	✓	✓	✗	✓	✗	✓	✓	✓	25.16
Conflator with StableLM	✓	✓	✗	✓	✗	✓	✓	✓	29.06
Conflator with Alpaca	✓	✓	✗	✓	✗	✓	✓	✓	29.89
Conflator with LLaMA	✓	✓	✗	✓	✗	✓	✓	✓	**30.15**

Table 4: Results of position sensitive experiments for ***Machine Translation*** on CM text. Higher BLEU is better.

Normalization. In addition, we apply dropout and normalization to the sums of the word embeddings and the positional encodings in both the encoder and decoder layers. We use a rate of $P_{drop} = 0.2$.

Intrinsic Evaluation: The perplexity scores of baseline language models in comparison with CONFLATOR on code-mixed language modeling task are shown in 2. We see that our model performs much better than other models.

Extrinsic Evaluation: We evaluate our model on two downstream tasks: (i) sentiment analysis, and (ii) machine translation. For sentiment analysis, (Table. 3) we use the data provided by Patwa et al. (2020a). CONFLATOR achieves 76.23% F1 score and outperforms the SOTA (Ali et al., 2022). The main reason for this is learning SP by aggregating with the help of rotary positional encoding with a variable length MHA framework. For the machine translation (Table 4), we use the data provided by (Dhar et al., 2018). We achieve 29.1 bleu score and outperform the SOTA (Dhar et al., 2018) using the Unigram SPRoPE model which is able to learn the patterns of language mixing with the help of switching point based rotary positional encoding.

8 Conclusion & Takeaways

In this work, we report experiments on *Hinglish* sentiment analysis and Machine translation problems through the lens of language modeling. Our contribution could be seen as following:

(i) We introduce the idea of switching point based rotary positional encoding. Whenever a switching point is encountered, we incorporate rotation change to learn the patterns of language mixing.

(ii) We introduce CONFLATOR, a neural language modeling approach for code-mixed languages. CONFLATOR tries to learn better representations by means of switching point-based rotary positional encoding, initially at unigram level and then at bigram level.

(iii) We empirically prove that CONFLATOR is learning the patterns of code-mixing which other models with different positional encodings prove unsuccessful, as shown in Figure 5.

(iv) It is also noteworthy that CONFLATOR achieves comparable to SOTA results even without any pre-trained heavy language model.

9 Limitations

Although our bigram model achieves SOTA on sentiment analysis using unigram, it is slightly behind the bigram model when it comes to machine translation, where using bigram at the decoder level resulted in poor performance. Despite conducting extensive experiments, there lacks a detailed explanation on why the bigram-based approach for MT fails. Future experiments will focus on exploring or understanding the issue of bigrams for MT and coming up with a solution for the same.

References

Mohsin Ali, Sai Teja Kandukuri, Sumanth Manduru, Parth Patwa, and Amitava Das. 2022. Pesto: Switching point based dynamic and relative positional encoding for code-mixed languages (student abstract). In *Proceedings of the AAAI Conference on Artificial Intelligence*, volume 36.

Segun Taofeek Aroyehun and Alexander Gelbukh. 2018. Aggression detection in social media: Using deep neural networks, data augmentation, and pseudo labeling. In *Proceedings of the First Workshop on Trolling, Aggression and Cyberbullying (TRAC-2018)*, pages 90–97, Santa Fe, New Mexico, USA. Association for Computational Linguistics.

Shubhanker Banerjee, Bharathi Raja Chakravarthi, and John P McCrae. 2020. Comparison of pretrained embeddings to identify hate speech in indian code-mixed text. In *2020 2nd International Conference on Advances in Computing, Communication Control and Networking (ICACCCN)*, pages 21–25. IEEE.

Utsab Barman, Amitava Das, Joachim Wagner, and Jennifer Foster. 2014. Code mixing: A challenge for language identification in the language of social media. In *Proceedings of the First Workshop on Computational Approaches to Code Switching*, pages 13–23, Doha, Qatar. Association for Computational Linguistics.

Yoshua Bengio, Réjean Ducharme, Pascal Vincent, and Christian Janvin. 2003. A neural probabilistic language model. *J. Mach. Learn. Res.*, 3:1137–1155.

Aditya Bohra, Deepanshu Vijay, Vinay Singh, Syed Sarfaraz Akhtar, and Manish Shrivastava. 2018. A dataset of hindi-english code-mixed social media text for hate speech detection. In *Proceedings of the second workshop on computational modeling of people's opinions, personality, and emotions in social media*, pages 36–41.

Eyamba G Bokamba. 1988. Code-mixing, language variation, and linguistic theory:: Evidence from bantu languages. *Lingua*, 76(1):21–62.

Bharathi Raja Chakravarthi, Vigneshwaran Muralidaran, Ruba Priyadharshini, and John P McCrae. 2020. Corpus creation for sentiment analysis in code-mixed tamil-english text. *arXiv preprint arXiv:2006.00206*.

Arindam Chatterjere, Vineeth Guptha, Parul Chopra, and Amitava Das. 2020. Minority positive sampling for switching points - an anecdote for the code-mixing language modeling. In *Proceedings of The 12th Language Resources and Evaluation Conference*, pages 6230–6238, Marseille, France. European Language Resources Association.

Amitava Das and Björn Gambäck. 2014. Identifying languages at the word level in code-mixed indian social media text.

Jacob Devlin, Ming-Wei Chang, Kenton Lee, and Kristina Toutanova. 2018a. Bert: Pre-training of deep bidirectional transformers for language understanding. *arXiv preprint arXiv:1810.04805*.

Jacob Devlin, Ming-Wei Chang, Kenton Lee, and Kristina Toutanova. 2018b. BERT: pre-training of deep bidirectional transformers for language understanding. *CoRR*, abs/1810.04805.

Mrinal Dhar, Vaibhav Kumar, and Manish Shrivastava. 2018. Enabling code-mixed translation: Parallel corpus creation and MT augmentation approach. In *Proceedings of the First Workshop on Linguistic Resources for Natural Language Processing*, pages 131–140, Santa Fe, New Mexico, USA. Association for Computational Linguistics.

Björn Gambäck and Amitava Das. 2016. Comparing the level of code-switching in corpora. In *Proceedings of the Tenth International Conference on Language Resources and Evaluation (LREC'16)*, pages 1850–1855, Portorož, Slovenia. European Language Resources Association (ELRA).

Vinay Gopalan and Mark Hopkins. 2020. Reed at semeval-2020 task 9: Sentiment analysis on code-mixed tweets. *CoRR*, abs/2007.13061.

Madan Gopal Jhanwar and Arpita Das. 2018. An ensemble model for sentiment analysis of hindi-english code-mixed data. *arXiv preprint arXiv:1806.04450*.

Abhishek Laddha, Mohamed Hanoosh, Debdoot Mukherjee, Parth Patwa, and Ankur Narang. 2020. Understanding chat messages for sticker recommendation in messaging apps. *Proceedings of the AAAI Conference on Artificial Intelligence*, 34(08):13156–13163.

Abhishek Laddha, Mohamed Hanoosh, Debdoot Mukherjee, Parth Patwa, and Ankur Narang. 2022. Large scale multilingual sticker recommendation in messaging apps. *AI Magazine*, 42(4):16–28.

Guillaume Lample and Alexis Conneau. 2019. Cross-lingual language model pretraining.

Xuanqing Liu et al. 2020. Learning to encode position for transformer with continuous dynamical model. In *ICML 2020*.

Yili Ma, Liang Zhao, and Jie Hao. 2020. Xlp at semeval-2020 task 9: Cross-lingual models with focal loss for sentiment analysis of code-mixing language. In *Proceedings of the fourteenth workshop on semantic evaluation*, pages 975–980.

Ravindra Nayak and Raviraj Joshi. 2022. L3cube-hingcorpus and hingbert: A code mixed hindi-english dataset and bert language models.

Braja Gopal Patra, Dipankar Das, and Amitava Das. 2018. Sentiment analysis of code-mixed indian languages: An overview of sail_code-mixed shared task @icon-2017. *CoRR*, abs/1803.06745.

Parth Patwa, Gustavo Aguilar, Sudipta Kar, Suraj Pandey, Srinivas PYKL, Björn Gambäck, Tanmoy Chakraborty, Thamar Solorio, and Amitava Das. 2020a. SemEval-2020 task 9: Overview of sentiment analysis of code-mixed tweets. In *Proceedings of the Fourteenth Workshop on Semantic Evaluation*, pages 774–790, Barcelona (online). International Committee for Computational Linguistics.

Parth Patwa, Srinivas Pykl, Amitava Das, Prerana Mukherjee, and Viswanath Pulabaigari. 2020b. Hater-O-genius aggression classification using capsule networks. In *Proceedings of the 17th International Conference on Natural Language Processing (ICON)*, pages 149–154, Indian Institute of Technology Patna, Patna, India. NLP Association of India (NLPAI).

Alec Radford, Jeff Wu, Rewon Child, David Luan, Dario Amodei, and Ilya Sutskever. 2019. Language models are unsupervised multitask learners.

Niloofar Safi Samghabadi, Parth Patwa, Srinivas Pykl, Prerana Mukherjee, Amitava Das, and Thamar Solorio. 2020. Aggression and misogyny detection using bert: A multi-task approach. In *Proceedings of the second workshop on trolling, aggression and cyberbullying*, pages 126–131.

Ayan Sengupta, Sourabh Kumar Bhattacharjee, Tanmoy Chakraborty, and Md Shad Akhtar. 2021. Hit: A hierarchically fused deep attention network for robust code-mixed language representation.

Peter Shaw, Jakob Uszkoreit, and Ashish Vaswani. 2018. Self-attention with relative position representations. In *NAACL 2018*.

Rajendra Singh. 1985. Grammatical constraints on code-mixing: Evidence from hindi-english. *Canadian Journal of Linguistics/Revue canadienne de linguistique*, 30(1):33–45.

Vivek Srivastava and Mayank Singh. 2020. Phinc: A parallel hinglish social media code-mixed corpus for machine translation. *arXiv preprint arXiv:2004.09447*.

Jianlin Su, Yu Lu, Shengfeng Pan, Bo Wen, and Yunfeng Liu. 2021. Roformer: Enhanced transformer with rotary position embedding. *CoRR*, abs/2104.09864.

Tiancheng Tang, Xinhuai Tang, and Tianyi Yuan. 2020. Fine-tuning bert for multi-label sentiment analysis in unbalanced code-switching text. *IEEE Access*, 8:193248–193256.

Debapriya Tula, Prathyush Potluri, Shreyas Ms, Sumanth Doddapaneni, Pranjal Sahu, Rohan Sukumaran, and Parth Patwa. 2021. Bitions@DravidianLangTech-EACL2021: Ensemble of multilingual language models with pseudo labeling for offence detection in Dravidian languages. In *Proceedings of the First Workshop on Speech and Language Technologies for Dravidian Languages*, pages 291–299, Kyiv. Association for Computational Linguistics.

Debapriya Tula, MS Shreyas, Viswanatha Reddy, Pranjal Sahu, Sumanth Doddapaneni, Prathyush Potluri, Rohan Sukumaran, and Parth Patwa. 2022. Offence detection in dravidian languages using code-mixing index-based focal loss. *SN Computer Science*, 3(5):330.

Ashish Vaswani, Noam Shazeer, Niki Parmar, Jakob Uszkoreit, Llion Jones, Aidan N Gomez, Ł ukasz Kaiser, and Illia Polosukhin. 2017a. Attention is all you need. In *Advances in Neural Information Processing Systems*, volume 30. Curran Associates, Inc.

Ashish Vaswani, Noam Shazeer, Niki Parmar, Jakob Uszkoreit, Llion Jones, Aidan N. Gomez, Lukasz Kaiser, and Illia Polosukhin. 2017b. Attention is all you need. *CoRR*, abs/1706.03762.

S.K. Verma. 1976. Code-switching: Hindi-english. *Lingua*, 38(2):153–165.

Yogarshi Vyas, Spandana Gella, Jatin Sharma, Kalika Bali, and Monojit Choudhury. 2014. Pos tagging of english-hindi code-mixed social media content. In *Proceedings of the 2014 conference on empirical methods in natural language processing (EMNLP)*, pages 974–979.

Unified Model for Code-Switching Speech Recognition and Language Identification Based on Concatenated Tokenizer

Kunal Dhawan, Dima Rekesh, Boris Ginsburg
NVIDIA, Santa Clara, USA
{kdhawan, drekesh, bginsburg}@nvidia.com

Abstract

Code-Switching (CS) multilingual Automatic Speech Recognition (ASR) models can transcribe speech containing two or more alternating languages during a conversation. This paper proposes (1) a new method for creating code-switching ASR datasets from purely monolingual data sources, and (2) a novel Concatenated Tokenizer that enables ASR models to generate language ID for each emitted text token while reusing existing monolingual tokenizers. The efficacy of these approaches for building CS ASR models is demonstrated for two language pairs, English-Hindi and English-Spanish, where we achieve new state-of-the-art results on the Miami Bangor CS evaluation corpus. In addition to competitive ASR performance, the proposed Concatenated Tokenizer models are highly effective for spoken language identification, achieving 98%+ accuracy on the out-of-distribution FLEURS dataset.

1 Introduction

Automatic Speech Recognition (ASR) systems are moving from specialized monolingual models to ASR architectures capable of handling multiple languages simultaneously (Weng et al., 1997; Waibel et al., 2000; Kannan et al., 2019; Li et al., 2022; Pratap et al., 2023). Code-Switching (CS) is a special category of multilingual speech in which two or more languages or varieties of languages are used in the same utterance. It can further be divided into two categories: *inter-sentential* code-switching where the switching between languages happens predominantly at the sentence boundaries and *intra-sentential* code-switching, which happens within the sentence (Myers-Scotton, 1989).

Most of the work in code-switching ASR is dependent on the availability of a good quality code-switching speech corpus (Sitaram et al., 2019). One of the questions that we explore in this paper is: how to better utilize the readily available monolingual speech corpora and train CS ASR systems that can perform well in real-world code switching scenarios.

Text post-processing after ASR, e.g. punctuation and capitalization (Guerreiro et al., 2021) and inverse text normalization (Sunkara et al., 2021), is another important problem for multilingual and CS speech systems. Such post-processing is harder than the monolingual scenario as it requires accurate language identification in addition to transcript generation. Traditionally, separate Language Identification (LID) and ASR models have been trained for the task, usually with a common acoustic encoder. Li et al. (Li et al., 2019) was one of the first few works to propose an end-to-end architecture for intra-sentential CS ASR. They trained two separate monolingual ASR systems and a frame-level LID model. The posteriors of ASR models were adjusted with the LID scores and greedy decoding was used without any language model rescoring. In (Ali et al., 2021), the authors proposed to use multi-graph weighted finite state transducers, which was shown to be more effective than Transformer-based systems for the intra-sentential CS. Recent works (Seki et al., 2019), (Radford et al., 2022) approach this problem differently by introducing special LID symbols such as [EN] [ES], that are added to the vocabulary for language identification. These symbols are predicted either at the start of the utterance to identify which language the decoded text belongs to (Radford et al., 2022), or during the utterance to mark spans of decoded tokens belonging to each language (Seki et al., 2019).

In this paper, we propose a streamlined technique for learning token level language ID, which we term *Concatenated Tokenizer*. Unlike previous approaches of "aggregating" tokenizers that take the union of the per-language tokenizer vocabularies (Li et al., 2021) or create a shared sub-word token set across languages (Pratap et al., 2020a), in the concatenated tokenizer method we reuse monolingual tokenizers and map them to mutually ex-

Proceedings of the 6th Workshop on Computational Approaches to Linguistic Code-Switching, pages 74–82
December 7, 2023 ©2023 Association for Computational Linguistics

clusive label spaces for each language. This helps provide explicit language information to the ASR model while training and leads to inexpensive prediction of token level LID at decoding time.

The main contributions of the paper are as follows:

1. A scalable and extensible synthetic code-switching ASR data generation pipeline that allows us to generate a corpus of any size, online (e.g. during training) or offline, from strictly monolingual data sources.
2. The Concatenated Tokenizer method which can effectively utilize pre-existing monolingual tokenizers and provide token level LID information while learning multilingual and CS ASR models.
3. We demonstrate CS speech recognition capabilities of the proposed unified ASR model on real world data for two language pairs and spoken language identification capabilities on the out of distribution FLEURS evaluation dataset.

2 Multilingual and Code-Switching ASR

Modern Natural Language Processing (NLP) and ASR models use tokenizers to represent text (Kudo and Richardson, 2018). The traditional approach requires that a new tokenizer is learned for each language and domain. In ASR, this tokenizer is also used to reduce the target sequence length to satisfy CTC requirements under aggressive downsampling with respect to original audio length (Graves et al., 2006). In this section, we discuss the proposed concatenated tokenizer and the synthetic code-switching data generation pipeline.

2.1 Concatenated Tokenizers

When training multilingual ASR models, monolingual training sets typically have significantly different characteristics (e.g. total size, quality, noise levels, etc.), requiring experimentation of combining them with different ratios for an optimal outcome. Training a different tokenizer on the combined mixture of datasets for each experiment becomes a logistical challenge, while the resulting model must always use the exact same tokenizer with which they it was trained. Synthetic code-switching training datasets present an additional challenge since the tokenizer learns the purely synthetic co-occurrence of adjacent tokens from dif-

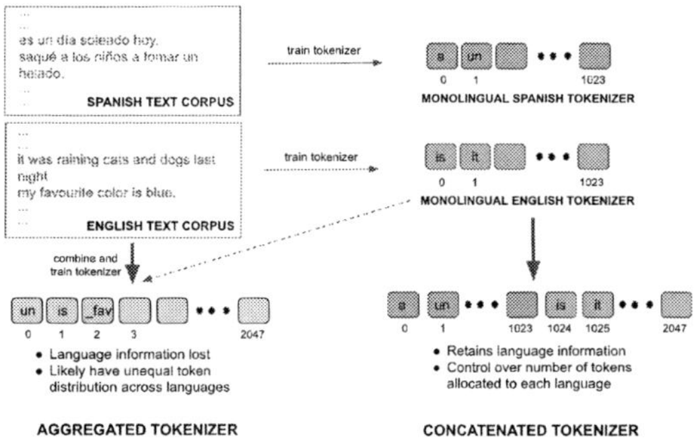

Figure 1: Aggregated vs Concatenated (proposed) tokenization approaches for a bilingual English-Spanish example. Spanish text and tokenizer is represented in red, English text and tokenizer in blue.

ferent languages, which is unlikely to occur in real code-switching data. Finally, when training a single tokenizer on multilingual data, we must disregard the LID information for each token and need to rely on an external technique if retention of LID is desirable.

We propose the concatenated tokenizer technique to mitigate the above issues. Fig. 1 illustrates this approach when training a bilingual English-Spanish model with the vocabulary size of 2K. In the traditional approach, text transcripts are mixed in some proportion and a tokenizer is trained on the joint text corpus. LID information is lost and would need to be re-supplied if desired. For a CS use case, training a tokenizer on a synthetic code-switching dataset directly results in it learning arbitrary transitions between language samples, and is likely to be avoided.

In the concatenated tokenizer method, we train English and Spanish tokenizers with a 1K vocabulary size each on the corresponding monolingual datasets separately. We allocate the range of IDs from 0 through 1023 to English and 1024 through 2047 to Spanish. To achieve that, after tokenization, we shift each Spanish token by 1024 to ensure that it lands in its allocated range. The concatenated tokenizer has, therefore, also 2K tokens. During training, we use the English tokenizer (shown in blue) to tokenize each English sample segment, and the Spanish tokenizer (red) to tokenize each Spanish segment. At inference time, the model predicts a sequence of token ids. If the token ID is in the range from 0 to 1023, we know that it is an English token, and we use the English tokenizer to convert it to text. Similarly, tokens in the range from 1024 to 2047 are Spanish and are sent to the Spanish tokenizer for detokenization. Language ID information is embedded in the ID of each token and can be used in downstream processing of the resulting text segments. We name our method concatenated tokenizer because such tokenizer effectively contains more than one separate monolingual tokenizer with its preserved non-overlapping token space. In the above example, we chose to allocate the same number of tokens to English and Spanish, but that certainly does not need to be the case when dataset sizes are very different.

Note that the concatenated tokenizer method differs significantly from the standard technique of training an aggregated tokenizer on a mixture of transcripts and then re-injecting the language information into the tokenized sequences via special LID tokens (Seki et al., 2019), (Radford et al., 2022). In the latter approach, the special LID tokens indicate only the beginning and end of each monolingual span of text.

The design of the concatenated tokenizer allows us to easily suppress specific languages from inference when it is known that the audio does not contain them. We simply do not need to compute probabilities for token IDs in the ranges corresponding to the suppressed languages, simultaneously improving performance. Fig. 2 illustrates how this works with the CTC decoder. Conversely, when adding language(s) to the decoder, we can transfer existing token weights via weight surgery, initializing weights for the incremental language(s) from scratch. The same idea works with the Transducer decoder as well. This allows for a better decoder initialization while training multilingual model from monolingual checkpoints, while improving convergence time.

2.2 Synthetic data generation for Code Switching ASR

Synthetic code-switching data generation was an essential step in our work. It enabled us to effectively use the monolingual training data available at our disposal to generate a diverse set of CS speech training samples which then was utilized by our model for training. We had to be careful in the data generation strategy to ensure that we didn't introduce a bias of any kind that would make model training easier but would lead to poor performance on real world code-switching data. For example, if we simply stitched different speech samples together it would cause inconsistencies and the different amplitudes and background conditions can give the model easy clues for learning this generated data. Such inconsistencies would not be found in real life examples, and hence the model would not be able to generalize its performance. Furthermore, we didn't want to bias the generated samples to start from or end with a particular language, e.g. English.

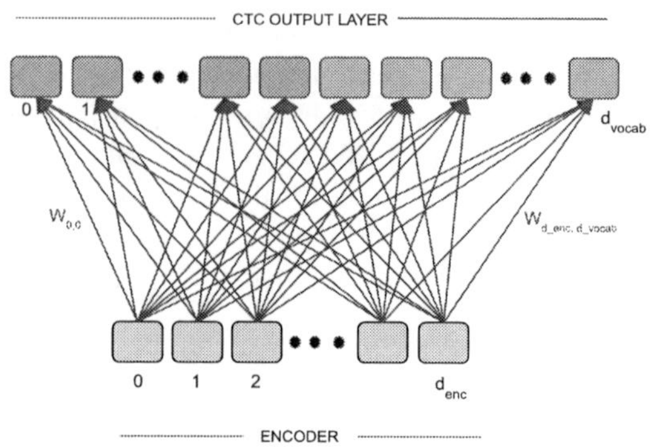

Figure 2: Diagram illustrating the benefits of concatenated tokenizers for easy addition/suppression of languages in multilingual ASR models. For simplicity, we show a single output step of a bilingual ASR model with a CTC decoder consisting of one feed-forward fully connected layer (FC) with weights W that maps encoder representation (dimension d_{enc}) to token logits (dimension d_{vocab}, blank symbol omitted). The concatenated tokenizer has two languages marked by red and blue. Due to the non-overlapping token mappings for different languages in the concatenated tokenizer, the FC weights can easily be separated and modified independently.

We used the algorithm detailed in Fig. 3 for generating synthetic CS speech data for two or more languages from their monolingual speech corpus. Each language was assigned a sampling frequency. For each synthetic CS sample we define a max and min duration, which are controllable parameters. This allows us to generate samples with a specific duration distribution and also ensures that the samples are of similar lengths which leads to lesser padding during batching, leading to more effective utilization of the data. To have a control over leading, trailing silences in the synthetic sample as well as the gap between concatenated samples, we introduce three parameters: duration beginning silence, duration ending silence, duration joining silence. In the current implementation we use silence, but this can easily be extended to adding noise with a desired SNR. The next step in the algorithm is removal of leading and trailing silences.

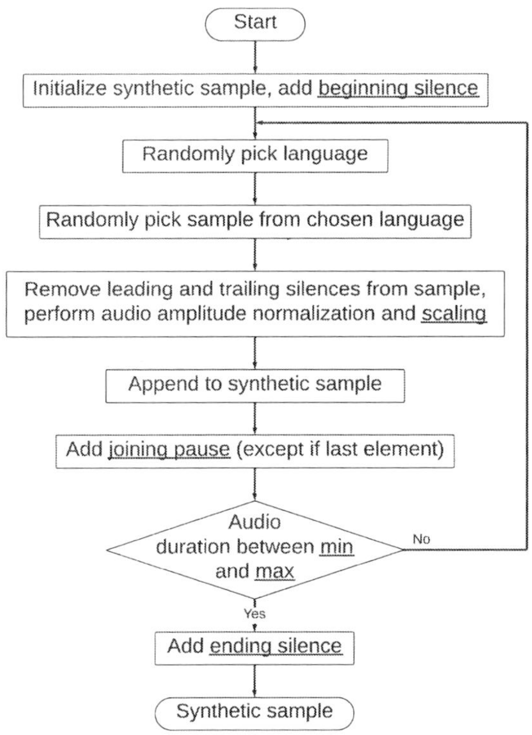

Figure 3: Flowchart of the synthetic CS sample generation process for two languages. The controllable hyperparameters have been underlined. The process can be used for both online synthetic data generation in the dataloader or offline creation of synthetic speech corpus as discussed in Section 2.2.

This ensures that we extract only the speech portion from the individual utterances and discard any silences in the beginning or end of the utterance. This allows us to have complete control over the leading, joining, and trailing silences in the generated sample using our tunable duration parameters explained earlier. In our current implementation we use an amplitude based threshold for removing silence, but this would be extended to voice activity detection (VAD) in the future iterations. Another important step in our algorithm is audio amplitude normalization and scaling. We perform peak amplitude normalization for each sample before concatenation and multiply the normalized sample with the controllable scaling parameter to ensure that all samples are in a similar amplitude range before joining, removing the amplitude bias from individual datasets that provide the monolingual samples. It should be noted that a similar synthetic speech data generation idea was proposed in (Seki et al., 2018), but our approach is more customizable and general due to the larger number of controllable parameters. We found this technique to be useful in generating synthetic samples that are longer and similar in duration, which accelerates training. Synthetic CS data generation approaches have also been explored in the text domain, for training multilingual language models (Winata et al., 2019) and translation models (Gupta et al., 2020; Tarunesh et al., 2021).

In our implementation, we provide both an offline and online version of the synthetic data generation pipeline. In the offline version, the generated synthetic corpus using the proposed algorithm is stored explicitly and can be used to train the ASR model. In the online version, the synthetic sample generation process happens in the dataloader, and is used to feed samples to ASR model for training. The online data generation approach provides the advantage of not having to save the generated synthetic corpus, and hence can be used to rapidly experiment with different language ratios and other parameter permutations, generating massive synthetic training CS ASR corpora with no disk space overhead. The code for the data generation process is open-sourced and available in NeMo toolkit[1].

2.3 Spoken Language Identification

Spoken language identification refers to the task of identifying the language of a given utterance directly from audio (Li et al., 2006). This task is critical for CS ASR because it enables us to reuse monolingual models to re-score CS decoded output if we can predict which language was spoken when. The proposed concatenated tokenizers fit in here perfectly as they also contain the information of the language that each predicted token belongs to. To calculate the efficacy of concatenated tokenizer for utterance level spoken language identification, we take the maximum over the predicted language for each token in the sentence. To ensure a fair comparison, we trained our models with the datasets described in Section 3.1 but evaluated spoken language identification performance on the blind test sets of the FLEURS [26] dataset.

3 Experimental Setup

3.1 Datasets

We used LibriSpeech (Panayotov et al., 2015)($\sim$ 960 hours) as the English corpus. For Spanish,

[1]https://github.com/NVIDIA/NeMo/scripts/speech_recognition/code_switching

we compiled a dataset ($\sim$ 1300 hrs after basic cleaning) consisting of Mozilla Common Voice 7.0 (Ardila et al., 2020), Multilingual LibriSpeech (Pratap et al., 2020b), Voxpopuli (et al, 2021) and Fisher (Graff et al., 2010) (all Spanish). For Hindi training we used the ULCA dataset (Dhuriya et al., 2022) ($\sim$ 2,250 hrs after basic cleaning).

For English-Spanish (en-es) and English-Hindi (en-hi) synthetic CS data generation we follow the approach outlined in Section 2.2 to generate a 10K hour training corpus with the following parameters: max sample duration 19 sec, min sample duration 17 sec, silence duration 0.02 sec, ending silence duration 0.02 sec, joining silence duration 0.1 sec. Using the same parameters, we generated 10 hour synthetic bilingual CS test sets using monolingual test sets for both language pairs. Language sampling probabilities were a parameter; we experimented with multiple ratios in the course of our experiments.

We chose the Miami Bangor corpus (Deuchar et al., 2014), which consists of full conversations, as the Spanish out-of-distribution CS test set. Individual interactions were extracted using provided timestamps. All utterances less than 2 seconds were removed. The final evaluation set has 16 hours with 16620 utterances and 35 unique characters. As the Hindi CS test set, we use the MUCS 2021 corpus (Diwan et al., 2021). We performed basic cleaning, leading to a 5 hour set with 3136 samples and 89 unique characters.

3.2 Models and Experiments

We used the Conformer-RNNT Large model (Gulati et al., 2020) ($\sim$ 120 M parameters, no external LM) and trained it for 200 epochs using the AdamW optimizer and Noam scheduler with a 20k steps warmup, 0.0015 peak learning rate and 10^{-6} minimum learning rate. We performed the following experiments:

- **Monolingual**: We trained monolingual English, Spanish, and Hindi ASR models (see Section 3.1). For each language, we trained an SPE unigram tokenizer (Sennrich et al., 2016) with a vocabulary size of 1024.

- **Bilingual**: We trained bilingual English-Spanish and English-Hindi models. We mixed the monolingual datasets in different ratios with the general idea of over-representing the smaller dataset. We trained two classes of models, one with the concatenated tokenizer (Section 2.1) and another with a regular (aggregate) tokenizer trained on the combined text corpus in the 1:1 ratio. We further performed an initialization study for both language pairs by training from scratch or starting from either monolingual checkpoint.

- **Code-Switching (CS)**: We trained CS English-Spanish and English-Hindi models using the synthetic code-switching data highlighted in Section 3.1. We experimented with training from scratch and also the corresponding bilingual (non-CS) model. Further, we investigated using both concatenated and aggregate tokenizers in all the scenarios.

- **Language Identification**: We used the English-Spanish and English-Hindi concatenated tokenizer trained during the bilingual CS experiments to perform utterance level language identification on the English (en_us_test, 647 samples), Spanish (es_419_test, 908 samples), and Hindi (hi_in_test, 418 samples) speech samples from the FLEURS set (Conneau et al., 2023).

4 Results and Discussion

In this section, we present results for the experiments outlined in Section 3.2. Table 1a shows performance of monolingual, bilingual and CS English-Spanish models with different tokenizers on the English Librispeech and Spanish Fisher test sets. We used dataset mix ratio (English to Spanish) of 2:1 for training the bilingual model in order to balance the training set. The Fisher test set was chosen to represent model performance on Spanish because it was the hardest (highest WER) out of the four Spanish datasets mentioned in Section 3.1. Similarly, Table 1b presents the results for the different models for English-Hindi language pair. We used dataset mix ratio (English to Hindi) of 2:1 as well for the bilingual model, again aiming to balance the training set. Results were averaged across three runs and averaged (Liu et al., 2018) over the five best model checkpoints.

The results for English-Spanish CS experiments are highlighted in Table 2a and for English-Hindi in Table 2b. The numbers for monolingual models are not reported on the code-switching evaluation datasets as they are relatively poor, as expected.

Table 1: Monolingual evaluation set results for the English-Spanish and English-Hindi models. We present WER(%) (lower is better) for multilingual (ml) and code-switched (cs) models trained with concatenated (con) and aggregate (agg) tokenizers vs monolingual baselines. We observe that the use of the concatenated tokenizer does not hurt model performance while adding the ability to predict LID for each token.

(a) English-Spanish results on the monolingual English Librispeech test-other and Spanish Fisher test sets.

Model	Tokenizer	English LS test-other	Spanish Fisher-test
en	mono	5.29	98.37
es	mono	85.68	16.14
ml	agg	5.00	16.37
ml	con	5.14	16.72
cs	agg	5.38	16.35
cs	con	5.28	16.42

(b) English-Hindi results on the monolingual English Librispeech test-other and Hindi ULCA eval sets.

Model	Tokenizer	English LS test-other	Hindi ULCA
en	mono	5.29	100
hi	mono	100	10.53
ml	agg	5.00	10.78
ml	con	5.14	10.73
cs	agg	5.42	11.35
cs	con	5.29	11.64

Table 2: Performance comparison of the code-switched (cs) English-Spanish and English-Hindi models trained with concatenated (con) and aggregate (agg) tokenizers on both synthetic and real world blind CS evaluation datasets. The performance of the multilingual (ml) models has also been reported as a benchmark. We observe that cs models significantly outperform ml models, highlighting the advantage of using the proposed synthetic CS data for training.

(a) Code-switched English-Spanish models: WER(%) on synthetic and Miami-Bangor CS evaluation sets.

Model	Tokenizer	synth	Miami
cs	agg	5.51	50.0
cs	con	5.50	53.3
ml	agg	16.52	58.78
ml	con	24.08	63.54

(b) Code-switched English-Hindi models: WER(%) on synthetic and MUCS CS evaluation sets.

Model	Tokenizer	synth	MUCS
cs	agg	6.55	30.3
cs	con	6.57	28.78
ml	agg	35.70	62.18
ml	con	53.01	100

When multilingual models are used to decode code-switched speech, we observe that they tend to stick with the language in which the utterance started and are not able to switch between languages as they occur within the utterance. This is evidenced by the correspondingly high WERs in Tables 2a and 2b, and is consistent with the fact that the models did not encounter code-switched data during training.

To illustrate, here are sample transcripts from one English-Spanish code-switched audio:
ML model output: con qué departamento puedo dejar fitbax sobre mi experiencia de compra en la tienda que estaba ubicada en one tú threforme ave
CS model output: con qué departamento puedo dejar feedbacks sobre mi experiencia de compra en la tienda que estaba ubicada en one two three fourth avenue
We can see that the ML model is not able to switch from Spanish (majority language) to English (underlined for easier visual comparison). On the other hand, the output of the CS model is 100% accurate.

Finally, the results of the Language Identification experiments for all the three languages are presented in Table 3. In the following, we dive deeper into the results and discuss the findings.

4.1 Bilingual models, effect of model initialization and tokenizers

From Tables 1a and 1b we observe that the bilingual and CS models achieve comparable performance to monolingual models on respective monolingual evaluation sets. This was seen for both the language pairs considered: English-Hindi and English-Spanish. It is an interesting result as this allows us to use a single bilingual code-switched model instead of creating two separate monolingual models for each language. Initializing training from either monolingual checkpoint, while accelerating training, did not improve the final WER for both language pairs considered. Using either a concatenated or an aggregate tokenizer led to similar performance. However, the concatenated tokenizer provides additional benefits, such as language identification and multilingual LM rescoring,

Table 3: Spoken language identification using English-Spanish and English-Hindi concatenated tokenizers on the FLEURS dataset.

Language	# of samples	LID accuracy
English (en_us_test)	647	98% (632/647)
Spanish (es_419_test)	908	100% (908/908)
Hindi (hi_in_test)	418	99% (414/418)

as discussed in the Section 4.3.

4.2 Code-Switching models, effect of model initialization and tokenizers

Table 1a presents the performance of the English-Spanish CS ASR models on monolingual test sets: Librispeech and Fisher. Table 2a presents the corresponding results on the code-switched sets: synthetic and the Miami Bangor corpus. Similarly, for the English-Hindi code-switched ASR models, Table 1b presents the performance on monolingual test sets: Librispeech and ULCA, while Table 2b summarizes the results on the code-switching test sets: synthetic and MUCS. For both language pairs, we observed that initializing the code-switched model from the multilingual checkpoint leads to better results and faster convergence as opposed to initializing the model from scratch or from either monolingual checkpoint. We also experimented with different language dataset mix ratios and determined that the best results are achieved when the code-switched dataset is roughly balanced. This may require oversampling of the smaller language.

In (Weller et al., 2022), the authors reported a performance of 53% on the Miami Bangor corpus, which shows that our code-switched models perform competitively with the state-of-the-art on real world samples, while being trained purely from synthetic code-switched data. Another important observation is that the concatenated tokenizer performs just as well as the aggregate tokenizer for the CS models and therefore should be preferred given the additional benefits that it provides. Concluding the discussion, we now have a single model that performs well on monolingual, bilingual, as well as code-switched data.

4.3 Concatenated Tokenizers and Language identification

Table 3 presents utterance-level spoken language identification performance of the English-Spanish and English-Hindi models trained with the concatenated tokenizer on the test sets of the FLEURS dataset. We observe that these models are very accurate at predicting the language of the utterances directly from speech samples. We find it to be significant, since these samples are out of distribution and were not seen by the model during training.

5 Conclusion

In this paper we investigate training of bilingual and code-switching models using purely monolingual datasets. We propose two novel techniques: (1) a real-time and offline synthetic code-switching data generation pipeline and (2) the concatenated tokenizer method, which allows the model to predict language ID directly at the level of individual tokens. We use these two techniques to train CS ASR models and find that they match monolingual model performance on monolingual evaluation benchmarks while performing significantly better on code-switching data. We evaluate model performance against synthetic CS test sets as well as real world Engish-Spanish Miami Bangor and English-Hindi MUCS corpora. In addition, we find that the models display strong performance on LID detection, which we measure using the FLEURS dataset. Performance of models trained with the novel concatenated tokenizer is similar to models trained with the regular aggregate tokenizer, while offering the additional benefit of LID detection. The results suggest that these approaches could be extended to additional languages without increasing model architecture complexity. Further, the excellent LID capabilities of concatenated tokenizer models can enable us to use monolingual language models to rescore and further improve code-switched model predictions. All of this has implications for further research. The code and model weights have been released publicly in NeMo[2].

Limitations

In this work we present techniques that enable the development of code-switching speech recognition models exclusively from monolingual data sources. To validate the efficacy of the proposed work, we

[2]https://github.com/NVIDIA/NeMo

experimented with two language pairs: English-Spanish (en-es) and English-Hindi (en-hi). We selected en-es due to the prevalent bilingual nature of English and Spanish, while en-hi was chosen as Hindi and English possess distinct character sets, thereby allowing us to assess the robustness of our approach. However, we would need to perform experiments with a more diverse set of language pairs to validate if the methods work in general. Furthermore, more experiments are warranted to see if the concatenated tokenizer expands to more than two languages used at a time. As the concatenated tokenizer assigns mutually exclusive token spaces for each language, its size increases with the inclusion of additional languages. This scalability challenge may potentially impede the construction of massive multilingual models. By addressing these limitations through future research endeavors, we can enhance the comprehensiveness and applicability of our findings in the realm of code-switching speech recognition.

Ethics Statement

We adhere to and endorse the principles outlined in the ACL Ethics Policy. Our work on synthetic code-switched ASR holds the potential to offer far-reaching benefits across a spectrum of languages, spanning from widely spoken to less common ones. By alleviating the challenges associated with data collection, our research contributes to the advancement of a more diverse and equitable linguistic landscape. Furthermore, our exploration of multilingual models not only streamlines the computational demands of training and deployment but also fosters resource efficiency by consolidating the utility of numerous monolingual models. Finally, we affirm our commitment to transparency and openness by sharing all code and models used in this study, which were exclusively trained on publicly available datasets, and making them accessible online.

References

Ahmed Ali, Shammur Absar Chowdhury, Amir Hussein, and Yasser Hifny. 2021. Arabic Code-Switching Speech Recognition Using Monolingual Data. In *Interspeech*.

R. Ardila, M. Branson, K. Davis, M. Henretty, M. Kohler, J. Meyer, R. Morais, L. Saunders, F. M. Tyers, and G. Weber. 2020. Common voice: A massively-multilingual speech corpus. In *LREC*.

Alexis Conneau, Min Ma, Simran Khanuja, Yu Zhang, Vera Axelrod, Siddharth Dalmia, Jason Riesa, Clara Rivera, and Ankur Bapna. 2023. FLEURS: Few-shot learning evaluation of universal representations of speech. In *SLT*.

Margaret Deuchar, Peredur Davies, Jon Russell Herring, M Carmen Parafita Couto, and Diana Carter. 2014. Building bilingual corpora. In *Advances in the Study of Bilingualism*, pages 93–110. Multilingual Matters.

Ankur Dhuriya, Rishabh Gaur, et al. 2022. Ulca-asr-dataset-corpus. https://github.com/Open-Speech-EkStep/ULCA-asr-dataset-corpus.

Anuj Diwan, Rakesh Vaideeswaran, Sanket Shah, Ankita Singh, Srinivasa Raghavan, Shreya Khare, Vinit Unni, Saurabh Vyas, Akash Rajpuria, Chiranjeevi Yarra, et al. 2021. Multilingual and code-switching asr challenges for low resource indian languages. *arXiv preprint arXiv:2104.00235*.

Changhan Wang et al. 2021. VoxPopuli: A large-scale multilingual speech corpus for representation learning, semi-supervised learning and interpretation. In *ACL*.

David Graff, Shudong Huang, Ingrid Cartagena, Kevin Walkera, and Christopher Cieri. 2010. Fisher spanish speech. https://catalog.ldc.upenn.edu/LDC2010S01.

A. Graves, S. Fernández, F. Gomez, and J. Schmidhuber. 2006. Connectionist temporal classification: labelling unsegmented sequence data with recurrent neural networks. In *ICML*.

Nuno Miguel Guerreiro, Ricardo Rei, and Fernando Batista. 2021. Towards better subtitles: A multilingual approach for punctuation restoration of speech transcripts. *Expert Systems with Applications*, 186:115740.

Anmol Gulati, James Qin, Chung-Cheng Chiu, Niki Parmar, Yu Zhang, Jiahui Yu, Wei Han, Shibo Wang, Zhengdong Zhang, Yonghui Wu, et al. 2020. Conformer: Convolution-augmented transformer for speech recognition. *Interspeech*, pages 5036–5040.

Deepak Gupta, Asif Ekbal, and Pushpak Bhattacharyya. 2020. A semi-supervised approach to generate the code-mixed text using pre-trained encoder and transfer learning. In *Findings of the Association for Computational Linguistics: EMNLP 2020*, pages 2267–2280.

Anjuli Kannan, Arindrima Datta, Tara N Sainath, Eugene Weinstein, Bhuvana Ramabhadran, Yonghui Wu, Ankur Bapna, Zhifeng Chen, and Seungji Lee. 2019. Large-scale multilingual speech recognition with a streaming end-to-end model. *Interspeech*.

Taku Kudo and John Richardson. 2018. Sentencepiece: A simple and language independent subword tokenizer and detokenizer for neural text processing. In *EMNLP: System Demonstrations*.

Bo Li, Ruoming Pang, Tara N Sainath, Anmol Gulati, Yu Zhang, James Qin, Parisa Haghani, W Ronny Huang, Min Ma, and Junwen Bai. 2021. Scaling end-to-end models for large-scale multilingual asr. In *ASRU*.

Haizhou Li, Bin Ma, and Chin-Hui Lee. 2006. A vector space modeling approach to spoken language identification. *IEEE Transactions on Audio, Speech, and Language Processing*.

Ke Li, Jinyu Li, Guoli Ye, Rui Zhao, and Yifan Gong. 2019. Towards code-switching ASR for end-to-end CTC models. In *ICASSP*.

Xinjian Li, Florian Metze, David R Mortensen, Alan W Black, and Shinji Watanabe. 2022. ASR2K: Speech recognition for around 2000 languages without audio. *arXiv:2209.02842*.

Yuchen Liu, Long Zhou, Yining Wang, Yang Zhao, Jiajun Zhang, and Chengqing Zong. 2018. A comparable study on model averaging, ensembling and reranking in NMT. In *NLPCC*, pages 299–308.

Carol Myers-Scotton. 1989. Codeswitching with english: types of switching, types of communities. *World Englishes*, 8(3):333–346.

Vassil Panayotov, Guoguo Chen, Daniel Povey, and Sanjeev Khudanpur. 2015. Librispeech: an ASR corpus based on public domain audio books. In *ICASSP*.

Vineel Pratap, Anuroop Sriram, Paden Tomasello, Awni Hannun, Vitaliy Liptchinsky, Gabriel Synnaeve, and Ronan Collobert. 2020a. Massively multilingual ASR: 50 languages, 1 model, 1 billion parameters. *Interspeech*.

Vineel Pratap, Andros Tjandra, Bowen Shi, Paden Tomasello, Arun Babu, Sayani Kundu, Ali Elkahky, Zhaoheng Ni, Apoorv Vyas, Maryam Fazel-Zarandi, et al. 2023. Scaling speech technology to 1,000+ languages. *arXiv:2305.13516*.

Vineel Pratap, Qiantong Xu, Anuroop Sriram, Gabriel Synnaeve, and Ronan Collobert. 2020b. MLS: A large-scale multilingual dataset for speech research. In *Interspeech*.

Alec Radford, Jong Wook Kim, Tao Xu, Greg Brockman, Christine McLeavey, and Ilya Sutskever. 2022. Robust speech recognition via large-scale weak supervision. *arXiv:2212.04356*.

Hiroshi Seki, Takaaki Hori, Shinji Watanabe, Jonathan Le Roux, and John R Hershey. 2019. End-to-end multilingual multi-speaker speech recognition. In *INTERSPEECH*, pages 3755–3759.

Hiroshi Seki, Shinji Watanabe, Takaaki Hori, Jonathan Le Roux, and John R Hershey. 2018. An end-to-end language-tracking speech recognizer for mixed-language speech. In *ICASSP*.

Rico Sennrich, Barry Haddow, and Alexandra Birch. 2016. Neural machine translation of rare words with subword units. In *ACL*.

Sunayana Sitaram, Khyathi Raghavi Chandu, Sai Krishna Rallabandi, and Alan W Black. 2019. A survey of code-switched speech and language processing. *arXiv:1904.00784*.

Monica Sunkara, Chaitanya Shivade, Sravan Bodapati, and Katrin Kirchhoff. 2021. Neural inverse text normalization. In *ICASSP*.

Ishan Tarunesh, Syamantak Kumar, and Preethi Jyothi. 2021. From machine translation to code-switching: Generating high-quality code-switched text. *arXiv preprint arXiv:2107.06483*.

Alex Waibel, Hagen Soltau, Tanja Schultz, Thomas Schaaf, and Florian Metze. 2000. Multilingual speech recognition. In *Verbmobil: Foundations of Speech-to-Speech Translation*, pages 33–45. Springer.

Orion Weller, Matthias Sperber, Telmo Pires, Hendra Setiawan, Christian Gollan, Dominic Telaar, and Matthias Paulik. 2022. End-to-end speech translation for code switched speech. In *ACL*.

Fuliang Weng, Harry Bratt, Leonardo Neumeyer, and Andreas Stolcke. 1997. A study of multilingual speech recognition. In *Fifth European Conference on Speech Communication and Technology*.

Genta Indra Winata, Andrea Madotto, Chien-Sheng Wu, and Pascale Fung. 2019. Code-switched language models using neural based synthetic data from parallel sentences. *arXiv preprint arXiv:1909.08582*.

Multilingual self-supervised speech representations improve the speech recognition of low-resource African languages with codeswitching

Tolúlọpẹ́ Ògúnrẹ̀mí **Christopher D. Manning** **Dan Jurafsky**

Stanford University
tolulope@cs.stanford.edu

Abstract

While many speakers of low-resource languages regularly code-switch between their languages and other regional languages or English, datasets of codeswitched speech are too small to train bespoke acoustic models from scratch or do language model rescoring. Here we propose finetuning self-supervised speech representations such as wav2vec 2.0 XLSR to recognize code-switched data. We find that finetuning self-supervised multilingual representations and augmenting them with n-gram language models trained from transcripts reduces absolute word error rates by up to 20% compared to baselines of hybrid models trained from scratch on code-switched data. Our findings suggest that in circumstances with limited training data finetuning self-supervised representations is a better performing and viable solution.

1 Introduction

Over half of the world's population uses at least two languages regularly (Ansaldo et al., 2008). Despite this common occurrence, automatic speech recognition (ASR) models don't work well with speech that includes **code-switching**: when a speaker alternates between two or more languages or varieties within utterances (Myers-Scotton, 2017). For low-resource languages, we encounter two issues when attempting to address this problem: insufficient data for end-to-end-training and insufficient data for language modelling.

Recently, self-supervised pre-training of speech such as wav2vec 2.0 (Baevski et al., 2020) have proven to give very low error rates for English ASR. Although very costly to pre-train, the English models and cross-lingual (XLSR) representations (Conneau et al., 2020) are available for finetuning to efficiently make speech recognisers for many languages.

In this work we ask: *Does fine-tuning XLSR improve recognition of code-switched data over traditional training on code-switched data?* To test this phenomenon, we look at four African languages (isiZulu, isiXhosa, Sesotho, Setswana) code-switched with English. We also explore three questions about how to go about this fine-tuning process. We first experiment with different types of data to add to the codeswitched dataset in order to improve ASR performance, asking *1. Should we add monolingual data?* Many other methods incorporate language identification (language ID) into models, so we ask: *2. Does it help to add language identification in our pipeline (either explicitly or implictly)?* . We test this by augmenting utterances to implicitly identify the language and use a multi-task learning setup to learn frame-level language ID and ASR simultaneously. Finally, we ask: *3. Does a simple n-gram language model trained on the code-switched data improve performance despite the tiny amount of data?*. We use the codeswitched corpus to train bigram and trigram models which we use when decoding the models.

We find that finetuning multilingual pretrained models, augmented with a simple trigram language model, works well for recognizing code-switched data in low-resource languages, significantly better than prior methods of training bespoke models (CNN-TDNN-F acoustic model + LSTM language model) from scratch. We find that neither language ID nor adding monolingual data adds further performance gains and perhaps surprisingly, that adding monolingual data worsened model performance. Our findings suggest that in circumstances with limited training data, finetuning self-supervised representations are likely a better performing and viable solution.

2 Related Work

In speech processing, work on code-switching can be divided into code-switching detection (Rallabandi et al., 2018; Yılmaz et al., 2016; Wang et al., 2019) using language identification (Choud-

Proceedings of the 6th Workshop on Computational Approaches to Linguistic Code-Switching, pages 83–88
December 7, 2023 ©2023 Association for Computational Linguistics

hury et al., 2017) and end-to-end recognition (Indra Winata et al., 2018). In this work, we look at both methods via finetuning of self-supervised representations, namely wav2vec 2.0 (Baevski et al., 2020). Language identification methods either identify the language before doing the ASR on the speech or have language ID trained in tandem with the acoustic model of representations. End-to-end recognition splits into two main approaches: a multilingual modelling with cross lingual representations (Li et al., 2019a; Luo et al., 2018; Zhang et al., 2022) and parallel modelling generating multiple transcriptions which are interpolated to result in one transcription with the highest likelihood (Ahmed and Tan, 2012; Lyu et al., 2006).

For low-resource languages, we encounter two issues when attempting to apply these methods: a lack of sufficient data for end-to-end training and a lack of sufficient data for neural language modelling in the low-resource language or the codeswitched language pair. The absence of a language model for the codeswitched pair leads to prior less computationally expensive methods to fail and the lack of sufficient data for the model to generalise, resulting in poor performance of models.

In our work, we focus on leveraging a pre-trained self-supervised acoustic model, wav2vec 2.0 (Baevski et al., 2020) to finetune an existing multilingual acoustic model for our chosen language pairs. We incorporate language identification to see if this additional signal can improve performance given the small datasets.

3 Background

3.1 Languages

The languages used in this work are four South African languages and English. The South African languages are all Southern Bantu (SB) languages, in the Nguni and Sotho-Tswana branches. The English used in this work is English spoken with a South African accent.

3.2 Data

We use the South African corpus of multilingual code-switched soap opera speech (Niesler et al., 2018). It is a corpus of speech collected from 626 South African soap opera episodes, with utterances from four South African languages: isiZulu, isiXhosa, Sesotho and Setswana codeswitched with English.

Language	No. speakers (millions)	Language Family
isiXhosa	11.6	SB: Nguni
isiZulu	8.2	SB: Nguni
Sesotho	4.0	SB: Sotho-Tswana
Tswana	3.8	SB: Sotho-Tswana
English	380	IE: Western Germanic

Table 1: An overview of the languages used in this work. The South African languages are in the Nguni and Sotho-Tswana branches of the Southern Bantu (SB) language family and English is in the Western Germanic branch of the Indo-European (IE) language family.

For additional monolingual data in the languages, we use the isiZulu, isiXhosa, Sesotho, Setswana and English portions of the NCHLT Speech Corpus (Barnard et al., 2014) to add as monoingual supplementary finetuning data. We use the *NCHLT-clean* partition of the dataset. The datasets used in this work are summarised in Table 2.

	Lang(s)	No. utts	Duration (hrs)
Soap Opera Corpus	Eng-Zul	9347	5.45
	Eng-Xho	7941	3.14
	Eng-Sot	6303	2.86
	Eng-Tsn	6563	2.83
NCHLT Corpus	isiZulu	44673	56.2
	isiXhosa	46651	56.3
	Sesotho	57539	56.3
	Setswana	58414	56.3
	English	77412	56.4

Table 2: Summary of the data used in experiments from both the South African corpus of multilingual code-switched soap opera speech (Soap Opera Corpus) and NCHLT-clean Speech Corpus (NCHLT Corpus).

3.3 Baseline Model

We compare our models to those trained from scratch on this data by Biswas et al. (2022). Their best performing acoustic model is a Kaldi-based (Povey et al., 2011) CNN-TDNN-F trained on all 5 languages and finetuned for each language pair. For language model decoding, the authors used a bidirectional LSTM architecture with a 256-dimensional embedding and 256-dimensional matrices. The LSTMs are trained on language pairs, resulting in four separate language models. We compare our methods to the best performing model for each language pair in this work.

4 Which additional data is helpful?

Given the low-resource natural of codeswitched speech datasets, we ask which type of data can best supplement the codeswitched dataset to improve downstream results. To test this, we "pre-finetune" the model with additional data other than the Soap Opera Corpus data for each language pair, before finetuning it on the codeswitched language pair.

To test whether in-domain data is most useful, we pre-finetune the model with Soap Opera Corpus data from all four language pairs for 42000 steps. This model is then further finetuned with the Soap Opera Corpus data for each individual language pair alone for 12000 steps, resulting in the **+all 4 pairs** models.

To test whether adding monolingual data improves performance, we use NCHLT monolingual data from each language in a language pair, plus the data from the corresponding language pair in the Soap Opera Corpus data to pre-finetune models for 42000 steps. We then further finetune these models with Soap Opera Corpus data from that specific language pair, resulting in **+monolingual** models.

To compare the proposed methods with finetuning with solely Soap Opera Corpus data in the desired language pair, we finetune the model for 15000 steps with the Soap Opera Corpus data for that language pair, resulting in the **One pair** models.

Table 3 shows the results for these experiments with greedy decoding.

Lang pair	Model type	WER
xho-eng	One pair	72.2
	+all 4 pairs	**59.0**
	+monolingual	77.5
zul-eng	One pair	60.8
	+all 4 pairs	**50.8**
	+monolingual	67.6
sot-eng	One pair	59.4
	+all 4 pairs	**50.2**
	+monolingual	63.3
tsn-eng	One pair	51.4
	+all 4 pairs	**42.7**
	+monolingual	60.4

Table 3: Effects of additional data used in "pre-finetuning" on ASR performance. WER is word error rate of models. **+all 4 lang pairs** is "pre-finetuned" with in-domain codeswitched data from the Soap Opera Corpus and **+monolingual** is "pre-finetuned" with monolingual data in each language in the lamguage pair along with the Soap Opera Corpus data for that specific pair.

We see that across languages, using codeswitched-data from all four languages (i.e., "pre-finetuning" with Soap Opera Corpus data from all 4 languages) gives the best results on each South African language pair. The fact that adding data from three different languages helps on the 4th language is somewhat surprising, and points both to the importance of the similarity of the 4 languages, and to the fact that all data are from a single Soap Opera genre. By contrast, the genre difference from the monolingual read speech data is enough to severely hurt performance. In summary, when finetuning multilingual, self-supervised ASR models on low-resource codeswitched data, we find that matching domain and genre properties (such as the presence of codeswitching) is more important than adding monolingual data from the same language if the genre is a mismatch.

5 Does adding implicit or explicit language id information help?

Prior work has shown that for codeswitched ASR, simultaneously learning the language identification (language ID) and ASR improved the ASR performance (Luo et al., 2018; Li et al., 2019b; Zeng et al., 2019). Here we try to add language ID information in two ways: by augmenting the data and by training a classifier.

We experiment with augmenting the Soap Opera Corpus utterances to encapsulate the bilingualism in the utterances in lieu of explicit language labels or timestamps. For each language pair, we use two methods: language specific casing and language specific tags. For language specific casing, we double the vocabulary size by giving each language a specific case, e.g., English in uppercase and isiZulu in lowercase. We then finetune wav2vec 2.0 XLSR 300M with this data for 12000 steps resulting in **+casingID** models for each language pair. For language specific tags, we put opening and closing tags on either side of the text in a specific language. We then finetune wav2vec 2.0 XLSR 300M with this data for 12000 steps resulting in **+tagsID** models for each language pair.

> Casing: **WHAT IF etholwa amaphoyisa kuqala**
>
> Tags: ***<eng>* what if *</eng>* *<zul>* etholwa amaphoyisa kuqala *</zul>***

Example 1: Demonstration of implicit addition

of language information to our models through language-specific casing and language-specific tags.

To train a language ID classifier on our data, we add a frame-level classification head to the wav2vec 2.0 XLSR encoder. We use the timestamps in the corpus to label frames with either English or the South African language, and train a model with cross-entropy loss. The results of the language ID models are in Table 4.

Language Pair	Lang ID Accuracy
English-isiZulu	97%
English-isiXhosa	98%
English-Sesotho	96%
English-Setswana	97%

Table 4: Results from frame-level language identification of the four South African languages and English

The frame-level language ID models work well, so we try a multi-task setting in hopes of improving the model performance. We learn language ID and ASR at the same time, summing the weighted loss of the two tasks. The loss calculation is summarised in Equation 1. As ASR is the priority, we always keep the CTC weight higher than the language ID weight. The resulting models are the **+multitaskID** models, with each language pair finetuned for 12 00 steps. The model architecture is visualised in Figure 1 .

$$Loss_{CTC+LID} = \lambda_{CTC} L_{CTC} + (1 - \lambda_{CTC}) L_{LID} \quad (1)$$

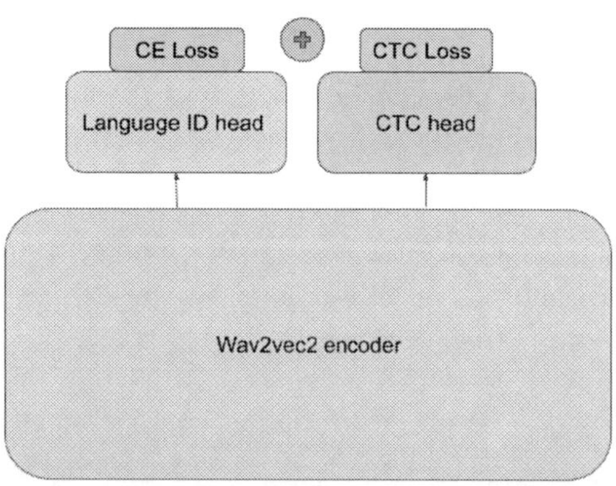

Figure 1: Our multi-task learning setup for combining frame-level language ID with CTC by a weighted sum of the losses.

Lang pair	Model type	WER
xho-eng	One pair	72.2
	+tagsID	83.4
	+casingID	87.9
	+multitaskID	75.2
zul-eng	One pair	60.8
	+tagsID	80.8
	+casingID	80.9
	+multitaskID	64.2
sot-eng	One pair	59.4
	+tagsID	76.3
	+casingID	89.4
	+multitaskID	65.6
tsn-eng	One pair	51.4
	+tagsID	72.6
	+casingID	86.6
	+multitaskID	64.5

Table 5: Effects of incorporating language ID on ASR performance. WER is word error rate of models. **+tagsID** uses language specific tags around utterances in the dataset and **+casingID** uses one case per language (e.g. uppercase for English and lowercase for isiZulu). Models trained to learn both language ID and ASR at the same time during finetuning are referred to as **+multitaskID** models. The **+multitaskID** models work better that **+tagsID** and **+casingID**. But none of the language ID models work as well as the baseline of not using Language ID at all (the "One pair" row).

The results of our experiments are in Table 5. For the multi-task setup, the results with the best language ID and CTC weights are reported.

The multi-task learning setup improves performance downstream over language specific casing and tags, but not over further fine-tuning, possibly due to the model being hindered rather than helped trying to learn two tasks at once.

Language specific casing does not improve model performance, it actually worsens the models compared to the baselines. This is likely due to the unnecessary doubling of the vocabulary.

Language ID tags work better than the casing across languages, however they do not outperform finetuning without tags. This is likely due to the fact that the tags do not correspond to any speech, so the introduction of them creates initial confusion.

In summary, adding language identification information does not improve ASR performance on our code-switched dataset. This could be due due to the lack of data available for training, the fact that the character sets for our 5 languages are all overlapping, or the fact that our experiments consist of finetuning and not end-to-end pretraining. Other work that uses multitask learning for code-switched speech recognition (Li et al., 2019b; Zeng et al., 2019; Song et al., 2022; Winata et al., 2018) has shown success with a language pair with an non-overlapping character set: English and Mandarin Chinese. Those English/Chinese models are also trained from scratch end-to-end, so it is possible that incorporation of language ID is more useful during training and less useful at later stages such as finetuning.

6 Does a language model improve performance?

For our experiments thusfar, we do greedy decoding from the wav2vec 2.0 model finetuned with a CTC head. Could adding language model information improve performance? The baseline system with which we are comparing used an LSTM language model, suggesting that this information might be useful.

In this section, we study whether using the transcripts from the Soap Opera Corpus as training data for a small n-gram language model could improve accuracy. We train separate bigram and trigram (word) language models using KenLM (Heafield, 2011) from each of the 4 language-pair datasets, and then use this language model in decoding.

The language model results for the best finetuned models per language pair are presented in Table 6.

	xho-eng	zul-eng	sot-eng	tsn-eng
Baseline	48.7	43.3	48.5	43.5
Greedy	59.0	50.8	50.2	42.7
2-gram	26.7	25.5	30.6	28.9
3-gram	**22.1**	**22.3**	**23.4**	**21.7**

Table 6: Effect of language modelling on ASR performance (measured in WER). The numbers in the baseline raw are taken from (Biswas et al., 2022); their system (which includes an LSTM language model) is compared to wave2vec 2.0 finetuned on the Soap Opera Corpus data, using greedy decoding (no LM) as well as bigram, and trigram n-gram models trained with the Soap Opera Corpus data. Without n-gram language models, the baseline model outperforms finetuning wav2vec 2.0. However, training an n-gram language model with the ASR data improves over the baseline.

Although greedy decoding does not work better than the baseline (CNN-TDNN-F acoustic model plus a bidirectional LSTM model) since the baseline has a language model, we find that the fine-tuned models equipped with a simple n-gram language model consistently beat baseline models. These results suggest that fine-tuning large pre-trained models with only very simple language model support can be a better solution in low-resource scenarios.

7 Conclusion

In this work, we have finetuned wav2vec 2.0 XLSR with codeswitched data of South African languages and English. We found that this system augmented with a simple bigram or trigram language model beats baseline models trained with LSTM language models. We also found that it helps to add data from other languages, albeit very related languages and in the exact the same genre/domain.

We were not able to improve the model with various kinds of language ID information; these methods may see more success for languages with character sets that overlap less, or when there is enough data to train an end-to-end model from scratch.

This work demonstrates a method to train ASR models on codeswitching data with relatively minimal computation and a very basic n-gram language model, suggesting a direction for addressing an important task in the low-resource settings that characterise many of the world's languages.

8 Acknowledgements

We would like to thank the reviewers for their comments and suggestions. This research was funded in part by NSF award number IIS-2128145 and in part by a Stanford School of Engineering Fellowship to TO. CM is a fellow in the CIFAR Learning in Machines and Brains program.

References

Basem H.A. Ahmed and Tien-Ping Tan. 2012. Automatic speech recognition of code switching speech using 1-best rescoring. In *2012 International Conference on Asian Language Processing*, pages 137–140.

Ana Inés Ansaldo, Karine Marcotte, Lilian Scherer, and Gaelle Raboyeau. 2008. Language therapy and bilingual aphasia: Clinical implications of psycholinguistic and neuroimaging research. *Journal of Neurolinguistics*, 21(6):539–557. Acquisition, Processing and Loss of L2: Functional, cognitive and neural perspectives.

Alexei Baevski, Yuhao Zhou, Abdelrahman Mohamed, and Michael Auli. 2020. wav2vec 2.0: A framework for self-supervised learning of speech representations. In *Advances in Neural Information Processing Systems*, volume 33, pages 12449–12460. Curran Associates, Inc.

Etienne Barnard, Marelie H Davel, Charl van Heerden, Febe De Wet, and Jaco Badenhorst. 2014. The NCHLT speech corpus of the South African languages. In *4th Workshop on Spoken Language Technologies for Under-resourced Languages (SLTU 2014)*, pages 194–200.

Astik Biswas, Emre Yılmaz, Ewald van der Westhuizen, Febe de Wet, and Thomas Niesler. 2022. Code-switched automatic speech recognition in five south african languages. *Computer Speech & Language*, 71:101262.

Monojit Choudhury, Kalika Bali, Sunayana Sitaram, and Ashutosh Baheti. 2017. Curriculum design for code-switching: Experiments with language identification and language modeling with deep neural networks. In *Proceedings of the 14th International Conference on Natural Language Processing (ICON-2017)*, pages 65–74.

Alexis Conneau, Alexei Baevski, Ronan Collobert, Abdelrahman Mohamed, and Michael Auli. 2020. Unsupervised cross-lingual representation learning for speech recognition.

Kenneth Heafield. 2011. KenLM: Faster and smaller language model queries. In *Proceedings of the Sixth Workshop on Statistical Machine Translation*, pages 187–197, Edinburgh, Scotland. Association for Computational Linguistics.

Genta Indra Winata, Andrea Madotto, Chien-Sheng Wu, and Pascale Fung. 2018. Towards end-to-end automatic code-switching speech recognition. *arXiv e-prints*, pages arXiv–1810.

Ke Li, Jinyu Li, Guoli Ye, Rui Zhao, and Yifan Gong. 2019a. Towards code-switching asr for end-to-end ctc models. In *ICASSP 2019 - 2019 IEEE International Conference on Acoustics, Speech and Signal Processing (ICASSP)*, pages 6076–6080.

Ke Li, Jinyu Li, Guoli Ye, Rui Zhao, and Yifan Gong. 2019b. Towards code-switching asr for end-to-end ctc models. In *ICASSP 2019 - 2019 IEEE International Conference on Acoustics, Speech and Signal Processing (ICASSP)*, pages 6076–6080.

Ne Luo, Dongwei Jiang, Shuaijiang Zhao, Caixia Gong, Wei Zou, and Xiangang Li. 2018. Towards end-to-end code-switching speech recognition. *arXiv preprint arXiv:1810.13091*.

Daucheng Lyu, Ren yuan Lyu, Yuang chin Chiang, and Chun nan Hsu. 2006. Speech recognition on code-switching among the chinese dialects. In *2006 IEEE International Conference on Acoustics Speech and Signal Processing Proceedings*, volume 1, pages I–I.

Carol Myers-Scotton. 2017. Code-switching. *The handbook of sociolinguistics*, pages 217–237.

Thomas Niesler et al. 2018. A first south african corpus of multilingual code-switched soap opera speech. In *Proceedings of the Eleventh International Conference on Language Resources and Evaluation (LREC 2018)*.

Daniel Povey, Arnab Ghoshal, Gilles Boulianne, Lukas Burget, Ondrej Glembek, Nagendra Goel, Mirko Hannemann, Petr Motlicek, Yanmin Qian, Petr Schwarz, et al. 2011. The kaldi speech recognition toolkit. In *IEEE 2011 workshop on automatic speech recognition and understanding*, CONF. IEEE Signal Processing Society.

SaiKrishna Rallabandi, Sunayana Sitaram, and Alan W Black. 2018. Automatic detection of code-switching style from acoustics. In *Proceedings of the Third Workshop on Computational Approaches to Linguistic Code-Switching*, pages 76–81, Melbourne, Australia. Association for Computational Linguistics.

Tongtong Song, Qiang Xu, Meng Ge, Longbiao Wang, Hao Shi, Yongjie Lv, Yuqin Lin, and Jianwu Dang. 2022. Language-specific characteristic assistance for code-switching speech recognition. *Interspeech 2022*.

Qinyi Wang, Emre Yılmaz, Adem Derinel, and Haizhou Li. 2019. Code-switching detection using asr-generated language posteriors. *Proc. Interspeech 2019*, pages 3740–3744.

Genta Indra Winata, Andrea Madotto, Chien-Sheng Wu, and Pascale Fung. 2018. Towards end-to-end automatic code-switching speech recognition. *arXiv preprint arXiv:1810.12620*.

Emre Yılmaz, Henk van den Heuvel, and David van Leeuwen. 2016. Code-switching detection using multilingual dnns. In *2016 IEEE Spoken Language Technology Workshop (SLT)*, pages 610–616. IEEE.

Zhiping Zeng, Yerbolat Khassanov, Haihua Xu Van Tung Pham, Eng Siong Chng, and Haizhou Li. 2019. On the end-to-end solution to mandarin-english code-switching speech recognition. *Interspeech 2019*.

Shuai Zhang, Jiangyan Yi, Zhengkun Tian, Jianhua Tao, Yu Ting Yeung, and Liqun Deng. 2022. Reducing multilingual context confusion for end-to-end codeswitching automatic speech recognition. In *Proc. Interspeech*, pages 3894–3898.

Author Index

Association for Computational Linguistics
209 N. Eighth Street
Stroudsburg, Pennsylvania 18360

ISBN 978-1-7138-8597-9

CURRAN ASSOCIATES INC.
proceedings.com